also by Julianna FreeHand

The Westchester Treasure Hunt Tour, Guide 1:
Treason in the American Revolution

A Seafaring Legacy

Julianna FreeHand

A Seafaring Legacy

The Photographs, Diaries, Letters
and Memorabilia
of a Maine Sea Captain
and His Wife

1859-1908

Random House New York

Library of Congress Cataloging in Publication Data

FreeHand, Julianna, 1941–
    A seafaring legacy.

    Bibliography: p.
    1. Drinkwater, Sumner. 2. Seafaring life.
3. Yarmouth (Me.)—Social life and customs.
4. Yarmouth (Me.)—Biography. I. Drinkwater, Alice.
II. Drinkwater, Sumner. III. Title.
F29.Y2F73   910.4′5′0924 [B]   81– 40240
ISBN   0–394–51771–7   AACR2

Manufactured in the United States of America
98765432
First Edition

This truly happened: a lady who had moved out of the State of Maine to the Boston area experienced some difficulty recently in locating some dividend checks that had not been forwarded to her. She telephoned several places in Boston before she was finally referred to the correct bank. After she called there and stated her case, the banker told her, "Anyone who moves away from the State of Maine deserves to lose their checks." Amen.

To the State of Maine from a prodigal daughter. In particular, to: Florence McAlpine Free, my beloved "Grammy"; Edith McAlpine Free, my mentor; and Dinky, to whom I owe so much.

ACKNOWLEDGMENTS

I enjoy writing nonfiction because the truth is so much better than anything I could make up. However, it would have been impossible for me to have written this story without the help of those people who remembered its pieces. I am deeply indebted to Irene Arbo, Frances Bucknam, James Romeo Bucknam, Iva Burgess, Carolyn Christie, Mr. and Mrs. Maurice Colesworthy, Doris Dean, Phyllis Drinkwater, Eunice de Sanchez, Malcolm Drinkwater, Mabel Harrigan, Philip Knight, Richard Long, Mr. and Mrs. Joe Pullen, Marion Knight Reed, William S. Rent, Charles G. Rice, Jessie Simonton, Mildred Soule, Alfreda and Leon Thurston. I feel fortunate to have been able to talk with Robert Stephen Collins, the grandson of Sumner's first skipper and the last surviving commercial pilot to tow sailing vessels up Yarmouth's Royal River. I hope Mr. Collins succeeds in publishing his book about Yarmouth, *Westcustogo and Aucocisco.* Finally, I should indeed be remiss if I didn't express my deep gratitude to Winifred Glover Blanchard, who remembered roughly half of the Drinkwater family stories that appear in this book.

Many individuals and institutions lent me invaluable research assistance. I am especially indebted to Karl Kortum, Chief Curator of the National Maritime Museum at San Francisco, and Andrew J. Nesdall. Among others I should like to thank are Wally Buxton, George F. Campbell, Roger Campbell, Charity Cole, Clifford M. Collins, Tom Frankel, Richard Lederer, Velma Oliver, Dorothy Schupp, Robert J. Thomson, Edith Towne and Robert A. Weinstein. Thanks also to Paul Wish and Marie Bigliante of the Atlantic Company, E. B. Berlinrut of the Bonaire-Dutch Antilles Tourist Information, Dr. Harry Krulewitch of the Community Health and Education Center, the Dental Society of New York State, Ruth Nevendorffer of the Historical Society of the Tarrytowns, Sidney Mund, Grand Secretary and New York State Executive Officer of the Knights of Pythias, the Library and Museum of the Masonic Hall in New York, Charles Brown, Grand High Priest of Grand Chapter of Maine Royal Arch Masons, Ralph C. Rackliff, Grand Recorder of the Grand Commandery of Maine Knights Templar, Arthur Gerrier and Cynthia Murphy of the Maine Historical Society, Nathan Lipfert of the Maine Maritime Museum, Ardie L. Kelly of the Mariners Museum, the Mystic Seaport Library staff, Harlen Soeten of the National Maritime Museum, Kathy Flynn of Peabody Museum, Edith H. McCauley of Portland Public Library, Norman Brouwer of South Street Seaport Museum, Harvey Dixon of the Statue of Liberty Library, Susan Trevitt-Cark of the University of Oregon Library Map Room, Muriel Sanford of the University of Maine Library and Claire Page of the Yarmouth Historical Society.

Jean Bennett, Carole Breen, Gail Brewer, Ainslie Gilligan, Doris Hathaway, Craig and Harriet Miller, Charles Newman, Michael and Susan Pease and Anthony Scholl all helped at sensitive moments as the book took form, while Charlotte Mayerson and Nancy Banks did everything they could to ensure that the book *would* take form.

And Ruth Crull, Brendan, Darrow, Elizabeth and John Hand? They made it all possible—in their own special way.

J.F.

CONTENTS

THE DISCOVERY
JULY 1978

*"If it were a bear,
it would bite you."*

The legend of the Yankee sea captain has long appealed to the American romantic imagination. Captain Sumner Pierce Drinkwater and his wife, Alice Gray Drinkwater, lived the latter legend and recorded it, leaving a collection of photographs, letters and diaries that are unparalleled in American maritime history. At the time I discovered their collection at my family's home in Maine, I had acquired a local reputation for publishing historical photographs of Westchester County, New York, where I lived with my husband and three children. While I immediately recognized the importance of the material, I was dumfounded to discover it on a bookcase back home.

I was not in Yarmouth, Maine, in any professional capacity, that July of 1978. Rather, I had gone there to settle the estate of my maiden aunt, Edith McAlpine Free, who had died some months earlier at the Drinkwater place. After Captain Drinkwater passed away in June of 1942, his second wife, Mabel, continued to rent rooms in their house as a means of income. My aunt left her parents' home in Portland, Maine, to stay at the Drinkwaters' in Yarmouth. It was the autumn of 1942, during World War II, and she was driving a bakery truck for Cushman's. The bakery had hired fourteen women for this traditionally male job during the war, but my aunt was the only one they kept on after the men returned.

Aunt Edie realized even greater success with the Drinkwaters. Initially a boarder, she became a member of their household, and when she was appointed my legal guardian at my mother's death, she brought me there as well. It was all one to the Drinkwaters; they also had an affection for dogs and cats.

My aunt's life enthusiasm was photography and I came to share it because she force-fed me progressively difficult cameras from the time I was six. I remember balking as a teen-ager when she decided to replace the Retina she had given me with a 35mm Argus camera. My protests were ignored; she traded the Retina in. The Argus was the last camera she gave me before I left my teaching career, committed myself to professional photography and purchased my own equipment. Edie meant to have the last word, however: she left me her Leicas when she died.

Yet in all our years of discussing photography, my aunt never once mentioned the photographs or the papers of the Drinkwater collection. Neither, for that matter, did the Drinkwaters. I found out about this treasure only after Aunt Edie died when her friend Dot Hathaway came by the house to take me berry picking, something she had promised to do for years. As Dot was one of the most prodigious berry pickers in the State of Maine, it wasn't long before we were returning home loaded with strawberries. We decided to stop at the store for some whipping cream before going to Riverside Cemetery to visit Edie's grave. Riverside Cemetery hadn't been on the afternoon agenda. It was just something we decided to do.

Sumner and Alice's monument.

My aunt was buried in Sumner's family plot beside its monument, topped with the globe Sumner had specifically designed to commemorate his and Alice's voyage around the world together. I share the popular antipathy to graveyards, but Sumner had chosen to lie with his Alice in a spot that charmed me—on the bank of the Royal River which flows into Casco Bay and the Atlantic Ocean.

In choosing a site in Riverside Cemetery, Sumner had broken with tradition because his family's gravestones stand in formation half a mile away in old Ledge Cemetery looking out toward Casco Bay. He may have brought Alice to Riverside when she died in 1915 because they had spooned in this cemetery during their courting years, or maybe he chose it because her family was buried there. In any case, I was enchanted by this plot on the bank of the Royal River. Bordered by pines, the site seemed more like a picnic grove than a burial ground, though those same pines have grown so over the years that they now block the view that Sumner had at the turn

The Drinkwater family plot.

of the century. Then he would have seen the Yarmouth shipbuilding yards and the wharves where he had docked to discharge his cargoes. Perhaps, though, it doesn't matter that the pines have grown, because Sumner wouldn't recognize the somnolent harbor now.

Dot broke the silence as we looked at the Drinkwaters' globe. "By the way, Julie, you like history. What do you think of Alice's journal?"

"Alice's journal?"

"Alice Gray, Sumner's wife, kept a journal on one of their sailing voyages. Haven't you ever read it?"

"No." I was tired from the strawberry picking and the emotions of visiting my aunt's grave. This information couldn't be as important as it seemed.

"Well, I read it," Dot continued, ignoring my lack of response, "and it's real interesting. You should ask your family to let you read it."

I promised I would as we turned back to the car. Not until much later would I wonder at the psychic connection that led me to the journal as I stood by Alice Gray Drinkwater's grave.

I asked about the journal when I got home and was dismayed to find that it had been lent months earlier with some other material to a neighbor, a teen-ager who was working on an independent history project at her school. She had been admonished to return it within a few weeks. Fortunately, I didn't grumble and groan as I wanted to, about how much this development alarmed me, for once we asked the student about the things, she readily returned them.

But the incident had served to shake the complacency, the take-it-for-granted attitude, that inevitably prejudices the familiar —if it's been lying on our own bookshelf, how important can it be? Retrieving the journal had aroused my professional instincts, but at first glance its appearance was anticlimactic. Alice's journal, written in an ordinary composition book certainly didn't look like much. I remember taking it out to the backyard, where I stretched out in a lawn chair in the sun.

Occasionally, in the course of my research, time thins and I brush an earlier consciousness; history comes alive. Such moments

Yarmouth Shipyard, late nineteenth century.

are more a product of academic ecstasy than of the occult, and they don't happen daily or even once a year. Certainly, I wasn't expecting one to happen that afternoon when I opened Alice's journal.

The nondescript cover was deceptive; reading Alice's account of her long sea voyage with Sumner was one of the most thrilling moments of my life. Although her shipboard routine was foreign to me, she drew me to her with her candid voice and her womanly concerns. Her syntax seemed surprisingly modern; she wrote in a clear, feminine hand; and her dry understatement tickled my funny bone in a spot only a Yankee can reach. At some point in her narrative, I began to feel urgently that this experience was something I must share. Alice's account gave me a greater sense of history than all the lists of Presidents and dry facts I had memorized in school. Long before I had finished reading her journal, I was committed to getting it published—if the family would agree. Darkness drove me inside to supper.

"Why haven't you ever shown me Alice's journal before?"

"Didn't suppose you'd be interested."

"But you know that I've been doing almost exactly this kind of work during the last two years in Westchester."

"Well, you've been in Westchester mostly in the last two years. Anyway, just didn't happen to think about it. Since you're interested, would you like to see the photographs Alice and Sumner took on that trip?"

I was already having a hard time concentrating on supper. "Photographs? From their voyage, the same ones she mentions in the journal? Do you know how *rare* that is?" And I twitched through the rest of supper.

"Sure think it's funny how excited people get over things like this. Not my cup of tea t'all." A manila envelope full of photographs was produced, as well as two boxes of glass-plate negatives.

"You've got the original glass plates as well? My God, I don't believe this is possible. Do you know what a treasure this is?"

A glance noted my invocation of the Lord. "Thought those were important. That's why I've always taken good care of them."

I had to wait until the following day to get on the telephone. Although I was sure that this material was significant, Maine historians would have to verify the importance of my find. Even at that early stage of my research, the museums I called were very encouraging. They had inherited a number of personal diaries which Yankee captains kept concurrently with the official ship's log. Understandably, however, these are filled mostly with technical details about the voyage and hold very little interest for the general public. Far fewer women had left journals, and none that they were aware of had left an account of a voyage with accompanying photographs. The uniqueness of this material and its historical impact derives from the sum of its parts. While diaries, photographs and letters exist in maritime archives, none of them correlate one to another as extensively as they do in the Drinkwater memorabilia.

After I had spoken to several Maine historians and reported their interest to the family, the fact that Sumner's fifty-three diaries were stored away in a Girl Scout cookie box carton was suddenly "recalled." Looking through them I saw, firsthand, the type of captains' logs that the museums had warned me about. Sumner's diaries, which began shortly before he courted Alice, were no more than daily outlines, devoid of human-interest detail. The only way I could use them was as a framework for Alice's journal.

At that point focus for the book was still on Alice. Because of the material available, Sumner remained in the shadows, although, perhaps, a tinge of feminism also was influencing me. After a perfunctory inspection when I separated out those diaries that had become mildewed over the years, I stacked them back in their cookie carton.

Two years elapsed before an interested publisher urged me to look for additional material because the journal was too short for a book-length work. On May 3, 1980, I returned to Maine to search for more information about Alice. I wasn't optimistic because none of my attempts to learn more about her in the meantime had produced anything substantial. Only Alice's journal gave her human dimension. Without it, she might never have existed. I spent most of that May day interviewing the various branches of the Drinkwater family, but I had reached a dead end and Alice was still an enigma. That evening, preparing to go over Sumner's diaries again, I found a worn manila envelope tucked into the box the family had set aside for me while they were selling off and moving out of Sumner's house.

Sumner as a boy.

Christmas came in May that year; the envelope was crammed full of Sumner and Alice's correspondence.

Forty of the letters were Sumner's; five were Alice's. As I pored over them, my bias for Alice collapsed and Sumner moved center-stage. I was enthralled to find letters that he had saved from his childhood. Sumner had kept one particular letter all his life, which showed how long he had cherished his determination to go to sea. This letter, apparently sent to Sumner from an older friend of the family's, Carrie Soule, was enclosed with a letter from his brother John. John, four years his elder and already at sea, was to be Sumner's lifelong friend as well as his favorite brother.

There is no year next to the date on Carrie Soule's letter, but the vessel he and John Drinkwater sailed on, the *Carrie Bertha,* was a 487-ton brig built in Yarmouth in 1869. Sumner, born January 11, 1859, would have had to receive it sometime after he was ten, but

before he was sixteen and a cabin boy at sea. The "Aunt Sallie" Carrie speaks of may be one of his relatives and Sumner's teachers. The Soules were one of the founding families of Yarmouth. "Josh" in this letter was Sumner's younger brother.

Savannah Dec 9th   Brig Carrie Bertha
Dear Summie
I am going to write you a few lines and send it [in] John's letter. How do you do this winter? I suppose you go to school and study like fun. Do you get any lickings. I guess you deserve them if you don't get them. I must write to Aunt Sallie and tell her she must pound you twice a day. Don't you miss Joshie poor little boy down sick and can't take any comfort. I expect one of these days to see a smart little fellow by the name of Sumner flying round on the deck of some thousand ton ship giving orders to do this and that and to see folks taking of their hats to him Aye Aye Cap'n. wouldn't that be nice. You are going to be a sailor aint you Summie. But I mustn't write anymore so good bye. your affec. friend.

                                    Carrie B. Soyle
                                    (An old sailor)

Although he recorded his financial earnings in an account book from the age of fifteen, Sumner did not begin keeping a diary until 1879, when he was twenty. Therefore, most of the notes I give about his childhood are interpolations from later diary entries or from my interviews with family descendants and old-time residents of Yarmouth. Because my adopted aunt was Sumner's daughter from a later marriage, I found everyone very courteous and responsive to my research. Indeed, the Drinkwater descendants were quite patient with me as I sorted them out, since, though I had known a few of them, I found the huge family roster overwhelming. To understand the privilege they showed me, you have to understand something about the State of Maine.

Establishing residency in America is fairly straightforward. It's straightforward but stringent in Maine; you have to be born there. While moving there entitles you to pay taxes, you're still "from away." The state has always stood apart from the rest of the continent, although more than one Yankee noticed that the Civil War was happening when the cost of cotton went up. Actually, they should have—Maine contributed proportionately more sons to that war than did any other Northern state.

You don't even get to coastal Maine the way you go to most other places; you go down East instead of up north or northeast. The expression arose because ships sailed downwind to Maine on the prevailing westerlies and beat upwind to Boston on the return. "Downwind to Maine" became abbreviated to "down East."

Maine folk mistrust strangers and quickly peg someone who is putting on airs. While tourists definitely boost the Maine economy, that seasonal visitor is often referred to as a "summer complaint." The only thing lower than a New Yorker to Maine folk is a Massa-chusetts driver, but the exception only applies to driving. Since I am a transplant, born in Portland but bred in New York, I became aware of this attitude at a very young age. My New York accent often grated on my Yankee grandmother and she retaliated by exaggerating my pronunciation of the vowel *a,* reciting:

> I saw a *c*alf,
> Go down a p*a*th,
> And I l*a*ughed and l*a*ughed,
> For an hour and a h*a*lf.

As a result of her drills in pronunciation, to this day my *aunts* aren't *ants.*

I belatedly realized some benefit from my position between two worlds with the Drinkwater materials. I was Yankee enough to command the confidence of Maine people; living in New York made it easier to find a publisher.

THE FORMATIVE YEARS
1859-1878

"Eat it up
wear it out
make it do
& do without."

Of the papers I successfully ferreted from the descendants' family archives, the earliest were two letters from Nicholas, Sumner's father, dated 1868. Nicholas Drinkwater was highly respected in the town of Yarmouth. He held the office of selectman for eleven years, six of which he served as chairman of the board. His first five years in this municipal office, a triumvirate mayoralty, were from 1859 to 1863. The six terms as chairman of the board came much later, after the age of sixty-two in 1887–1890 and 1893–1894. Additionally, he was prominent in his Masonic lodge and served nine terms in their highest office, Worshipful Master, in the years 1855 –1867. Nicholas evidently went to sea at an early age, as had his father before him. However, the dates of his terms in office suggest that he retired from the sea around the age of twenty-five to farm, marry Margaret Hannah Gray, beget children and, simultaneously, become influential in his community affairs. The vocational information he supplied for his Masonic records lists Nicholas Drinkwater as a mariner and farmer.

His election to selectman would have been the first matter of business at the town meeting, an annual affair in Yarmouth. Although prior to the success of the suffrage movement women did not vote at this event, they were encouraged to voice their opinions and serve a potluck dinner to the men. The town meeting sometimes occupied an entire day depending on how many items were up for discussion or whether the election of the three selectmen who served as municipal officers was prolonged.

The most exciting meeting in town memory occurred thirteen years before the Civil War, when Yarmouth "seceded" from North Yarmouth. The area known as Yarmouth today was the cradle of North Yarmouth. Settlers came first to Cousins Island and then leap-frogged to the mainland. The Ledge area was an early center of North Yarmouth: the first meeting house stood on present-day Gilman Street. As the settlement grew, the town's center shifted to an area around the mills built on the Royal River. Eventually, two interest groups evolved: the people of the northern portion devoted themselves almost exclusively to farming while those in the southern part were involved in mercantile, manufacturing and shipbuilding pursuits. The southern faction, the "Southers," became incensed when the "Northers" refused to replace a thirty-two-year-old fire engine that was supposed to protect the village area of North Yarmouth. This issue snowballed into talk of secession and a special town meeting was convened on June 18, 1849. Over 450 voters crowded into the old town house. There were so many people, it was impossible to take an accurate count, so the moderator moved the vote to the street; 275 men in favor of division stood on one side of the road and 175 lined up on the other. Yarmouth and North Yarmouth were officially divided by an act of the Maine legislature on August 20, 1849.

One of Nicholas' obituaries rather colorfully described his first voyage at the age of fourteen when he supposedly served as a cabin boy on a slave ship. Within the same sentence the writer quickly added that later, as a captain, Nicholas returned to Africa with "the first shipload of manumitted slaves sent out from Baltimore" by the American Colonization Society.

The slave trade was outlawed in this country in 1808, a year after Great Britain took that step. The American Colonization Society began settling Liberia, West Africa, with freed slaves around 1822. As Nicholas was not born until 1825, it is impossible to credit this information. However, this obituary might have confused incidents from his sea career with those of his father, Nicholas, for whom he was named. Born in 1794, the elder Nicholas would have been just fourteen at the end of the slave trade and most certainly was a captain by the age of twenty-eight, which was about the time the American Colonization Society began to send freed slaves to Liberia. The Drinkwater descendants corroborated that "a Nicholas" had served on board a slaver.

The following letter was written by Sumner's father, Nicholas, in 1868. Since the Yarmouth town records show that Nicholas had been town postmaster in 1866 and head of his Masonic lodge in 1867, this letter apparently arrived shortly after he had returned to the sea. It was not addressed to Sumner, but to his eldest son, John, age thirteen, whom he had left in charge of the family and whom he would take to sea within a few years. "Lay days" refers to a contracted time the vessel had to be in port for loading or discharging cargo. If at the end of this period she still lay idle, a daily monetary penalty called "demurrage" was imposed on the firm chartering the vessel by the shipowner.

New York March 18th 68

My Dear Son.

I received your letter when I arrived here & was glad that I had a son who could write me. you write & spell very well, as well as any boys of your age & advantages.

You must try & improve in writing. I received Mother's letter today & was glad to hear you were all well. You must be a good boy & saw the wood & take good care of the cow & horse.

I have sent a barrel of sugar home & if it gets there safe it will be left to Capt Prince's. & you can go up next week & get it. Mrs. Prince will pay the freight on it, & you can pay her. I don't know how much it will be you can ask her. it will be about one Dollar. I wrote mother last week & sent her a check. I will enclose a dollar to pay the freight on it & when you get it you can have a pint a piece to eat. It cost me $14.00 in gold & I was offered 28 Dollars to day for it. It will be worth when you get it home 15 cents a lb. & mother can sell part of it if she wants to, at that price   I shall bring some more next voyage   You must not tell every body about it. I sent you a paper & will send you another, & the rest, one each, before I go.

We discharged our cargo Monday. & hauled to the wharf to load. Our lay days commenced yesterday morning so we have two days the less to lay in Cuba. We may be loaded this week.

Be a good boy & do the work & mind your mother & you shall have a big lump of sugar, if you ain't a good boy Mother mus'nt give you any.

Give Fathers love to all your brothers & sisters & Grandmother & write me again to cuba & put in with mothers.

Father.

Commonly, seamen wrote letters home addressed to one member of the family that were intended to be shared by all. Thus, although the letter was received by John, it most certainly circulated throughout the family. The second letter that Nicholas sent his son is a marvelous example of how tradition is perpetuated. Nicholas is preparing John, and also his second son, Sumner, to follow in his career. Nicholas' comment about "the captain" in the April-fool incident is a third-person reference to himself. Undoubtably, he was master of the vessel.

I loved reading this letter from Nicholas as I felt it was geared to my level of understanding of maritime matters. Not only would it have greatly simplified my research if his children had saved more of Nicholas' letters, it would have markedly reduced my eyestrain. Unfortunately, Sumner was not his equal in penmanship or in English composition. Nicholas believed in punctuation, indenting paragraphs and writing legibly.

"Old dandy" may be the dog, as a letter written to Nicholas by Sumner only two years later refers to "old Dorbin"—presumably the horse.

"The Highlands of Neversink" are on the northern New Jersey coast and mark one of the bearings for the New York harbor entrance. Going to or returning from Cuba, the Highlands would be an expected sight, and a well-known one for East Coast mariners. They would have been more than that for Nicholas because his father had died within sight of this landmark. The elder Nicholas had contracted an infection sometime during a voyage from Santo Domingo. A newspaper report indicated that one of his sons who was serving as first mate on the voyage had been stricken by the same illness but had survived to reach New York. This son could only have been Nicholas, Sumner's father, as the next son in line, John Gray, was fifteen at the time and too young to have been first mate. His father's death on August 16, 1847, aboard the vessel *Don Nicholas,* was only three years before Nicholas took up his community involvement. The proximity of these dates suggests that his father's death and his own illness may have led to Nicholas' decision to leave the sea and stay home for a while.

His mothers death in 1853 probably increased his family obligations as some of his siblings were still youngsters. Nicholas' mother, Mary White Drinkwater, was directly descended from Peregrine White, the first child born in Plymouth to the passengers of the *Mayflower*.

Havana Cuba April 1868

My Dear Son,

I received your letter with Mothers, the next day after we arrived here, & was glad to hear you were all well. & that old dandy was so smart.

I suppose it will interest you most to hear about our passage out. & the sunny isle where we now are. So I will tell you something about it.

We left New York Saturday the 28th day of march & got down to the Highlands of Neversink at dark, when it fell calm & we were obliged to anchor to keep from drifting ashore. Just before midnight a breeze sprung up from North East & we hove up our anchor & proceeded on our voyage & at 4 o'clock Sunday morning we lost sight of Highland lights. At noon we were 810 miles from the Hole in the wall & 1150 from Havana. Monday the 30th we had light airs from N & calm. At noon we were 630 miles from the Hole in the wall.

Tuesday 31st we had strong gales from the north East & North with much rain. We scud before it under a single reefed foresail going 8 & 9 miles an hour. The night was very dark & stormy & the wind blew very hard, & the sea ran higher but we ran before it safe, although we were obliged to run off of our course to keep before the sea; for I must tell you that when the sea is mountains high, a vessel must be kept right before it, or it will break over her & sweep the decks & often it will break over the stern & deluge the decks. Many seas broke over us, while we were running before that fearful storm, but as we were light loaded, & high out of water, none done us any damage. Once we got considerable water into the cabin, by the door & windows being carelessly left open, but after that we were more careful to keep the doors & windows closed. April 1st the gale continued though with less fury & the rain squalls were not so frequent. We had crossed the Gulf Stream & the weather was warm. The rain ceased & the clouds broke away. When the captain called the cook in the morning he told him to take his tin pan & go forward & pick up the flying fish for breakfast. So Frank got up & built his fire. & took his tin pan and marched forward & hunted around. & came back & said he could not find any, & then he thought it was April fool day, & he had been badly fooled.

April 2nd the weather was fine & pleasant & by observation I found we were in the lat of 31°09′N & long 71°54′ W. 410 miles from the Hole in the wall & 750 from Havana.

From the 2nd to the 6th we had light head winds & calm weather so that we made but 30 miles towards our port. Tuesday the 7th day of April we had Strong breezes from East to S.E. and made 165 miles. At noon we were in the lat of 27°10′ & Long of 73°12′ & 225 miles from the Hole in the wall. Wednesday the 8, we had squalls of wind & rain with the wind all around the compass but we made 68 miles.

Thursday the 9th we had moderate breezes but a very bad sea running. We made 77 miles & were at noon, 80 miles from the Hole in the wall. & here perhaps I ought to tell you that a sea day commences 12 hours before the civil day. So that Sunday commences Saturday at noon & ends Sunday noon. When Monday begins the first 12 hours are marked P.M. & the last 12 A.M.

Friday the 10th sea account at 10 P.M. we made the Hole in the wall light & passed it about 2 o'clock in the morning: last voyage we passed it in the day time & saw the Hole in the wall. It is on the South east corner of the island of Abaco near the light. A narrow point of rocks makes off a little way & through there is a hole with an arch overhead large enough for a boat to pass through. The wind was light that day & we did not get over to the Stirrup Cay (pronounced Key) until after dark, a distance of 40 miles. The Stirrup Cay on which there is a light house is the western most of a group of small islands

called the Berry islands lying on the northern edge of the great Bahama Bank. There are 5 or 6 hundred people on them, all negroes except the light keeper. They belong to England & speak English.

When we were most over to the Cays we were boarded by two men (negroes) & a little boy about as large as you: his father called him Theophilus: they had some fish to sell, & we bought them & paid for them in flour & pork & had a nice supper & breakfast. They said it was good friday & the people were all to church. We gave them some papers to read & after they had spent an hour or more on board they rowed away for their island home.

The next day, April 12th, we were sailing over the Bahama Banks with light winds. The distance from the Stirrup Cays to the Southern Edge of the bank is 90 miles & we did not get over it until half past 3 Sunday morning. The water is from 15 to 24 feet deep the bottom is white sand & some parts of the way it is so clear that everything on the bottom can be distinctly seen while on other parts the water looks like milk. when we leave the bank the water deepens from 4 or 5 fathoms to no bottom in the vessels length. From the Great Bahama bank to the Salt Cay Bank the course is S.W. by S. 50 miles. We made the Dog Back on the N.W, part of it, at noon & were all the rest of the day until midnight getting by the bank, The Gulf Stream being against us. The salt Key Bank is not so large as the Great Bahama, but the water on it is deeper. All the next day, Monday, we had strong breezes from East & at 5 PM we made the Pan of Matanzas, a mountain 1260 feet high in cuba back of Matanzas. At 10 PM we made the light on the Moro Castle at Havana & at 2 next morning we hove too off the Moro to wait for sunrise as no vessels are allowed to go in or out between sunset & sunrise. At sunrise we hoisted the Stars and Stripes & Stood in, but the moment we shot in by the high point on which the moro castle stands the wind struck us ahead & would have blowed us out again had there not been a steam tug ready to take us in tow & we were soon anchored in the beautiful harbor of Havana. The entrance is very narrow. The port hand is bold [drops off steeply] & you can go within the vessels width of the rocks, while far above the masts heads is the Moro Castle & the lighthouse. The other side is shoal, but the moment you pass the moro point you are in smooth water. The harbor then opens out broad, & runs back several miles & is large enough to hold a thousand ships. The city of havana lies on the western side & on the Eastern side is a little town called Regla built on a point which projects into the harbor & divides it in to East & West Regla. We anchored at the west Regla & the next day a tug boat was sent & towed us into the Quay. There are no wharfs in Havana but one strait wharf or Quay in front of the city a mile long or more & to this the vessels of all nations are moored bows on & an anchor out astern. & all cargo is discharged over the bow on a stage.

We were squeezed in between a Bark & a brig. Each of the Captains had their wives & children. One had two little girls about as large as Lucy & looked as though they were both born in one year. The other had a boy as large as Sumner & a little tow headed girl as large as Lucy. The noise of the children reminds me of home. Havana is a large city. The streets are very narrow just room enough for two carriages to pass, & the side walks are just wide enough for one. There are no very handsome buildings, as there are in New York & Boston but some are quite large.

The governors Palace is quite large but not very handsome. it is only a short distance from the shore, & the garden in front of it called in Spanish Plaza de Arma, is oposite Cabanga's store. it is surrounded by a row of trees called the Royal india laurel. the branches & leaves are so thick that a dozen men might hide in the branches. in the center is a statue of King Ferdinand of Spain, for you know Cuba belongs to Spain. Every evening a band of music plays in the garden.

Elizabeth Port [N.J.] May 14th 1868

I have not had time to finish telling you about Havana now. We are loaded with coal for Yarmouth & shall be home in a few days.

You must fix up the fences what you can & be a good boy & help mother all you can. I got mothers letter yesterday.

I hope to be home in a few days
From your father

This next letter written to Nicholas two years later by Sumner is frustrating because of what it leaves unsaid. Lillian, Nicholas and Margaret's last child, was born three days after it was written. "Janie Snell," who was about Margaret's age, was no doubt helping in the household during his absence. She may even have been the midwife. "The Falls" where she went with Sumner is still a designation for lower Yarmouth village. The name comes from the first fall in the Royal River, an abrupt drop formed where the river's fresh water meets the salt of the sea. "Nicholas Bucknam" was a first cousin. "May" was Sumner's elder sister, Mary. "Maggie," named for their mother, Margaret, was three years younger than he.

Yarmouth Me lower village Post office small building with sign M.C. Merrills Drug Store & Cong. Church taken in early -80's

Dear Father   July 13 1870

I am glad answered the few lines that I wrote you the peice down in the feild has not got hardely any weeds in it only a few roman-worm wood and wee have got them bout all out We have got the peice in the little feild most hoed but it is petty weedy and it is petty hard hoeing for the ain't much soile the hens do not lay very well now the chickens are growing nicly they are all alive but one maggie killed that one with the hoe it was one of the little banties old Dorbin is as well as when you went but he is lazy as ever Janie snell and I went to the falls with him saturday afternoon I am going up & after the washwo in the morning and I shall carry this letter to the office I an afraid the straw berries will bee all

July 13 1870

Dear Father

I am glad [you] answered the few lines that I wrote you. The peice down in the field has not got hardly any weeds in it only a few roman-wormwood [ragweed] and wee have got them bout all out. We have got the peice in the little feild most hoed but it is petty weedy and it is petty hard hoeing for the[re] ain't much soil. The hens do not lay very well now the chickens are growing nicely. They are all alive but one maggie killed, that one with the hoe. It was one of the little banties. Old Dorbin is as well as when you went but he is lazy as ever. Janie snell and I went to the falls with him Saturday afternoon. I am going up & after the washwoman in the morning and I shall carry this letter to the office. I am afraid the strawberries will bee all gone before you get back. The blueberries are very plenty and mary had a blue bery pudding for diner yesterday. She says she is going to have another when you get home. One of the tomatoes is blowed and the rest is all budded. I have not got any chance out [to work] a haying though nicholas bucknam might want me afternoons. I hope we shall see you in a few days. I can't think of anything more to write so I will go to hoeing good by from sumner

From the tone of Sumner's letter we can assume that either Nicholas had returned from a deepwater voyage and had remained with his vessel for unloading or that he was coasting. A coaster, as distinguished from a ship that sailed the seven seas, carried cargo, port to port, along the Eastern seaboard with, now and then, a voyage to the West Indies. If Nicholas was, in fact, coasting, the family could easily anticipate his itinerary and send him letters to the ports on his schedule. The mail delivery between New York City and Yarmouth apparently took only one day.

It does seem likely that Nicholas did not reach home in time for his daughter's birth. Unfortunately, forty-year-old Margaret Drinkwater had tired of bearing children by the time her eighth arrived and Lillian apparently always felt somewhat rejected. In talking with her daughter, I learned that Lillian had enjoyed few privileges as the youngest of the family; at age six she was given a stool so that she could reach to wash dishes. She had much fonder memories of the time spent in the kitchen when she walked around the table hand in hand with her father while he memorized his part for Masonic rituals. Nicholas, and Sumner after him, were celebrated for their ability to perform Masonic ceremonies from memory. Lillian attributed her own love of language to these kitchen parades with Nicholas and later often entertained her own children with a fiery recitation of "The Charge of the Light Brigade."

May, two years older than Sumner, was an epileptic and suffered from seizures all her life. One physician, Dr. Thomas, attended her to his sorrow. Returning home from the call, his horse fell down, and when Dr. Thomas got out of his carriage, the horse got away from him. Since no one could find him, the doctor was forced to return home on a borrowed steed. His own horse and carriage were discovered later in an apple orchard, with only one shaft of the carriage broken.

The following letter is one that May wrote to their brother John. Possibly Sumner, at eleven, was old enough to replace John as the head of the family because Nicholas seems to have taken John to sea sometime this year. John, at fifteen, would have been aboard in the capacity of "boy." While he had such duties as making up the officers' berths, cleaning their quarters, and assisting the steward in any way he could, he was actually on the bottom rung of the ladder which led to being mate and captain. He was given such duty on deck as would prepare him for officer's station. Because the highest sails were the smallest, the ship's boy was sent aloft to furl them. This chore would quickly accustom him to moving about in the rigging. Possibly, his father Nicholas cautioned him the first time, "One hand for yourself and one for the ship. Keep your eyes on your job and don't look down."

The "grandmother" May mentions was their maternal grandmother, Lucy Gray, born on December 19, 1790. Several anecdotes are still told about this grandmother. She used to remark, "I've found that if I live through January, I'll live through the rest of the year." Although she was bedridden for years, she didn't remain idle and tried to ease her daughter's burden by sewing on buttons and mending tears in the children's clothes. One day when Sumner's brother John went in to see her, he suggested that she open up a window. Evidently she was "allergic" to the outdoors, for she answered, "If you don't like the air in here, Johnnie, you can run right out."

Although Lucy Gray never left her town of birth, legally she was born in North Yarmouth and died in Yarmouth (because of the division of the town in 1849). Lucy was a member of the congregation of the first church the town had built in 1729–1739, the Meeting House under the Ledge. When the center of the parish population shifted to the village of the "Falls," a new Congregational church was built. Lucy Gray was a member of a small group of loyal parishioners who refused to abandon the original church. This renegade group continued to worship at the old meeting house, calling itself the Chapel Church, until it finally dissolved in 1833. Its members united with other churches—Lucy left in 1831—and the meeting house was sold and destroyed in 1839. According to legend, its oak and yellow pine timbers were broken up and used to build three vessels, each of which met with a calamity.

"Bronswick" refers to Brunswick, a town about twenty miles north of Yarmouth. Bowdoin College, one of the nation's older colleges, which lists Nathaniel Hawthorne and Henry Wadsworth Longfellow among its alumni, is located there.

"Eunice" was the next to the last Drinkwater child, three years older than Lillian. She married a twin, William Oscar Doyle, and was considered an exceptionally good cook. Eunice treasured the memories of those days when her father came home from the sea. He would forewarn them of his arrival so that the children could take turns being "lookout." When at last he was spied coming along the road, the lookout signaled the others and they would all fly pell-mell down the lane to greet him.

Yarmouth Nov 23 1870

Dear Brother

I reiced your letter today & was glad to here of your arival and I expect to see you comeing home before long. When Summie went over to take care of the horse to night he asked about Jane but she had forgotten but his store is on federal street 146. That story you sent me about the gamblers daughter is continued in a saturday night no 6 vol 8 and i wish you could get it for me.

you wanted to know wether Carrie was going to school this winter she is not a going. She is going to recite [her lessons] to her mother and oncle alvin. They expect augustos home to thanksgiving.

Charles Tenley went to bronswick last friday and is going to spend thanksgiving. Hodd Winslow was down to meeting week ago friday night and spoke and i expect he will be down again. How is old John this cold weather does he go barefooted yet? i expect your cook will give you some thing extra for thanksgiving. i have been cooking all day and i got my chicking pie baked and that is all we are going to have except some minsepies.

Cad and Mrs royal are geting up some taberlose [tableaux] and i expect they will be next wensday night i expect to be in some of the plays.

i hope you will be able to go and see eddie longby as he wanted you to if you ever came there.

Eunice wants you to buy her a little picture boock and bring it home to her.

i can't think of anything more to write but Josh is seting here almost asleep and don't want to go to bed

from your Sister
MA D

Grandmother and the boys send there love
to you and father

Josh was the youngest of the three brothers as he was born fourteen months after Sumner. Even when they were very young, the Drinkwater boys were expected to take a great deal of responsibility for the family farm, especially when their father was at sea, but they apparently had enough energy to spare to play some dangerous jokes on each other. John forced Sumner to learn to swim one day when he toppled him off a dock into Casco Bay, but a prank Sumner pulled on Josh alienated him forever. According to family legend, when they were teen-agers Sumner fired a gun at Josh, wounding him in the arm and Josh never spoke to him again. Such memories aside, however, Josh is mentioned in Sumner's notes until apparently a permanent rift occurred after their mother's death in 1914.

Margaret had tried to forestall family disputes over the disposition of her household goods after her death. Having a set of eight chairs, she broke it up to give one to each of her eight children. To every grandchild she willed a glass goblet, an egg cup and a blue willowware dish. Although her intention was to keep her family happy, everyone was upset because no one had a complete set of anything. In addition, a dispute arose over the ownership of the family home and Josh was ousted. The house was sold off and destroyed. Sumner may have sided against Josh at this time. In any case, although their womenfolk remained civil, Josh's name rarely appeared in Sumner's diaries after that date and I am told that they both would "just as soon walk on the opposite sides of the street from each other."

Josh was a rugged individualist for the Drinkwater family. He had to be; he grew up to be a mailman. He alone of Nicholas' three sons disliked the sea and only ventured on it in a rowboat from time to time. Perhaps the farthest he ever traveled from Maine was to Chicago, when he went to the World's Fair on his honeymoon in 1894. His wife, Harriet Robie, was from Boston and the only "outsider" to marry into the Drinkwater family. She had been vacationing in Maine with two girl friends from her job as a clerk in J. Arthur Stowell's Jewelry Store in Boston when they met. In those years the Drinkwater family home was in the middle of a very celebrated resort area.

Josh was renowned for his wit. Unlike other brands of humor which have a long build-up to the punch line and are accompanied by a jab of the elbow—"Get it?," Maine wordplay is subtle and over quickly. The best jokes are the ones delivered, absolutely deadpan, in as few words as possible. Josh's audience might be in convulsions over what he'd said, but he'd remain sober as a judge. Of course, none of the Drinkwaters seemed to be slouches in this department. Josh's favorite sibling, Lucy, always "gave as good as she got."

Josh mentions their sister's suitor, "Woodbury" Dyer Hamilton, who lived across Casco Bay on Cousins Island, where he was brought up by a relative, Captain Lorenzo Hamilton. Woodbury and May got married in 1875 and were so devoted that the family feared for his sanity after she passed away in 1923 at the age of sixty-three.

The A. H. Lennox

Yarmouth Feb 5 1872

Dear Brother

You have been away quite a number of times and as I have never written to you I thought I would write to you this evening. I and Mother are a lone. Sumner has gone up to the Falls, and May is gone to ride with Woodbury. now I will tell you how I get along with my studies. I get along quite well with my arithmetic and most through my geography. We don't read but once a day. The teacher has got sharp eyes and quick ears   we can't throw many spit balls   she does not lick us but puts us under the desk when we do any mischief.

We haven't had much slideing this winter and we don't have much fun. The boys have had one or two parties on the island and May went with Woodbury. Charles Royal went to school the first half term and since has been hauling hay to Portland. I was glad to hear you had a pleasant voyage and were all well. Sumner is expecting Sarah Larribee every day. i can't think of any thing more to write. Grandmother and all the rest send their love to you. I want you to write to me if you have time.

From your Brother.
Joshua A G Drinkwater Esq.

Margaret Hannah Gray had married Nicholas Drinkwater in 1855. A spry little woman, she often said that hers had been a life of shirts. When Nicholas left for foreign voyages, he would take with him fifty-two white shirts, with fine pleats and ruffles. Thus supplied, he had one clean shirt for every Sunday service that he conducted on shipboard. She made the shirts by hand, stitching the tiny tucks with her needle. Nicholas' arrival home inevitably meant fifty-two shirts to wash, starch and iron before he left on the next long voyage.

Margaret's life lacked such modern conveniences as piped water. The Drinkwater homestead depended on a well close by the house until December 1903, and even after the town water was connected to the house, the pipes froze. In any event, Sumner's mother didn't care for the taste of plain water and drank primarily a diluted warm tea. She would save the tea leaves to sprinkle on her carpets before sweeping them in order to keep the dust down.

ALFREDA THURSTON

Hattie Josh and Josh outside Sumner's family homestead.

Women had little time to make social calls or to undertake community volunteer work. Each and every household task was hard as well as time-consuming. Water had to be lugged from the well, usually by the women. If hot water was needed, it had to be heated. Although wood stoves were an improvement over cooking in the fireplace, since food didn't get sprinkled by the ashes as much, it took a while to get a good fire burning in a wood stove. Most food was made from scratch and either grew in the garden or had been "put by" in preserve jars. Two staples in Maine are lobster and baked beans. Baked beans and brown bread were traditionally served every Saturday night. There was no set timetable on lobster; usually it was eaten as often as the supply allowed. Margaret even boiled fresh lobster and salted it down in a barrel. Though this sounds like a waste of good lobster, without refrigeration the family couldn't be particular.

Children's clothes were sewn by hand, and shoes were cherished. The same year that Nicholas held the highest political office in his community, his daughter Lillian walked to church with her shoes tucked under her arm. If she didn't carry them most of the way, not only would they be unpresentable for Sunday service, they'd wear out too fast. One woman I interviewed had been born in 1890. She remarked, "Didn't we work hard then in those days! I don't really know how we did it. Why, kings in those days couldn't live the way folks take for granted today."

Margaret's letter to her first-born could be any mother's letter to her child. Timeless and universal, except for certain phrases, it might have been written in this century.

Again, "Mary" is May's given name; "Nick" is Nicholas Bucknam, a first cousin.

By "improving" the sleighing, Margaret means that it is being packed down by the sleigh's runners. In those years, snow wasn't plowed but rolled down by a team of four to six horses pulling a roller. Everyone using the road after the roller came through "improved it." Even so, the wind might blow snowdrifts across the road, blocking it "in solid" and forcing the driver to take his chances in

an adjacent field. The town eventually started putting up snow fences, which alleviated this problem.

Yarmouth Feb 9th 1873

Dear Son Johnny,

As Joshy did not fill this sheet I thought I would write you a few lines so that you might know your Mother had not forgotten you. I was glad to hear you was well and I hope you will be this voyage. We have had a very cold winter but I hope we shall have it more moderate now. I expect your clothes are getting ragged and your stockings have neither heels or toes. But I shall get some knit for you and your father before you get back. but as you are going into warm weather you won't mind it so much.   though we all like to have whole clothes when we can. It is is a very pleasant day with us today and I expect you are having warm and pleasant weather now in New York and I am thinking you may be looking around N York today.   it is good sleighing with us now and everyone that has a team or can get one is improving it. We have considerable passing especially since <u>Mr. York</u> got home. He is down about every day to see Cad and Friday night he carried her to a dance. She was in yesterday she said she did not get home till two or three in the morning. She does not think so much of the Island boys this winter as she did last. Mary has gone up to Nick's to take care of the baby so they can go to meeting. She is going to the Sabbath School consert this evening. She will write to you tomorrow. The children write with me in love to you all.   from Your affectionate Mother.   M.D.

A letter from Sumner accompanied the packet going to John. However, while the two previous letters were sent to his brother, Sumner wrote to his father. The contrast between Josh's and Sumner's description of school is striking. Even without the salutation, it is obvious which letter is meant for a brother's eyes, and which for a father's.

Sumner and his siblings attended a one-room school across the lane from their home. It was a shingled building with few windows and was well suited for its later use as a shed. A few of the family descendants initially thought a photograph taken by the Drinkwaters of the Doyles' bunkhouse was one of this District #5 schoolhouse. Except for the door placement and the much larger windows, the two buildings were similar to each other. School was only open from December through February, when the pupils weren't needed by their families to work on the farms. Sumner recalled school as being cold but pleasant. He enjoyed his studies but body temperature depended on proximity to the stove. Girls often received more education than boys, who couldn't be spared from the family work as easily.

Apparently a distant relative of Sumner's, one of the Bucknam girls, died in school a few years after he stopped his schooling. The child hadn't felt well in the morning before she left for school, but had gone anyway. When the teacher sent the class out for recess, her head was down on her desk; she'd died that morning without a word.

The town of Yarmouth abandoned the little schoolhouse across from the Drinkwater homestead before the turn of the century, and Nicholas and Josh brought it across the lane and attached it to their home to use as a shed. This wandering school was finally burned on a neighboring property around 1950.

Sumner was thirteen when he wrote the following letter to his father. In it he refers to the area of Yarmouth in which they lived overlooking Casco Bay as the "foreside." This term is all but forgotten in Yarmouth, although Falmouth, a town to the south of Yarmouth, still calls its shoreline by that name. Several neighbors are mentioned: "Charles Royal," "Alvin and JD Cleaves." Sumner later sailed under Captain J. D. Cleaves. Perez G. Drinkwater was a member of another branch of the Drinkwaters. I puzzled over Sumner's mention of a "bridge" to Cousins Island because there wasn't one at that time. Then I realized that he was referring to the ice bridge that used to form between the Yarmouth Foreside and Cousins Island each winter until sometime in the 1930s, when the weather was no longer cold enough. Often people who grew hay on Cousins Island harvested it and left it there until the ice bridge formed, permitting them to bring the crop across with horses. That method was a great deal easier than shipping by boat across to the mainland. In 1955, at the time it installed a hydroelectric plant on the island, Central Maine Power built a bridge, which has provided a more reliable connection to the mainland.

Yarmouth Feb 9th 1872

Dear Father

As I have never writen to you before this Voyage I thought I now would take the opportunity to write to you. As there is not much to write I will tell you how I get along with my studdies. I have begun to studdy History this winter and have got along quite well with it.

The Doyles' camp on Cousins Island. Eunice, Sumner's sister, sits next to the door. Her husband, Will, is at the far left.

And have got along quite well with my Grammer. I have got so I can tell a Verb from a Noun or wether a verb is transitive or intransitive. school is done next week and I am sory for I have got quite interested in my Grammer & History. I have got over to percentage in my arithmetic & have got along quite well in my Geography. Nicholas Bucknam has carried 7 loads of hay in to Portland for you & I have helped him load them & have helped him load 6 loads of his own hay & helped PG Drinkwater load 2. Charles royal has hauled in a number of loads & Alvin & JD Cleaves are hauling hay & that is about all that

is going on here on the foreside. There is a nice bridge on to the island & there is considerable going back & forth. Josh & I have been so exceedingly smart that we have not got those bricks over to the barn yet but are going to after school is done. Josh & I have managed to saw grandmothers wood & as mother burns coal it does not take much for her. We got most of the alders up. Woodbury is over quite often. I can't think of any thing more to write. Please write soon from your son.

SPD

Marian, Eunice's daughter, sits on a stool. Will Doyle is behind her. Others not identified.

The letters from Sumner's childhood gain interest when compared with the ones he wrote Alice at the age of forty. Sumner had received something between a fourth- and eighth-grade education by the time he was twenty, but he compensated for this handicap by becoming a voracious reader. Both he and his brother John could recite poetry and long passages from Plato and the Bible from memory.

Perhaps his lack of formal education added to the freedom of his language, because his later writings are lyrical in expression with delightful flashes of sexuality and humor. He's inconsistent in his spelling: some words, correct at times, are incorrect at others. Except when his spelling interferes with the sense of his sentences, I have left it undisturbed and confined my corrections to punctuating his sentences or inserting a forgotten word. He wrote the old-style contraction, a raised letter rather than an apostrophe. I have substituted apostrophes. Also, I have retained one idiosyncrasy that initially confounded me. Sumner used *& co.* in place of *etc.*

At the onset, I had no idea of the beauty and power of Sumner's letters. They interested me primarily because of their historical context. I was amazed to discover in this sea captain so sensitive though unlettered a writer.

Sumner sent his father the following letter at age sixteen, and already his advancing maturity and even literary proficiency can be noted in this letter over the previous ones.

Yarmouth Aug 1st 1875

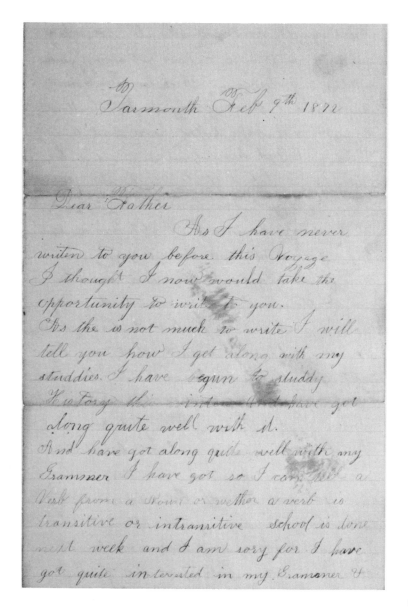

Dear Father

I thought I would write to you to knight to let you know that we are all well & hope that these few lines will find you in as good health as we are, it is know about nine oclock & they are begining to disperse so I thought I would write know so that mother [could] write & she don't want [to] write till we all get to bed.

John & myself are to work for Mr. Royal & we shal finish next week if we have good weather & I hope we shal for I have had about haying enough for one season though we have not had any more days than usual but the re has been so much stormy weather that we have got along rather slow but Mr Moccy [the harvester] has gone through ours awful quick. He was only 7 days cutting & getting in both fields. He began a week ago yesterday morning on yours & finished geting in Grandmothers last nigt about nine oclock. He got the whole of Grandmothers yesterday & he got in 14 loads between ten oclock in the forenoon & nine in the evening. Mr. Soule has got done & Nicholas has only got one more mornings mowing & he will be done but most everybody is late about haying this year except those who had the courage to smash write through without minding the weather. There is considerable more hay on yours this year than there was last & I beleive Mr Moccy thinks there is about 11 tons. Our planting peice looks first rate & is rather beating Mr. Soules. The corn has begun to spindle & the most of the beans have poded & there is pumpkins & squashes as large as an egg & the turnips & peas are doing well & allso the potatoes over there are as large as an egg.

I got the saddle boards down from the scaffold carried them round into the shed & hauld a load of sand & put down front of the door for the horse to go out on, & hauld over those bean pods & planks from the barn & laid the plank where you told me to. One thing I haven't done yet & that is to fix the fence but the old horse has never got out yet. But I shal fix it after haying. I haven't seen uncle william since

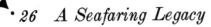

Yarmouth Aug 1ᵗʰ 1875

Dear Father

I thought I would write to you to knight to let you know that we are all well & hope that these few lines will find in as good health as we are, It is know about nine oclock & they are begining to disperse so I thought I would write know so that mother write & she dont want write till we all get to bed.

John & myself are to work for Mr Royd & we shal finish next week if we have good weather & I hope we shal for I have had about haying enough for one season though we have not had any more days than usual but the has been so much stormy weather

you went away so I haven't told him to sell the old horse if he can but the old horse has got quite alot of fat on him.

There was a house burnt down on Chebeague [Island] this afternoon on the hill right over Capt Lorenzo's house [Woodbury's home on Cousins Island] from here & we could see it real plain with a spyglass & could see the men around it & we could see them put wet quilts on the barn or what we soposed to be quilts & they saved the barn. But we don't know where it caught but thought it must have caught somewhere near the roof as it seemed to burst out there first.

As I have been writing little over a hour & cannot think of anything more to write I will bid you good & retire

From your affectionate son

S.P. Drinkwater

P.S. I wish you could get some segars to bring home if you could get them cheap but I don't know as you can get them any cheaper there than here.

S.P.D.

This letter was possibly the last Sumner sent his father before he ran off to sea himself. No Drinkwater could ignore the dangers inherent in following the sea; the family burial plot was a grim reminder. Adam Gray, Sumner's cousin, fell to his death from aloft at the age of seventeen. Sumner's grandfather, Nicholas Drinkwater, was only fifty-three when he died off the Highlands of Neversink returning from Santo Domingo. Seven years later, in 1854, Sumner's father's twenty-two-year-old brother John was mate of the ship *Moses Taylor* when he was murdered in the English Channel by "a Spanish mulatto" on the passage from Le Havre to New Orleans. Only his name reached the family graveyard in Yarmouth; he lies buried in Plymouth, England. Sumner's brother John, born the year following this family tragedy, was named for Nicholas' brother.

Now, in 1875, John had already been at sea for five years. Sumner could wait no longer. At the age of sixteen he began his

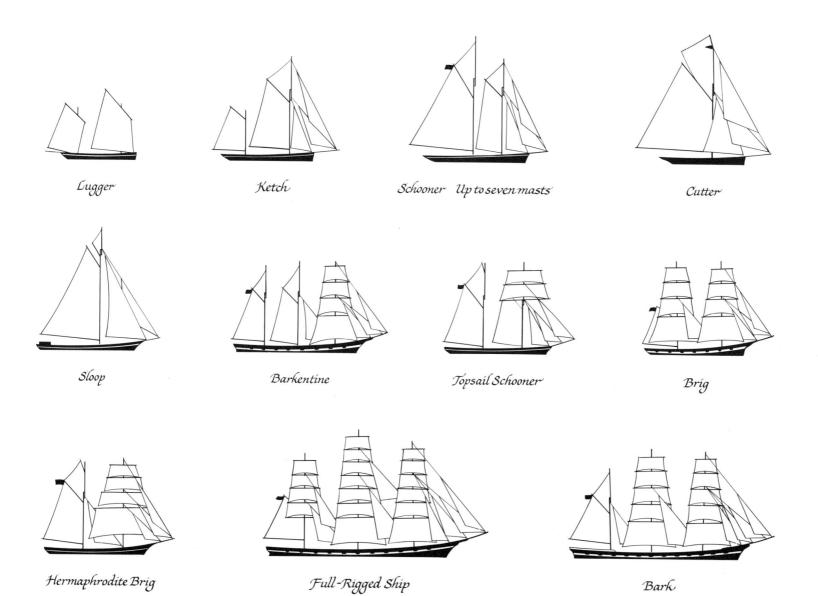

Lugger

Ketch

Schooner Up to seven masts

Cutter

Sloop

Barkentine

Topsail Schooner

Brig

Hermaphrodite Brig

Full-Rigged Ship

Bark

career as a ship's boy, earning $15 a month under a Yarmouth skipper, Captain Darius Collins. His diary noted that his first voyage was to Philadelphia, omitting the name of the vessel. However, since he shipped again two years later with the same captain on the *Ruth H. Baker,* presumably that was the schooner on which he made his maiden voyage.

His first passage could not have been a great surprise to his family. He smoked "segars"; he was a man. The *Ruth H. Baker* was a 371-ton schooner built in Yarmouth in 1863. If he was on her with a Yarmouth skipper for a month's passage, he wasn't far from home.

Captain Collins was about eleven years younger than Sumner's father, Nicholas. He would retire after fifty years at sea having "never lost a man," although when he was a young sailor, he himself had had a narrow escape. The sea washed him overboard somewhere near the bow of the ship, but luckily, his captain, who was standing aft, was observant. While Darius Collins struggled, the ship passed by him and he heard the captain shout, "Watch out for a coil of rope!" The rope was well aimed and struck him square on the head, nearly ending the tale. But somehow the lad managed to tie it around himself and he was towed back aboard, half dead. Thus, Darius Collins survived to become Sumner's first captain. He had a reputation for being a God-fearing man. Since Sumner shipped on with him again, the Drinkwater family must have given their approval. There is no record that Sumner ever sailed under his father, as his brother John obviously had.

The year before Sumner wrote that last childhood letter to his father was the high-water mark for Yarmouth shipbuilders. Within the short space of an eighth of a mile, along the present sleepy harbor of Yarmouth, eight vessels stood in the stocks at the same time. Twelve ships in all were built that year. In 1875 the first ship to be fitted with iron masts made in New England was the *Admiral,* launched in Yarmouth in June 1875. At 2,209 tons, she was the largest ship ever launched from Yarmouth and she cost $150,000 to build. When she was wrecked twenty months after launching, the Yarmouth community was stunned.

The square-riggers built at that time in Yarmouth were large wooden ships and barks, now termed down-easters. About 70 percent of them were built in Maine.

The clipper ship, which preceded the down-easter, had only lasted about thirteen years because this vessel was designed for speed, not cargo. Although the clipper could sail faster than any steamboat at that time, she depended on wind and current. A steamboat could of course progress continuously in a straight line, and it soon became obvious that continuing to develop sail for speed was futile. In addition, much of the capital that had formerly been invested in shipping was at the end of the Civil War shifted inland to railways, factories and real estate.

Maine had no share in these new enterprises and continued to pursue wooden shipbuilding in order to maintain her economy and keep her skilled craftsmen at work. The down-easter, built to the profile of the clipper but with increased cargo capacity, handiness and lower operating costs is now considered by some sailing historians to be the highest development of the wooden sailing ship. These vessels could not compete with steam, but they were launched for long voyage, bulky carrying, which would prove them profitable in their lifetime. The down-easter extended the life of America's deep-water sail for a quarter of a century.

THE SEA AND ALICE
1878-1897

"In marriage we bear & forbear."

By the end of my interviews with family descendants and others who remembered the Drinkwaters, I had failed to add any statistics to my limited knowledge of Alice in her childhood and youthful maturity. Of necessity, I had to talk to people who were close to or over eighty. Even so, they had been youngsters when Alice was at the end of her life and their insights were not those of her peers. Furthermore, Victorian attitudes had censored their parents' conversation; "little pitchers have big ears." I loved watching the Drinkwaters' stern granite features relax and twinkle at me as I ransacked their memories for family detail. Everyone was eager to help but I had to figure out which questions were the triggers and learn to wait patiently for the answers. It was a slow, gradual process because the facts I wanted were buried under years of disuse and had

to be approached obliquely. Little by little, bits and pieces emerged to lend substance to the names in Sumner's journals. And how those names were loved after all this time.

But Alice remained elusive. She was described as an austere and composed personality who had commanded deep affection and respect. My heroine would have emerged with no more definition than a Victorian lady with false teeth and her hair in curlers every morning, except for one detail: everyone interviewed agreed that she had had brown *snapping* eyes. Fortunately, Sumner's record of Alice began prior to their courtship and presents a contemporary's view of her personality.

It was in 1878, when Alice was turning seventeen and Sumner a month from twenty, that they first took notice of each other—as far as we know. This entry is from Sumner's *Earnings and Expenses Book* in which he kept his accounts from the age of fifteen through nineteen (1874–1878).

Sunday Dec 8 1878
got Kicked by Cousin Alice G. Drinkwater
The effects of which will remain in my system for many a day
amen & bullfrog
signed & sealed By
S. P. Drinkwater
Yarmouth
Maine

Alice as a teen-ager.

Besides becoming sweethearts, Alice Gray Drinkwater and Sumner Pierce Drinkwater were related, but as they were cousins many times removed, there was no impediment to the match. Their common ancestral link went back five or six generations, over 125 years, to two sons born to Joseph Drinkwater and his wife, Jane Latham.

Joseph Drinkwater, whose father Thomas had emigrated from England, came to North Yarmouth from Taunton, Massachusetts in the fall of 1731. There he met and married Jane Latham. The couple

DEARBORN STUDIOS

BY THE NAME OF DRINKWATER.

settled on Cousins Island where they farmed and reared eleven children. Geneologists take special note of this union because Joseph was one of the first Drinkwaters born in America; thereafter the family line is descended from him.

Of Joseph and Jane's two daughters and nine sons, seven sons were sea captains—all of whom sailed into Boston harbor in their separate ships on the same day. When the port authorities heard that so many vessels commanded by men of the same name had arrived in Boston, the officer-in-command feared trouble and went to investigate. He was so relieved to discover the men to be brothers and their arrival to be coincidental that he gave a dinner in their honor.

Alice was the great-granddaughter of Joseph Drinkwater Jr., the eldest of that family, while Sumner was a descendant of the second son, John, who married Susanna Brown on March 4, 1761, having first left her standing at the altar. When some of the scandalized guests had proposed going to look for the absent groom, the bride said, "No, if he will not come of his own free will, he need not come at all." John presented his apologies the next day: while loading his vessel at nearby Chebeague Island, he had decided that he would stand by and finish rather than risk losing the run to Boston. Some other day would do just as well to get married.

Another story about this great-great-grandfather of Sumner's occurred during the Revolution. It appears in Nicholas Drinkwater's contribution to *Old Times in North Yarmouth, Maine.* John Drinkwater, with his elder sons as crew, was returning to Casco Bay from one of his voyages to the westward when he was spied and chased by a small British armed vessel (called a "pinque" because of her narrowed, or "pinqued," stern). When this vessel fired a gun for him to heave to, he ignored it as well as subsequent shots, and sending his boys below, kept on his course. His pursuer, much the faster sailor, approached him on his weather quarter thinking he would be an easy prize. However, just as they were in the act of boarding, Captain Drinkwater suddenly put his helm hard up and gibed over his mainsail so that his heavy main boom, driven by a strong breeze, struck his enemy's masts and left her a wreck. He kept on.

	JOSEPH DRINKWATER (1709–1784)	m.	**JANET LATHAM** (c. 1715–1794)	
Mary Leach (1739–1805)	m. Joseph Drinkwater, Jr. (1736–1822)		John Drinkwater (1738–1827)	m. Susanna Brown (1743–1819)
			John Drinkwater, Jr. (1764–1812)	m. Pamela Gray (–1816)
Mary Gardiner Mason (widow)	m. Allan Drinkwater (1768–1851)		Nicholas Drinkwater (1794–1847)	m. Mary White (1794–1853)
Sarah E. Staples (1830–1915)	m. Watson Gray Drinkwater (1830–1902)		Nicholas Drinkwater (1825–1908)	m. Margaret Hannah Gray (1830–1914)
	Alice Gray Drinkwater (1861–1915)	m.	Sumner Pierce Drinkwater (1859–1942)	

Cousins Island, where Joseph and Jane Drinkwater raised their family, is no more than a mile as the crow flies from Alice's and Sumner's birthplaces on the mainland. For well over a century, to Sumner's time, the Drinkwater descendants had not shifted their boundaries by very much nor had they changed their traditional preoccupation: most were mariners.

Alice's father, Watson Gray Drinkwater, was an exception. Although his father and grandfather had followed the sea, he did so for a very short time, enlisting in the United States Navy during the Civil War. His real vocation was farming and he was at home for most of his daughter's life. Alice Gray, his second child, was born on December 28, 1861; his first, Harriet, had preceded her on January 22, 1859; and John Allen, nicknamed Jack, was born on February 3, 1866. All three children trudged up Gilman Street to the Ledge schoolhouse. Harriet went on to become a stenographer, while Jack chose to be a carpenter. Only Alice would follow the sea—by marrying Sumner.

From Sumner's diaries of 1879– 1880 it is apparent that before he fell in love with Alice he courted Harriet, nicknamed Hattie. His romances developed gradually; he seems shy and a bit diffident with girls, although the octogenarians I interviewed seemed convinced that he had been quite a gay blade in his time.

His 1879 diary, apparently the first he ever kept, cost Sumner forty cents. The first few notations concern his return from Massachusetts on the coasting schooner *Essex,* skippered by J. D. Cleaves, his neighbor on the Foreside. Sumner was probably working as a foremast hand in this period, having outgrown the status of ship's boy. As he commented this year on being allowed to steer a course for the fifteen miles between Cape Elizabeth, Maine, and Cape Porpoise, it is likely that he was not yet rated an able-bodied seaman but as ordinary. An A.B. was expected to be proficient in steering a compass course, making a wide variety of knots and splices, and going aloft in rough weather to take in and furl sails—to "hand, reef & steer," as it was put.

Alice Gray Drinkwater, age three.

When the *Essex* arrived off the Foreside on January 8 at three-thirty, Sumner relaxed at home before going uptown for a shave and a haircut in preparation for school the next day. His schoolmarm, Mrs. Gurney, was definitely casual about his attendance during this term, which was to be his last. School had been in session for a month already, while Sumner was away at sea. Even so, he was permitted to leave class occasionally during morning recess to go into Portland

MALCOLM DRINKWATER

FAMILY REGISTER.

ALLEN DRINKWATER AND HANNAH GRAY WERE MARRIED JULY 13, 1790.		ALLEN DRINKWATER AND MARY MASON WERE MARRIED OCT. 17, 1826.

NAMES.	BIRTHS.	MARRIAGES.	DEATHS.
LUCY	Dec. 19, 1790	Dec. 28, 1812	Dec 30 1884
THEOPHILUS	Oct. 28, 1792	Jan. 29, 1822	Dec 15 1872
DEBORAH	Sept. 10, 1794	Jan. 27, 1818	Aug 21 1878
MARY GRAY	July 10, 1796	Feb. 29, 1820	Jan 4 1892
HANNAH	Aug. 28, 1798		Oct 6 1881
WATSON GRAY	Nov. 20, 1800	June 1, 1824	July 26, 1827
JOSEPH	Nov. 14, 1802	Sept. 21, 1826	June 21 1867
CHARLOTTE	Aug. 14, 1805		Jan. 22, 1807
HARRIET	Sept. 22, 1807	Nov 28 1841	Aug 14 1880
ALLEN	July 16, 1809	Sept 10 1840	Lost at sea 1848
MARTHA ANN	Oct. 27, 1811	June 4, 1833	Feb 22 1887
CHARLOTTE	Nov. 2, 1815		Aug. 17, 1818
WATSON GRAY	Feb. 7, 1830	Nov 19 1857	July 2 1902

with his friends. Possibly such truancy on the part of twenty-year-old scholars was a matter of course.

No grades were given in those years, and students had to take a qualifying examination to enter high school directly from grammar school. Perhaps Sumner was not able to pass the high school examination due to his haphazard schooling; perhaps he was not able to give over the time. Attending his one-room school at the age of twenty was no doubt Sumner's choice; many of his schoolmates had dropped out years before. When a week's recess was called after he had been home only two weeks, he seemed disappointed. But he probably had an ulterior motive for spending one of his recess days at the Ledge school in the next district where his cousins Hattie, age twenty, and Alice, age seventeen, were enrolled.

The following entries from Sumner's diary, written on a subsequent occasion, are in his handwriting and then in Alice's and then in Hattie's.

Thursday, February 27, 1879

[Sumner]   snowed during the night but Pleasant in the morning wind westerly
             at school [district] 2 such a giggling time, such giggling Girls I never saw.

[Alice]   [you] sat with Hattie of course and buzzed her like everything as a matter of fact.

[Hattie]   he did not set with me all the time and he buzzed Alice all the time.

[signed] Telegraph Poles

Placed in conjunction, the words "sailors" and "port" immediately conjure up a macho image—rowdy behavior and faithless, footloose men. Sumner's diaries record no such behavior. As far as I can tell, while in port he attended churches of various Protestant denominations, museums and plays, went sightseeing, called on relatives and family friends, saw a circus and often stayed on board ship to play euchre, a popular card game of the period. Perhaps, like his brother John, he spent a good deal of time in port browsing through secondhand book stores. Only once, in Salem, Massachusetts, did he mention a girl:

Thursday, July 3, 1879   Nice day though quite warm
         Sat a fly at the topmast head
         Went up town in the eve. Run acrost a young dame
         by the name of Cara Van. Went & had an ice cream & took
         a stroll. Turned in at midnight.

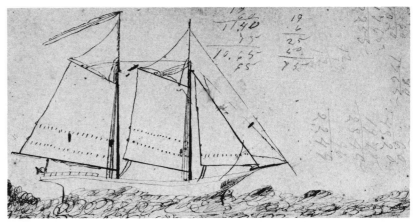

A sketch by Sumner on flyleaf of his diary.

Sumner seemed reticent with strangers. Most of his sweethearts were girls that he had grown up with back in Yarmouth. He noted in his diary that one of these, a coquette named Mamie, rebuffed him when he offered to see her home, so he turned to his cousin Hattie and left with her. Miffed, Mamie attempted to revive his interest in her. On July 30 he acquiesced to the point of walking "home with

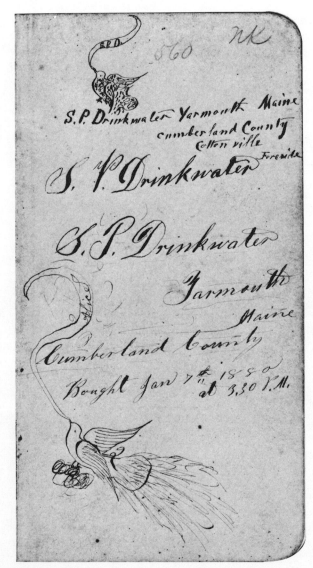

Flyleaf 1880 diary.

Mamie by her request" but it is clear from his subsequent entries that he had become more interested in Hattie. He devoted all his attentions to Hattie for the next six months.

Although Sumner's diaries outline his year's schedule, they are most uninformative about his attitudes. He either avoided confiding his feelings with such notes as "was much hurt by an occurrence today," "rather unpleasant news in regard to Family Affairs," "got a talking too" or worse yet, said nothing at all. Clearly, Hattie did not encourage his affection for she left Yarmouth for Upton, Massachusetts, on January 23, 1880, to learn to take shorthand. There must have been some unpleasantness between them at the time she left because when she wrote him five months before his wedding to Alice in 1882, he observed: "I guess she had concluded to like me a little better." Harriet Drinkwater never married. It might have proven complicated had she married Sumner, since both his brothers

DEARBORN STUDIOS

Universalist Chapel.

John and Josh married Harriets. The family eliminated some confusion by calling one wife Hattie John, and the other Hattie Josh. Had she married Sumner, Harriet Drinkwater undoubtedly would have been nicknamed Hattie Sum.

Sumner never loved any woman the way he loved Alice. His diary notations during their courtship, which began a month after her sister's departure, were the only ones that show such strong feelings, such extreme swings from joy to pain. None of the subtle wording of his later letters to her is apparent in the diary entries that recount their courtship.

Sumner did not bother to list Alice's other suitors. However, she had among her possessions a small golden thimble which had been given to her by Willard Baldwin Royal, one of Sumner's best friends and presumably a sweetheart of Alice's.

Throughout their courtship, they walked. He saw her home after prayer meeting, they dallied in the cemetery, and they spent long evening hours polishing the lamps in the Ledge schoolhouse. "Ha!"—his writing. During his nine months of courting Alice he shipped out twice on the schooner *Essex* and twice on the *Maggie Ellen,* constructed a weir to catch smelts and voted in his first election, on Tuesday, November 2, 1880. He observed on the momentous occasion:

> Election day dawns in beauty . . . an omen of good will. May it be such to this great nation. . . . It seems as though other than Justice & wisdom cannot rule the affairs of the universe. Will it rule the affairs of the nation? Time will tell.
> Down to the weir at 4 A.M. about 60 lbs [smelts]. Carried them to the depot & shipped them to Wallace & Kenney. Carried C. H. Palmer to the depot. Went up to the town house & voted my first party ticket for Gen. Hancock.

Sumner observed on the following day: "Election favors Garfield."

When Alice terminated their relationship three weeks later, on November 25, Sumner was devastated. His anguished diary entries clearly show how shallow his affection had been for Hattie. Sumner did not elaborate on the situation beyond noting that Alice thought the "end of their intercourse inevitable." At this point in their relationship he signed on the schooner *Elva E. Pettengill* under Captain J. York for $18 a month. He was sitting in Portland harbor aboard ship when his brother John married Harriet Frances Hamilton on December 20.

Sumner could not have been altogether unhappy about missing John's wedding; he was so forlorn at that time. The following poem, which appeared in the memoranda section of his diary that year, was evidently written on that voyage.

> When we are old we'll smile & say
> We had no care in Childhoods day
> But we'll be wrong; twill not be true
> I've this much care; I care for you.
>
> May flowerets of love
> Around thee be twined
> And the sunshine of peace
> Shed its joys o'er thy mind
> Like sweet music pealing
> Far o'er the blue sea
> Oft comes o'er me stealing
> Sweet memories of thee
> May your progress in lifes busy road
> Bring blessing in daily increase
> At its Close may your felings in fulness abound
> With harmony gladness & peace
>
> When counting o'er thy many joys
> Recalled by memory
> If twill not dim thy pleasure then
> Oh give one thought to me.

Casco Bay from the Ledge, Yarmouth, c. 1890.

Sumner became ill when they reached New York, and the captain discharged him and sent him back home. His condition apparently worsened on the arduous trip. He had to travel by train to Boston and then by steamboat to Portland. Coming out to Yarmouth by train, he got off at Cumberland station and nearly died crossing the ice over Broad Cove to the Foreside. He was so ill that Alice became concerned about him. She came for a short visit at his parents' home as he was convalescing which had a remarkable effect on his recovery. By February 28, 1881, they had reached a firm understanding.

The facsimile below is easier to read in the original because of the different-color inks the lovers used. On this date Sumner left his

diary with Alice on the condition that she could read it if she would also make entries. To further confuse future readers, this page contains an entry from the following year—1882. As a painter might paint over an old canvas, when Sumner found himself at sea and unable to buy a new diary at the turn of the year, he would simply write in any available space in the old one. The 1882 entry was made when he was returning from Cuba on the schooner *Canton* under Captain Henley.

Monday February 28, 1881

[Sumner]   Rainstorm   wind Easterly   held up in the afternoon but thick
Up to the villiage in the eve
No prayer metting [meeting] "to bad" [because he couldn't see Alice home afterward]

Wednesday February 1, 1882

this day begins with fresh gales N.W.
noon moderating & clearing off
4 P.M. made sail   set fore & main sail & spanker flying jib
Wind hauling westerly

Tuesday, March 1

[Alice]   Rainstorm part of the day. Sumner happened up (I knew he would.) staid to tea   went home early in the morn —evening. All the folks gone to N.Y. the happiest eve of my life thus far.   hope it was not very unpleasant to him.   A.G.D.

[Sumner]   Its memory will ever linger & brighten many a lonely hour

Wednesday, March 2, 1881

[Alice] I promised you I would write in this for the privilege of reading it. But I dont know what to write unless I tell you (Provided you let no one see it) what I am thinking of this lonesome rainy day. I cant imagine how I am ever going to get through the next 6 months which to me will seem years. without seeing you once not even Just once. but if it should be for ever what should I do. Alice

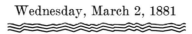

Thursday 3

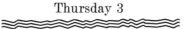

Snowed and Rained all day

Went up to Hattie Bucknam's to a party in the evening. Had a verry nice time. but the best of all was in the Parlor. for me at least.

[Sumner] by far S

[Alice] I never expect to have the headache again Alice [Alice suffered from severe headaches throughout her life.]

[Sumner] If I could only know you never would how happy twould make me

Friday, March 4, 1881

[Alice] Snow and Rain continued

I do hope it wont storm the rest of the winter. But it may for all the good it will do me. for I shan't want to go any where again until next Fall. Unless the Schr Ida should come back to Boston as I realy hope it will, and bring back the Angel it carries out.

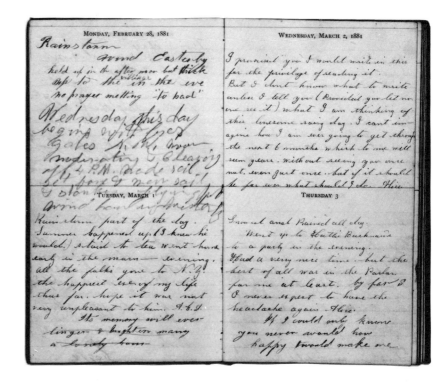

Saturday 5

Evening.

I have staid at home all day and made A "Shaving companion" for [you] but didnt make a pretty one because I dont exactly know how but hope you will like it and think enough of it to use it. hope I shall see you to morrow and [give] you this. for I cant seem to write anything "nice" as you told me to. Alice.

Alice's entry on March 4 seems to be anticipating how she will feel once Sumner ships aboard the schooner *Ida.* In fact, he did not leave on a voyage to carry granite down to Washington until April 7, and then it was on the *Manitou* under Captain Hamilton. His wages were increasing, as were his responsibilities. He earned $20 on this voyage and after returning for six days in July he shipped out almost immediately as mate of the schooner *Watchful* under Captain Gill. On their return from Norfolk, Virginia, Sumner was allowed a short leave while the schooner was anchored at Saco, south of Yarmouth. He used the time to buy Alice a gold ring which cost $5. The *Watchful* had finished discharging its cargo, but it was unable to get under way because of poor weather. While they were confined to port, the captain arranged that he and Sumner would take two local girls out in a sailboat. Sumner guiltily confided to his diary: "What would my darling say? But Heaven knows I would not be untrue to her. No My Own NEVER."

During the coaster's next run south, Sumner left the *Watchful* in Washington. On September 13 he took the train to Philadelphia, where he joined the crew of *Melissa Trask,* under Captain Trask, taking coal to Portsmouth, New Hampshire. He was heading home.

Remember me.

Though the nation was mourning President Garfield's assassination and burial on September 26, Sumner, reunited with Alice the next day, was ecstatic: "Passed the evening with my darling & need I say how happily."

He spent three months at home, then went to sea for the next eight. He made three trips to Cuba on the schooner *Canton,* with only ten days in Yarmouth during those eight months. That home leave came at the end of February after the *Canton*'s first voyage. His next passage from Cuba brought him to Baltimore, too far from Maine to see Alice. However, while he was in Baltimore, on May 5, 1882, she surprised him with a box of Mayflowers, "and such nice ones, smell just as fresh as can be. You knew darling how much I would prize them." Unfortunately, three days after Alice's box of posies arrived, his "Capt while passing the Hatch where they were loading . . . was knocked in to the hold & badly hurt though no bones are broken." A week later Captain Henley, still in great pain, was replaced by Captain Hamilton and the *Canton* got under way for Cardenas, Cuba. Sumner left the *Canton* at New York City after this third voyage. It was now mid-July. He had only one month at home before he left on the schooner *Fred Jackson* for Matanzas, Cuba. By then he was earning $40 a month as mate which would enable him to support a wife.

Sumner returned to Yarmouth in October and—obviously too busy—did not record anything for the remainder of that year. But according to family records, Sumner and Alice were married on November 21, 1882, almost four years after she had kicked him. Alas —nothing else is known about the wedding: not the name of the minister, the type of service nor whether the wedding was performed in Alice's home or at their minister's parsonage. For the next twenty years Sumner and Alice Drinkwater lived in her family's home, in their own apartment on the second floor. It cost them from $2 to $5 a month to rent.

In Sumner's diary of 1882, on the back pages intended for "Bills Receivable/Payable," there is an interesting entry about hand-tinting photographs written in an unfamiliar hand. Sumner and Alice would not purchase a camera for another fifteen years.

Alice's homestead.

Manzers, System of Photo painting

Put Photo in hot water to remove from card and dry.

Oil both sides of picture and let remain until picture is clear and transparant. Then wipe off oil CLEAN.

Paste face of picture smoothly to glass again. Dry.

Oil back of picture on it. Let remain until all white spots on back of picture disappear.

Again wipe off oil and paint on the back of the picture itself, everything except Hair, flesh, and light colored dresses which must be painted on last glass.

Materials Used
 Tube paints
 Eng. or Chinese
 Vermillion
 White
 Burnt Umber
 Emerald Green
 Permanent Blue
 Chrome Yellow No 2
 A N° 3 Sable pencil
 Convex Glass
 Starch for paste
 Castor-oil

Balt N° 5 North Charles
Philᵃ 63 Orch

Straw = White & Yellow
Lenore = same only more yellow
Brown = Burnt Umber & White and tint with red or yellow
Purple= Red White & blue

Flesh = Is a very light pink
Wine = Red, & blue
Light Green = Green & Yellow

From the time of his marriage until 1885 Sumner, practicing Yankee frugality, bought no new diary books but, instead, added bits and pieces of 1883 and 1884 to his diary for 1882. And in contrast to his industry prior to his wedding, he only made three voyages in 1883, two on the schooner *Odell* under Captain Winslow and one on his old friend the *Essex.* For half of the year he did odd jobs for the neighbors in Yarmouth while remaining home close to his bride.

Sumner and Alice entered Yarmouth's young married set. Socially as well as in religious matters, the churches were pivotal in the town's life. The Drinkwaters worshiped primarily at the Universalist Chapel and the First Parish Congregational Church, but they were "nondenominational" in their attendance at debates, picnics, concerts, plays, church suppers and lectures. The topics of these lectures included "Persian Customs and Habits," "Talk by A Survivor of the Jeannette Expedition," "Temperance," "Roman Catholism" and "The Imprisonment and Suffering of a Soldier." Sumner and Alice

"Attend your church" the Parson cries,
To Church each fair one goes;
The old go there to close there eyes,
The young to eye their clothes.

also attended the "pound parties," which were popular at that time, where guests would bring a pound of cornmeal, flour, sugar, etc., to the party. Quite often these events were given for the benefit of the parish minister.

Between them, Sumner and Alice seemed to be related to a large percentage of the Yarmouth population. Accordingly, a lot of their time was taken up by "social calls," although they spent most of their time with their immediate families. They didn't need to make much of an effort to visit Alice's family, as they lived with them. However, Alice's sister was rarely at home. She was working in an office in Boston and only came down East on her vacation. Hattie and Sumner had become reconciled after his marriage to Alice, and when she came home, Hattie was always included in the young couple's activities. As the handwriting of one diary entry showed, Alice enjoyed teasing him about his renewed friendship with her sister.

Wednesday, October 6, 1886

[Sumner]   Went to walk with Hattie in the eve.
[Alice]   Went in to the schoolhouse (<u>oh my</u>).

Sumner seemed to get along well with his in-laws, and she with hers. Sumner, with or without Alice, often walked down to the Foreside to visit his family. There seemed to be frequent opportunities for family get-togethers, and in just one month May and Woodbury threw two parties, entertaining sixty people at each. As Sumner's siblings married, the Drinkwaters became so numerous that when the family held a picnic, they took over the beach. Although Sumner's brother John did not attend the picnic photographed, his absence could not have been by choice. John was slim and wiry but throughout his life he had an immense appetite. After a huge Sunday dinner John would take his napkin and brush the crumbs off his vest and his close-trimmed beard, and then invariably lean back in his chair and say, "We Americans eat too much." In his later years John was bedridden; that is to say, he would go to bed after Christmas dinner and not get up again until it was time for Thanksgiving. Sumner observed in his diary, following a visit with John when they were both in their eighties: "Still eats the same."

Sumner received his master's license in 1883 and was presumably waiting for his own first command. In 1884, however, he sailed as first mate under his brother John's command, on the schooner *Grace Cushing.* The first mate was the ship's executive officer. The captain's position as the ship got under way was on the quarterdeck, or poop; the mate stood on the forecastle head. It was he who relayed the captain's orders to those lower in the chain of command and the crew. Sumner might be John's brother, but aboard ship and in front of the men, as well as in his diary, he would refer to John as "Captain." However, the crew of a coasting vessel was made up of friends and neighbors, and a general feeling of bonhomie existed on board. This was in sharp contrast to the atmosphere under deepwater command. There, the shipowners preferred cheap labor and exploited foreigners and incompetents. As a result, discipline had to be rigorously enforced and the "hell" ships were born. Officers were rarely punished for such misconduct as sending men aloft while they were too sick to hold on or beating sailors for minor infractions of discipline. However, deepwater sailors signed Articles (i.e., contracts) making them subject to their captain for the duration of the voyage. Coasting crews had no such contracts. Although Sumner would one day be a deepwater man, he would never run a "hell" ship.

In order to serve as first mate, for John or for any captain, Sumner would have had to be able to use a sextant, although supplementing the instrument, some mariners acquired an uncanny feel for their ship's position. Both the first and second mate had to possess sound judgment and the moral and physical courage from which leadership derives. A crisis didn't always leave time for these officers to place the situation in the captain's hands.

According to Sumner's diary, after the winter thaw of 1885 he helped John break the *Grace Cushing* out of the ice and sailed on her as first mate bound for New York on April 6. During the return voyage a crisis developed. The two brothers and their schooner were off Nantucket when the fog shut in thick. Faced with a rising gale

Standing: Lucy Drinkwater Bucknam, Woodbury Hamilton, Sumner Drink-water, Phebe Bucknam, Ethel Hamilton. Bucknam children: Muriel, How-ard, Eldon.

Seated, left to right: Allie Bucknam, Perez Bucknam, Everett Bucknam, George Bucknam, James Monroe Bucknam, Margaret Drinkwater Collie, Nicholas Drinkwater, Margaret Drinkwater, Mary Drinkwater Hamilton, Julia Longley, Hattie Josh Robie Drinkwater, Joshua Drinkwater, Alfred Drinkwater, Alice Drinkwater, Charles Lolley, (unknown), Carrie Miller.

and enclosed by land, they tried to anchor, but the anchors failed to hold the *Grace Cushing.* Since weighing anchor was a backbreaking job that took hours, in an emergency the crew would sometimes "slip" the anchor chain—that is, unshackle it, first attaching a buoy to the chain cable so it could be recovered later. In this case both chains broke and the anchors were lost before that could be accomplished. They attempted to get the vessel clear of the enclosing land, steering to pass a nearby point with a lighthouse on it but couldn't "fetch it," so, changing direction by "wearing ship," they tried to keep her off the shore on the other tack. Despite their best efforts, the storm pushed the vessel inexorably toward Nantucket. When it became evident that the ship could not avoid going ashore, they picked a spot that looked least threatening and drove the schooner onto the beach. This tactic, used on the sandy beach of Nantucket, succeeded in saving the ship as it could not have on the rocky coast of Maine. The account of the adventure as it was noted in Sumner's diary follows. Unlike his letters, which are often quite dramatic, his diaries—even in these extreme circumstances—are spare, and for those unfamiliar with nautical terms, seem to be written in another tongue.

Wednesday, April 29, 1885 This day comes in rainy with South winds strong
  4 am wind canting to west & clearing up a little
  8 am got underway [at Vineyard Haven] with fleet. Wind moderate all the forenoon, passed cross rip [light ship] at 1 pm. foggy. wind changing to northard & kept increasing all the afternoon & shut in thick worked to North Shore at
  6.30 let go both anchors, blowing a gale & tremendous sea running
  7 pm parted both chains. Lost whole of starboard chain. Got Jib & Piece of mainsail on her & run for cross rip. Made it bearing W.N.W. couldn't fetch it. Wore ship

& run for Great Point Light & made it about midnight bearing E. By S. Wore ship trying to keep off shore. Lost ground

& Thursday morning [April 30]
  1 am wore for the beach struck at 1.30 am. Vessel went quite easy but leaking some. Kept pumps going.
  4 am Life saving crew aboard

The wrecking crew arrived well supplied with anchors and other salvage gear. During the morning they set the anchors well off the beach and attached lines from the vessel to them, hoping that on the rising tide she could be refloated.

  forenoon crew came aboard & planted anchors off from 9 to 12 leaking 3000 strokes an hour on low water kept her free.

The vessel would not budge without the removal of some of her cargo. John's responsibility did not stop with his ship and crew, he had to safeguard her cargo until the underwriters arrived to supervise its removal.

Friday, May 1, 1885 Comes in with breeze from N.W., shifting to W.S.W. light & later shifting to Eastward.
  5 am Underwriters crew aboard. Went to lightering cargo and shoveling overboard.
  high water Hove on vessel but couldn't [move her] staid.
  pm Continued lightering vessel. Lightered about 20 tons & throwing overboard all they couldn't get on lighters [barges].
  pm wind E.N.E. rainy Day ends rainy. Wind Easterly.
  midnight hove hawser taunt. Kept vessel pumped.

This attempt to bring the vessel off proved successful. They might have borrowed an anchor from the wrecking crew. (A "fathom" is six feet.)

Saturday, May 2, 1885 Rainy, wind Easterly
    Soon after midnight, came off all right & made sail.
    2 am Wind canting to north & blowing up fresh & thick. Couldn't beat out. Went under Great Point Light & anchored with 50 fathoms Cable. Blowed a gale about North which lasted until noon when it moderated. Day ending calm & clearing weather.

The next day the *Grace Cushing* returned to Vineyard Haven and the wrecker's crew departed, leaving their bill for $700. Subsequent inspection indicated that the *Grace Cushing* had suffered no substantial damage, and that she was leaking only from the general strain of the grounding. The Drinkwaters purchased an anchor and 75 fathoms of chain in Vineyard Haven before proceeding to Portland, where they were able to purchase another anchor. By one-thirty in the afternoon on May 12, John and Sumner had anchored at the Foreside and come ashore. Although the voyage from New York had taken more time then anticipated, the brothers were unscathed and just in time for their sister Lucy's wedding two days later.

But they were very late by Alice's reckoning. She would have learned from the newspapers of the *Grace Cushing*'s beaching two weeks earlier and must have worried constantly since then. His diary doesn't detail their discussion, but when Sumner slept aboard the *Grace Cushing* at Walker's Coal Dock in Yarmouth the next night, Alice joined him, and when the schooner started on her next voyage, Alice and Hattie John were on board.

While women were a taboo according to early shipboard superstition, captain's wives routinely traveled on the down-easters, raising their families on board ship and entertaining in port. En-

couraging a captain to take his family on a voyage made good business sense to ship owners. A man living in domesticity would take better care of their property, operate it more efficiently and be less likely to take a hotel room ashore, leaving his responsibilities to the mate. Vessels carrying the captain's family were sometimes dubbed "hen frigates—particularly if the wife was a "take-charge" type. So many Yankee women chose to follow the sea with their men that the State of Maine passed a milestone education law that paid these women a teacher's wage if they taught their children at sea. Wives were on occasion on the Articles as "steward." In the pantry aft, the captain's wife might prepare and serve her husband's meals. She might supervise the galley, ordering and issuing the stores to the cook, but she would not fulfill the steward's other responsibilities of cleaning up after serving meals to the lower officers. Once in a great while a mate's wife might sign on as steward, but she would be expected to carry out all of the steward's duties. Alice probably sailed as a guest, however, since she was the sister-in-law of the captain.

Alice chose an exciting year to begin sailing with Sumner. Everyone on board ships moving in and out of New York harbor was beguiled by a statue known as Liberty Enlightening the World which had arrived from France in June of 1885. Construction of the pedestal started in late June and finished in April the next year, when construction of the statue itself began. The Statue of Liberty was dedicated at a ceremony on October 28, 1886.

After four voyages, however, Alice stayed home to prepare for the winter holidays. Their last run that year on the *Grace Cushing* was short and the brothers returned in two weeks, on November 30, 1885. Sumner immediately made an appointment to have a tooth extracted, the common remedy in those days for toothache.

He was fortunate to be living in Yarmouth at the end rather than at the beginning of the nineteenth century. In the earlier part of that century a dentist's instrument was fastened on the offending tooth and rotated first to the right, then to the left, then to the back, then to the front. If the tooth had not been broken in this process, it would have been successfully torn out. The dentist customarily cut around the tooth before securing the instrument, and on at least one

New York harbor, c. 1890.

occasion, when a knife was not available, the dentist substituted his thumbnail.

Sumner records being home for twenty days in December while he helped Alice tack the comforter she was making for him. Then, right before Christmas, he shipped aboard the schooner *Melaka,* under Captain Cattrell. The ship was bound for Norfolk in ballast and thence to load red-oak barrel staves and culls, pieces of low-grade lumber, for Barbados. The cargo went south where it was used to make hogsheads (casks). Rum, coffee and molasses were picked up and returned from these Barbados runs. Sumner hired on as second mate, who, though the lowest rank of the regularly certified officers,

EUNICE DE SANCHEZ

Eunice Drinkwater.

still lived in the afterhouse with a stateroom of his own. The second mate climbed aloft to work the sails, and he ate in the second sitting because he was standing the watch while the captain and the first mate were at table.

One of the advantages of the West Indies voyages was that contraband cargoes were plentiful. In addition to the cedar timber, mahogany, sugar and molasses that the *Melaka* brought back from Nuevitas, Cuba, her second mate noted in his diary that he smuggled in seven hundred cigars, which he sold in New York only hours before the customs officers searched through his things.

After stopping by to see John on the *Grace Cushing,* Sumner left New York and reached Yarmouth and Alice on May 26, 1886. The two of them promptly went out to buy a dress for Alice and a chamber set—a china bowl, pitcher, soap dish, hot-water pitcher, toothbrush holder, chamber pot and slop jar. Sumner "whitewashed over" their bedroom to set off the new chamber set.

Three weeks later, on June 18, they both left on the *Grace Cushing.* At the end of the year the coasting vessel was caught by the coal strike on her last voyage to New York that season. The schooner remained in New York while Sumner waited the strike out in Yarmouth. Hearing from John that the strike was over, the coal cargo loaded and the *Grace Cushing* preparing to get under way, Sumner returned to New York City on March 10 1887. His next voyage on the schooner was his last because W. S. Jordan, John's employer, offered him the command of a "sister" ship of the *Grace Cushing.*

On May 28, 1887, Captain Sumner Pierce Drinkwater bought a share in his new vessel, the schooner *Bramhall.* He was twenty-eight years old and the last in his line. Alice Gray Drinkwater was twenty-five. Their first trip on the *Bramhall* took them to Philadelphia, where he proudly gave his sister Eunice a tour of his vessel. Eunice had been "living in" with a Philadelphian family since 1886. She stayed with them for three years, only returning home shortly before her marriage to Oscar William Doyle.

Alice traveled with Sumner for eighteen and a half of the thirty-one voyages he would make in his schooner over the next five years.

(Her half trip occurred when, upon reaching New York, they received word that the sister of a member of their crew had died and Alice accompanied the sailor home.) Sumner was always much happier with her along.

Often Sumner and Alice would arrive in New York before John and his family had departed. Then John and Hattie John would come to spend the day and evening on the *Bramhall,* or Sumner and Alice would call aboard the *Grace Cushing.* On those occasions when the two brothers didn't have their womenfolk with them, John would usually stay aboard the *Bramhall* overnight.

The Drinkwater brothers would sometimes invite members of their families or friends to travel aboard their ships as guests. John delighted his kid sister Lillian when he took her to see the Statue of Liberty being assembled in New York harbor. Alice invited her girlhood friend Hattie Poole to come to New York with them on the *Bramhall.* Sumner's diary references to Hattie Poole are amusing because he progressed from writing about "Miss Poole" at the onset of the voyage to "Hattie" by the time they had reached New York. As the *Bramhall* was docked to discharge cargo at Yonkers, New York, on the Hudson River, the Drinkwaters and Hattie attended a Baptist church for Sunday worship and witnessed a baptism by immersion.

John rearranged his schooner's deck space to accommodate his son, Alfred, born in 1881, and his daughter, Edith, born in 1883. He rigged up a swing for them which skimmed low over the water. One summer day, when they lay at anchor, Edith was pumping away vigorously while John swam near the vessel. She giggled as he began teasing her whenever she swung over him. Suddenly he surged out of the water and tugged her off the swing and into the water with him. Edith learned to swim that day as abruptly as Sumner had years before.

Unfortunately, John lost command of the *Grace Cushing* when she was sold from under him on July 30, 1888. He could not find a new berth, and three months later signed on the *Bramhall* as Sumner's mate. Eventually his old employer, W. S. Jordan, made him captain of the *David Torey.*

Four of Sumner's five sisters, c. 1886: Lucy, Maggie, May and Lillian (seated).

WILLIAM S. RENT

Hattie John and John.

John and Hattie John had been very happy in the marriage that had, at the onset, scandalized at least one of Hattie John's relatives. "A Universalist and a Democrat?" the startled woman had said upon hearing that John Drinkwater was Hattie's prospective groom. Although John didn't wear his faith on his sleeve, he was very devout and often said that if he hadn't become a sea captain, he would have enjoyed being a Universalist minister.

He seems to have had a marvelous way of phrasing things. One evening after baby-sitting a crying infant, he greeted the dismayed parents on their return with the observation, "She opened her mouth so wide, she didn't have any face left." At one time his wife, Sumner and Alice pressed him to join their singing group which met informally at the members' homes. He resisted them, saying, "I'd sooner hear it thunder."

Hattie John is remembered as humorous and merry, always ready to make candy, cookies or popcorn for small fry. She made children feel as though she were a child herself, in spite of her serious health problems. On June 19, 1890, her left arm was amputated just above the elbow, and although she seemed to be doing well initially, she took an abrupt turn for the worse. John hurriedly left the *David Torey* in New York City, "Captain Munsie of Portland having come on to take her home." But Hattie John rallied and lived. She never seemed to others to be hampered by her handicap; however, when photographed, she always positioned herself so that her missing forearm would not show.

These were truly the days of Maine under sail, although there were already signs that the days of the down-easters were numbered. Yarmouth built its last vessel in 1890, and the *Aryan,* the last wooden down-easter built in the United States, was launched from Phippsburg, Maine, in 1893. However, Sumner and Alice could still travel in the company of fifty other vessels and know most of their captains. Even as they sailed with the fleet there would be vessels coming the other way to greet, among them, the *David Torey,* and the *Mattie B. Russell,* Captain Darius Collins' last command before retirement. Sumner must have been proud to greet his own first sailing master as an equal. It is possible that Captain Collins recommended Sumner succeed him because Sumner became captain of the *Mattie B. Russell* sometime during the 1890s.

It was in these years that Sumner joined the Knights of Phythias and the Order of Red Men, as well as his father's beloved Masonic lodge, Casco Lodge. The Order of Red Men was a patriotic organization which traced its origin to the rebels who disguised themselves as Indians for the "Boston Tea Party." This group was noted for its relief work among the widows and orphans of the town. Westcustogo Lodge, Knights of Pythias, was formed in Yarmouth on November 28, 1882, a week following Sumner and Alice's wedding. He joined the group, which adhered to principles of friendship, charity and benevolence, three years later.

Throughout their marriage Sumner and Alice held markedly different views on money. Sumner believed it should be spent. In 1888 Alice acquiesced to the purchase of a White sewing machine, and on January 25, 1889, they bought a pair of canaries. They were still without children after six years of marriage. Precisely one year later Alice and Sumner decided to add a horse to the household. They purchased a bay mare—$75, sleigh—$30, harness—$8, robe—$8, whip—$1, street and stable blankets—$4, for a total of $126. Not two weeks later, Sumner noted that the sleighing was "nearly all gone, bought a buckboard wagon—$42.50."

On Saturday, January 9, 1892, Sumner entered one of their canaries in a poultry show. It turned out to be a good investment because "Dick" won "5 lbs candy by Crombs Bros." Sumner took John's children, Alfred and Edith, to the "Biddy Show."

Winter is usually a time to stay tucked away indoors in Maine, but Sumner and Alice were among the many sidewalk superintendents to gather on Gilman Street on February 2 that same year. The old Ledge schoolhouse, which Alice had attended as a child and which held many romantic memories for them both, was being moved. A modern school had been built nearby on Prince's Point Road by Sumner's brother-in-law Will Doyle, and the old building had been left idle for some time.

Tuesday, February 2, 1892   Wind nearly calm all day   P.M. clouding up
11 A.M.   Went to hauling of the old School house District No 2, a Building some 150 years old. Hauled up under the old ledge at the top of the old meeting house hill where it was built, or near by. Day ends with Snow.

Politically, Sumner's beloved Grover Cleveland was very much in the public eye during this period. Sumner's diary recorded:

Wednesday, March 4, 1885
GROVER CLEAVELAND INAUGURATED
HURRAH FOR CLEAVELAND

Sumner and Alice.

The x to the far right shows where the old Ledge schoolhouse stood when Alice attended. The house and barn on the right were built in 1730.

Cleveland and Harrison entered a certain city on the same train the other evening. The Democratic and Republican politicians concluded that it would be a good opportunity to hear the two statesmen on the issues of the day. Arrangements were made to have them address the same meeting. The hall was crowded to suffocation, two-thirds of the audience being ladies. Harrison spoke first and said— As you are well aware my worthy opponent and I have mutually agreed that nothing personal should be uttered, but when I look at that glorious emblem (pointing to the American flag) my thoughts revert to the time of its peril. While I and my gallant comrades stood on the field of battle, where was my opponent? At home! When our martyred President called for troops, what did my opponent, Mr. Cleveland, do? He chopped off three fingers of his right hand to escape the draft, ladies and fellow citizens. Get up and show your hand you son of a bitch. Mr. Cleveland advanced to the front of the platform and stated that it was true that he amputated his fingers and that he remained home during the war. But, said he, I had a widow, Maria Halpin, and a child to take care of, and I appeal to your sympathy as to the righteousness of that deed. But was my opponent a patriot? Ask the war records. Where was he, ladies and gentlemen, while grape and cannister were tearing through the breasts of souls who knew no fear. I will tell you. He was strapped to a caisson wagon, with the letter "D" for desertion branded on his arse; get up and show your arse, you son of a bitch.

Sumner's loyalty to Cleveland and the Democrats is all the more interesting because the Republican presidential candidate in that election was James Gillespie Blaine of Maine. During the bitter campaign much had been made of Blaine's admitted paternity of an illegitimate child and his unconvincing denial of government graft in the "Mulligan letters" scandal. However, it was the loss of the New York Roman Catholic vote that cost Blaine the election. Grover Cleveland did not fare as well against his next opponent, Benjamin Harrison, and he was ousted from the White House—much to Sumner's disgust—but in 1892 he was again elected President.

The Panic of 1893 was the worst depression of the nineteenth century. There had been a steady decline in farm prices and a rash of strikes, which accounted for Sumner's glum notations: "No freight offering." The primary factors contributing to the depression were the overexpansion of the railroads and American business. By 1894, thousands of businesses had folded and four million people were out of work.

Long before the Panic of 1893, Sumner's diaries reflected the trouble the country was in. He was caught unaware when, in 1892, the shipping commission house of F. H. Smith & Co. went bankrupt. He was able to recover only half of the sum owed him—$52.68. As early as August 1891 he had written the owner of the *Bramhall*, W. S. Jordan, that he was considering selling his share in the schooner. Jordan only convinced him to continue by guaranteeing him $40 a month. By this time Sumner owned one eighth of the vessel, yet his dividend of $90 in 1889 had dropped to $50 in 1890. The drop was understandable; he had spent long frustrating intervals idling in port because there were so few cargoes available.

In addition, Sumner felt the *Bramhall* was in grave need of repair, but W. S. Jordan did not agree. Sumner didn't mention that she leaked, because that was the schooner's normal condition. Pumping was a regular part of the day's work on a wooden vessel and the hard, monotonous duty was performed routinely during the dogwatches, or if she was leaking more than usual, at the end of each four-hour watch. Indeed, the notation "leaking more than usual"

appeared frequently throughout his years of commanding her. Her collision with a steamer in 1890 had not improved her situation.

Monday, May 5, 1890

      9.30 a.m. fog lifting. Took Tow by Tug <u>Charles Runyon</u> through [Hell's] Gate
               Cast the Tow off Govenor's Island at 1 P.M.
               Made sail. Wind about S.W.

      2 P.M. off Staten Island was run down by Steamer <u>Helvetia</u>
               Had just tacked Ship to Southerd
               Was struck on starboard bow and dismasted.
               Decks ripped open. Forecastle stove [in]. Both rails broken. Starboard anchor taken from bow & forward bow stove in on starboard side. Employed steam tug <u>C. R. Stone</u> to Tow vessel to Pollions dock South Brooklyn. Telegraphed W. S. Jordan & Co. Stood watch during night.

The *Helvetia* had clearly been in the wrong, but the steamship company paid only $850 in damages, even though the repairs on the *Bramhall* came to slightly more than that. Evidently the steamship company never considered that the captain's "mental anguish" deserved remuneration.

The Drinkwaters' last voyage on the *Bramhall* at the end of May 1892 was notable. Alice and Sumner rode a gale in steamer time from Norfolk, Virginia, to Providence, Rhode Island. It was a nice way to say "goodbye." On June 21, back in Portland, Sumner noted: "Business dull, no freights offering. Concluded either to sell or repair vessel." Three days later when W. S. Jordan brought a Captain Gilchrist of Rockland, Maine, aboard "estimating cost of repairs & co.," Sumner tried to effect a sale with the newcomer. Then, on June 28, Sumner left the *Bramhall,* sending his things out to Yarmouth with his brother Josh. Sumner's first command had lasted five years.

Except for sailing the yacht *Tempus* down to New York City in October of 1892, Sumner did not go to sea for the rest of the year.

His records during 1893–1896—if, indeed, he kept any—did not survive, except for a six-week period from October 1 through November 12, 1895. At this period he was again in command of a coasting vessel near Bar Harbor, Maine, but he never identified her. However, when he resumed his diaries only sixteen months later, in 1897, he was just leaving the brigantine *Mattie B. Russell.* Therefore, she may have been the unidentified coaster of 1895.

In the fall of 1895 Sumner's brother John bought into the barkentine *John J. Marsh.* Captain John Drinkwater was to be the barkentine's last master: she sank 150 miles off the Highlands of

Schr. John J. Marsh of Portland, Me.   J.G. Drinkwater, Master.

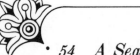

Neversink on April 4, 1896. John and his seven-man crew narrowly escaped with their lives.

It is curious that Nicholas' first-born son had such a close call with death in the very area on the Eastern seaboard where Nicholas' father had succumbed to sickness almost fifty years before. The ship's loss was explained as having been caused by a sudden leak. However, the *John J. Marsh* may have been plagued by a perpetual leakage problem comparable to that experienced by the *Bramhall.*

Shipowners walked a tightrope on vessel maintenance in order not to cut their profit margins. Thus, that "sudden" leak may have been one previously ignored by the managing owner which unexpectedly worsened in the storm.

In later years, John was often asked why he and his crew hadn't tried to make shore 150 miles distant. "Shore?" he'd say reflectively. "You don't go anywhere in the kind of sea we had that day. You're lucky if you stay afloat."

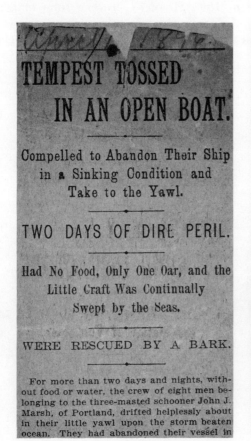

TEMPEST TOSSED IN AN OPEN BOAT.

Compelled to Abandon Their Ship in a Sinking Condition and Take to the Yawl.

TWO DAYS OF DIRE PERIL.

Had No Food, Only One Oar, and the Little Craft Was Continually Swept by the Seas.

WERE RESCUED BY A BARK.

For more than two days and nights, without food or water, the crew of eight men belonging to the three-masted schooner John J. Marsh, of Portland, drifted helplessly about in their little yawl upon the storm beaten ocean. They had abandoned their vessel in a sinking condition on April 5, and when picked up two days later by the Italian bark Africa were in an exhausted and half famished state.

They were landed safely in this port yesterday, but penniless and with only the scant clothing which they wore left of all their earthly possessions.

At the Sailors' Home I saw some of the unfortunate crew, and Able Seaman McDonald told me the story of their hardships.

The John J. Marsh, commanded by Captain Drinkwater, sailed from this port on April 3, bound for Jeremie, Hayti, with a cargo consisting of 39,000 bricks and 10,000 feet of lumber.

The Sandy Hook lightship had not disappeared below the horizon, when a strong northwest gale set in. All that day she scudded in the fierce storm, and as night was approaching it was discovered that she had sprung a dangerous leak. All hands were set to work at the pumps, but could not keep back the rapid influx of water. Shortly after dawn on Saturday morning nine feet of water was reported in the hold.

IN DIRE STRAITS.

The little yawl, the only small boat on the schooner, after being provisioned for several days, was with great difficulty launched in the heavy seas which were then breaking over the vessel. As the men were working their way over the rail into the small boat, those who were the first in were endeavoring to keep the little craft clear of the laboring schooner to prevent its being dashed to pieces. Then it was that a serious mishap befell them. All their oars save one were broken in pieces and the boat could only be propelled by sculling.

All hands got into the yawl safely, but as they shoved away from the deserted vessel a huge wave broke over them, nearly capsizing the boat and half filling it with water. Then, to their horror, they found that almost the worst had befallen them. The little stock of provisions and the remnants of the broken oars had been washed overboard.

Only three cans of butter were left in the bottom of the boat. Then began the desperate struggle for life. The little shell was put off before the wind, and was driven further away from land in a southeasterly direction.

They kept her scudding all night long, with the terrific seas breaking over them continuously, and the sufferers were drenched to the skin and chilled to the bone.

THE STEAMER PASSED THEM.

The red and green lights of a steamer were sighted dead ahead shortly before daylight on Saturday morning. The port and starboard lights showed alternately, denoting the approaching vessel was bearing almost directly toward them. As the steamer approached the occupants of the yawl, the dread that she might run them down gave way to the fear that she would miss them entirely. That was just what did happen. The steamer passed near enough to have heard their cries for help, but, although the despairing men yelled themselves hoarse in the vain effort to attract attention, and Captain Drinkwater fired his pistol, which he had brought from the schooner, those on the deck of the passing steamer were apparently oblivious of the proximity of the wave-tossed little craft, for they kept the steamer on her course.

During daylight on Sunday the previous day's battle with the elements was repeated. As darkness set in the wind moderated, but the weather became bitterly cold. The men kept themselves warm and alive bailing out the boat, while they stood knee deep in water, with every wave which struck the boat at short intervals dashing over them. To their intense joy, the white sails of the Africa were sighted about nine o'clock Sunday morning, dead ahead and bearing down on them. They were observed by those on the sailing vessel, and shortly afterward were safe in the snug little cabin, where a thawing out process was soon in operation.

Captain Cacace, of the Africa, did everything in his power to make the shipwrecked mariners comfortable, and they were loud in their praises of his hospitality while they were his involuntary passengers.

The John J. Marsh was built at Newburyport, Mass., in 1873, and was of 390 tons register.

The Grace Deering Years
1897-1901

"China is closer to Maine than St. Louis."

CALLIGRAPHY BY ANITA KARL

WOODEN BARK

GRACE DEERING

Daniel Brewer, Builder
Cape Elizabeth, Me.
1877

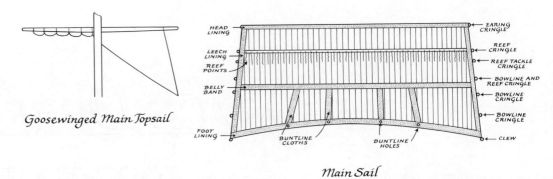

Goosewinged Main Topsail

HEAD LINING
EARING CRINGLE
LEECH LINING
REEF CRINGLE
REEF POINTS
REEF TACKLE CRINGLE
BOWLINE AND REEF CRINGLE
BELLY BAND
BOWLINE CRINGLE
BOWLINE CRINGLE
FOOT LINING
BUNTLINE CLOTHS
BUNTLINE HOLES
CLEW

Main Sail

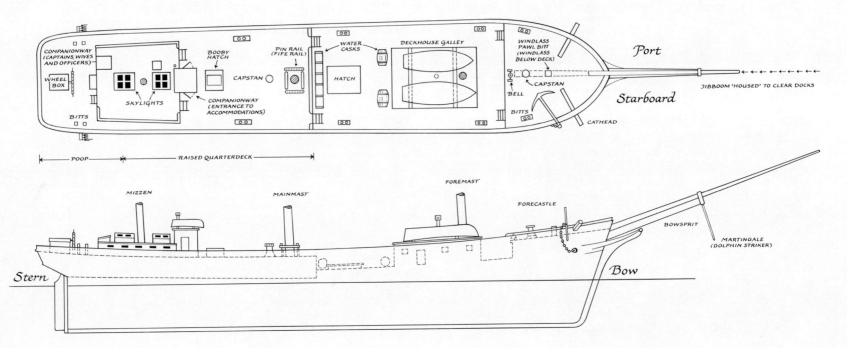

COMPANIONWAY (CAPTAINS WIVES AND OFFICERS)
BOOBY HATCH
PIN RAIL (FIFE RAIL)
WATER CASKS
DECKHOUSE GALLEY
WINDLASS PAWL BITT (WINDLASS BELOW DECK)
Port
WHEEL BOX
CAPSTAN
HATCH
CAPSTAN
Starboard
SKYLIGHTS
COMPANIONWAY (ENTRANCE TO ACCOMMODATIONS)
BELL
JIBBOOM 'HOUSED' TO CLEAR DOCKS
BITTS
BITTS
CATHEAD

— POOP —   — RAISED QUARTERDECK —

MIZZEN   MAINMAST   FOREMAST   FORECASTLE   BOWSPRIT   MARTINGALE (DOLPHIN STRIKER)

Stern   *Bow*

DRAWINGS BY ROGER CAMPBELL

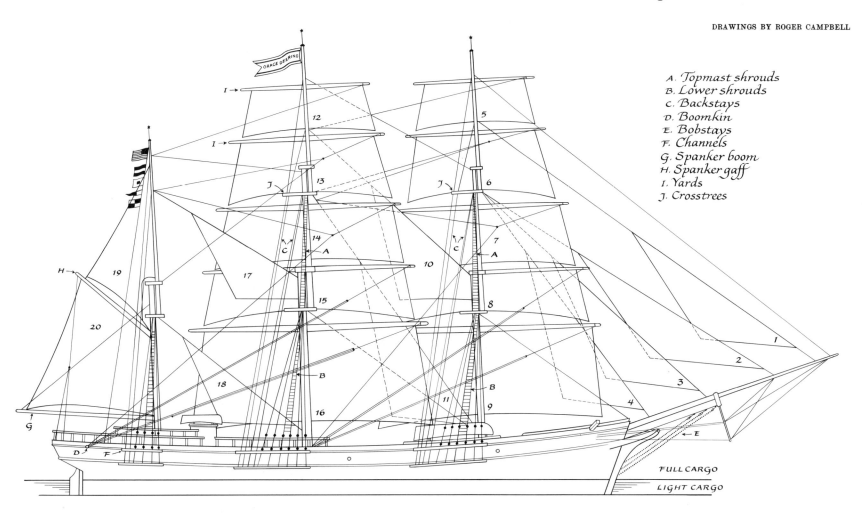

A. *Topmast shrouds*
B. *Lower shrouds*
C. *Backstays*
D. *Boomkin*
E. *Bobstays*
F. *Channels*
G. *Spanker boom*
H. *Spanker gaff*
I. *Yards*
J. *Crosstrees*

FULL CARGO

LIGHT CARGO

1. *Flying jib*
2. *Outer jib*
3. *Jib (or inner jib)*
4. *Fore topmast staysail*
5. *Foreroyal*
6. *Fore topgallant*
7. *Fore upper topsail*
8. *Fore lower topsail*
9. *Fore sail*
10. *Main topgallant staysail*
11. *Main topmast staysail*
12. *Main royal*
13. *Main topgallant*
14. *Main upper topsail*
15. *Main lower topsail*
16. *Main sail*
17. *Mizzen topmast skysail*
18. *Mizzen lower staysail*
19. *Spanker gaff topsail*
20. *Spanker*

March 11, 1897– December 7, 1897

In 1897, when he was thirty-eight years old, Sumner realized his own and every other seaman's dream—a deepwater command. Deepwater ships, the aristocrats of sail, crisscrossed the world unlike the "coasters," which ran port to port along the Eastern seaboard. While coasting schooners would continue to be built for three more decades, into the twentieth century, steam was successfully challenging the down-easters as the American foreign-going merchant marine. With fewer sailing ships on the sea all the time, many a man who had been a captain was now glad of a job as a second mate.

Despite these obstacles, on February 24, 1897, Sumner was offered the command of his own vessel, a down-easter three-masted bark. She was the *Grace Deering,* and her managing owner, Captain Benjamin Webster, proposed an around-the-world voyage to the Drinkwaters. The down-easter square-riggers were community enterprises, built and officered by local men, managed by a leading local citizen like Captain Webster. Shares in the boat were owned mostly by their builders, captains and prosperous townspeople. "When my ship comes in" was not an idle expression in Maine in that era; anyone in the community—doctor, dentist, ship chandler, grocer—was welcome to "take a venture" in the cargo of outgoing ships by investing $200 or more.

Captain Benjamin Webster was eighty-three and one of the best-known of Portland's sea captains. In fact, he had gone to sea at an early age. He commanded his first ship at nineteen and retired from active sailing thirty years later, in 1863. He became one of the few to manage the vessels he commanded and, thus, was free of the obligation of reporting to an owner. It was normal for a captain to own—as Sumner had in the *Bramhall*—1/64 to 1/8 of his ship, very rare, even foolish to own all of her. Insurance was expensive and people spread the risk by taking small shares in many vessels. A shipowner was simply a shareholder selected to be manager. In reality, his might not even be the controlling shares.

Among the vessels Webster managed were several he himself had commissioned to be built. One of these, the brig *Emma,* was the

boast of his career. He had contracted for her cargo in January 1865, when her frame was still being cut in the woods. On April 3, only ninety days later, she was launched from a Yarmouth yard and sailed fully loaded out of Portland harbor in time to get to Cuba and secure a return cargo home.

Captain Webster had "owned," in all, more than fifteen vessels at various times in his illustrious career, and on the day he called at Sumner's home he still had at least two ships: the *Grace Deering* and the *Onaway.* Although he lived in Portland, these two barks were registered in the port of New York.

Because it was not always possible to charter the vessel before she arrived in port, quite often the responsibility of finding her cargo fell on the captain of the vessel. The cargo arrangements that the captain made in some remote corner of the world were subject to the shipowner's approval only if he could be reached by cable or if there was time for an exchange of letters. When a captain was unable to get a cargo, he loaded ballast at the bottom of the hold in order to keep the ship upright. The weight of the masts, yards, rigging and the pressure of the wind on the sails would otherwise have capsized the vessel. The difference between a ship with a cargo and one in ballast is visually obvious—even to a child. The latter rides high, as if she were just getting her "sea legs."

Ballast was sand, rocks, rubble—anything that was worthless—and was dumped overboard at the end of the passage. There are many fables concerning ballast that found an unexpected use at the disembarkation port. The tea brought from China was a light cargo which by itself could not stabilize a vessel. Chinese "export-ware," heavier and sturdier than the fine porcelain used in China, was one of the things carried beneath a tea cargo to lower the center of gravity. The cobblestones which can still be seen paving some sections of New England streets were originally considered ballast as was the iron ore which found its way into the wrought-iron balustrades that Haiti incorporated into its unique architecture. Ballast often had to be bought, but if it had residual value and could be sold, it was not ballast but cargo.

In the following excerpts from Sumner's diaries he mentions that his wage will include a percentage on tobacco. He, like other captains, supplemented his income by carrying tobacco, which he sold at fifty cents a pound to members of his crew as well as to people in port. Sumner even recorded presenting a pound of tobacco to Mr. Lockie, a customs officer he and Alice befriended in Auckland. Giving such "gifties" was not an uncommon practice.

Wed. Feb 24, 1897 Ther= Cold wind N.W. Wea= Fine
    a.m. Captain Benjamin Webster called to offer me the Bark Grace Deering for a voyage to New Zealand & return to N.Y. A voyage round the world. Agreed to Call at his home at 296 Spring Street Portland tomorrow & decide
    p.m. Up to Brother John's

Thurs. Feb. 25, 1897 Ther= mild wind S.W. Fair
    Went to Portland to Capt Benjamin Webster to talk of taking charge of Bark Grace Deering at New York loading for New Zealand.
    Agreed to go the voyage & to take Alice.
    Wages $75.00 per month & board of wife Alice & per cent on tobacco.

On February 27 Sumner retrieved all his things from the *Mattie B. Russell,* his previous command.

After calling to say goodbye to his sisters Maggie and Lillian at their homes in North Yarmouth, Sumner spent the evening of March

The *Grace Deering* under repair in Brooklyn, c. 1897.

4 at Captain Prince's house. The Prince family was a respected seafaring family in Yarmouth. Prince's Point as it is still called, was named for them.

March 4, 1897

    Bought some charts & Books of sailing Directions & Co. of [Captain Prince] also Telescope in all $16.00 worth. North & south atlantic, Indian Ocean & South Pacific Ocean Charts, English Make, also 2 charts of Bass straights. Also Pacific Directory aids to Navigation. Also Australian Directory Vol- 1st South Coast

March 8, 1897 Mon. Ther=Milder Wea=Snowy Wind varrible

    Arrived N York at 6 a.m.

    Got to vessel at 9. Met by Capt Crickett

    Shipped crew [i.e., hired the crew for the voyage] & made other preparations for getting away.

    P.M. cleared from Custom House

        wrote Capt Webster

    finished loading at night.

The vessel got under way on March 11 and returned home on December 7. Because subsequent voyages on the *Grace Deering* are much more fully documented, only a few unusual excerpts from Sumner's diary are included here.

Sumner's first voyage on the *Grace Deering* was a period of adjustment as he learned her idiosyncrasies. Each vessel was an individual, and a new captain could not make any assumptions about her caprices based on his former commands. Her best balance could only be discovered by varying the amount of sail used under different circumstances. Sumner had to study and note the exact combination of canvas that caused her to sail most efficiently as the wind shifted. He probably carried on such calculations without even thinking about them. His response in a crisis would be instinctive, yet he would do the right thing in less time than it took to decide what that might be. Sumner blended into the *Grace Deering* and became the

mind of a living creature of wood and canvas that had the power to place him with the gods.

A ship's crew was a claustrophobic community, isolated from the rest of the world. Men and officers alike worked in the open, unprotected from the elements at all times. The seamen were on duty every day, in four-hour watches, for twelve of the twenty-four hours. No one was off duty in a crisis, when the call was "All hands on deck!"

Varying temperaments, varying levels of sophistication, national differences and language barriers made flare-ups among the crew unavoidable. To avoid violence the officers sometimes searched the sailors for firearms and liquor as they arrived on board. Now, at the end of the sailing era, there were few good men who wished to ship aboard for these long, arduous trips. Quite often the crews were a combination of greenhorns and an occasional real sailor.

Sat. June 5, 1897 Ther= 60 Barometer 29.80 Wea= Partially Cloudy

    All required sail set 86 days at sea

    1 P.M. A.M. Ship time 2nd mate refused to do work assigned to him by the chief mate resulting in the 2nd mate flatly refusing to taking orders from the mate & using abusive language & insults & threats to the mate after repeated orders from the master to desist & return to duty. Also threatening to shoot any one who should lay hand on him Proving him to be a dangerous man. The matter was quieted after a while & allowed to drop.

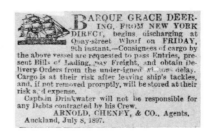

ALFREDA THURSTON

H. Whitnall-Smith

298, QUEEN STREET,

Auckland

Sumner is not specific about how he defused this volatile situation but it was clearly not in the interest of ship safety to confine the second mate to his quarters because that would have increased the captain's responsibility as well as the burden on the mate. No doubt the second mate was closely supervised, but if they could utilize him, they would. He was again insubordinate on July 4 and continued to be obstreperous the day after they reached Auckland.

Thurs.   July 8, 1897   2nd mate Dorman had trouble with Seaman James O'Neill striking him a severe blow on the cheek. Took them befor consul & 2nd mate Dorman was discharged from vessel.

Sumner's disciplinary problems did not end with the second mate's dismissal, for on Sunday, July 18, he noted:

11 PM   disturbance occurred on board between first mate, Steward & 3 seamen Frank, Chris & John by name.
Mate received bad scalp wound inflicted by Seaman Christian Nelson with capstan bar-Seaman John S——received several small scalp wounds by Mate with Iron stove poker. Seaman Frank K—— received blow from Steward with fists in Steward's Galley. Seaman Chris arrested & taken to lock up. Had Doctor to dress wounds of Mate [James McKimnon] and Seaman John.

The next day Sumner and the crew attended Seaman Nelson's trial in Auckland, where he was sentenced to fourteen days' imprisonment. On the following day Seaman Frank K——fell in the hold, injuring his right hip and joined the mate and Seaman John Seveson, who were already laid up. Then, to make things worse, when Seaman Nelson had served his sentence and returned aboard, he was demoted to night watchman but later found intoxicated in the forecastle when he was supposed to be on duty. All other hands were on shore.

Sat. Aug 7, 1897 Seaman Chris Nelson under the influence of Liquor committed depredations on shore Breaking a large window for which he is now in Jail. Broke Lamp & Table in forecastle, damage $2.00.

Sun. Aug. 8, 1897 Police officer on board to inquire relating to Seaman Nelson's wages.

Sumner's time in New Zealand was not entirely taken up by the "depredations" of the crew. He and Alice took time for sightseeing and making friends. Among their new acquaintances were Alfred Bailey and his wife, Clare, who will reappear during the voyage of 1899. They also met, on this trip, the customs official and his wife, the Lockies. The earliest dated amateur photograph from the Drinkwaters' travels was one of Alice on board with their new friends, the Lockies. Since the Drinkwaters had a camera only a few months later

on their next voyage, it is possible that their interest in photographing sprang from this experience.

On the flyleaf of his diary for this year, Sumner listed some of the stores opened during the voyage. (The figures in parenthesis indicate progressively the number of barrels used.) Supplies were commonly kept in the "lazarette," a belowdeck storage space right aft. A cursory look at the food they carried makes clear why catching and eating fresh fish was so important to them.

Sumner plainly relished being master of the bark *Grace Deering*. Rosco Davis, her former captain, had gone into retirement, and if Sumner proved himself competent on this first voyage, there was every possibility that Captain Webster would continue his command. Sumner had known the bark eleven years before he sailed on her. He had recorded calling aboard the *Deering* in Philadelphia when, at age twenty-seven, he was a mate on the schooner *Grace Cushing*. On that evening of August 10, 1886, the *Grace Deering* was only nine years old, and in her prime. The 733-ton down-easter had been launched

Stores used on [the] voyage New York towards New Zealand			
March 7th	1 10 lb. Pail Lard	June 24th	drew 15 gallons Kerosene oil
9th	opened 1 Barrel Beef	27th	Opened 1 Barrel Beef (5)
15th	drew 15 gal. Kerosene oil	30th	" 10 lb. Pail Lard
"	opened 1 Ell. Bread	July 12th	" 1 Barrel Flour (5)
23rd	" 1 Barrel Flour	Aug 8th	" 1 Barrel Flour (6)
20th	" 1 10 lb. Pail Lard	Aug 31st	" 1 Barrel Flour (7)
April 3rd	1 Barrel Beef (2)	Sept 7th	" 1 Barrel Beef (6)
21st	1 " Flour (2)	22nd	" 1 Barrell Flour (8)
28th	1 " Beef (3)	Oct 8th	" 1 " Beef (7)
29th	Drew 29 gal. Kerosene oil	13th	" 1 " Flour (9)
May 3rd	Opened 10 lb Pail of Lard	Nov 8th	" 1 " "(10)
May 10th	Opened 1 Barrel Flour (3)	Nov 8th	opened 1 Barrel Beef (8)
26th	" 1 Barrel Beef (4)	28th	" 1 " Pork
28th	" 10 lb. Pail of Lard	29th	" 1 " flour (10)
June 14th	" 1 Barrel Flour (4)		

by the JF Randall shipyards of Cape Elizabeth, Maine, in 1877 and was distinguished for having been designed by the well-known master shipbuilder Daniel Brewer. Her length was 152 feet, her breadth 33 feet, and her depth of hold was 18¼ feet. To the young mate this oceangoing lady must have been quite bewitching.

Sometime before their return to New York on December 7, 1897, Sumner copied into his diary from her ship's log the voyages of the bark *Grace Deering*. The last seven entries are in Alice's hand.

The Drinkwaters learned upon their arrival in New York that the barkentine *Mattie B. Russell*, the 370-ton coaster that Sumner

---

VOYAGES OF BARK <u>GRACE DEERING</u>

from July 1881	Boston to Melbourne	40 days to the line [equator] 116 days to Melbourne 10 days discharging at Melbourne took in 170 tons Ballast
	New Castle to Hong Kong	61 Days Drawing 18-04 aft 17' forward
	Hong Kong to Ililo	in Ballast, drawing 12 aft 11' forward
	Illilo to Sydney	34343 Bags Sugar Drawing 17-10 aft 16-10 forward Passage 86 days
	Sydney to New Castle	Towed with 70 Tons Ballast
	New Castle to Singapore	Coal Drawing 18-09 aft 18-01 Forward Passage 63 Days
	Singapore to Zebue	in Ballast 292 tons Drawing 11-10 aft 11-02 forward Passage 56 days
	Zebue to New York	Sugar 35144 Bags Drawing 19 aft 18 forward Passage not known Log book missing
1884	New York to Valaparaso	41 days to Line 86 to Cape Horn 105 to Valaparaso
	Valaparaso to Iquiqui	in Ballast
	Iquiqui to Baltimore	via Del. Breakwater 7199 Bags Nitrate Drawing 18.03 aft 17.5 forward Passage 97 days
1885	New York to Valapraiso	33 to the Line 91 to Val
	Iquiqui to Philadelphia	6583 Bags Nitrate Drawing 18.3 aft 17.9 Forward
1887–88	New York to Valapariso	42 Days to the Line 94 Days to Valapariso Drawing 16.8 aft 16-7 forward
	Pisagua to Philadelphia	cargo 7249 Bags Nitrate Drawing 18.3 aft 18.3 forward Passage 80 Days

1888	New York to Valapariso	47 Days to the Line 96 to Valapariso
1889	Pisagua to N. York	Passage about 80 days
1890	New York to Talcuhana Pisagua to Philadelphia	32 Days to the Line Passage 115 Days 7736 Bags Nitrate Drawing 18.10 aft 18.6 forward Passage 83 Days to Bkwter-
1890	New York to Talcuhana Talcuhana to Huanila, thence to Hampton Rhoades	25 Days to Line Passage 97 Days Draft 16-9 aft 16.5 forward 144 tons ballast thence to Hampton Rhoades Passage 86 days
1891	New York to Valapariso thence to Antofasta thence to Caleta Buena for N. York	29 Days to Line Passage 87 Days with part of cargo in Ballast cargo 8010 Bags Nitrate Passage 111 Days Draft 19 aft 18.3 Forward
1892	New York to Valapariso thence to Iquiqui thence to Caleta Buena Caleta Buena for Boston	32 Days to Line Passage 85 Days with coast freight [cargo probably nitrate] Passage 92 days
1893	Philadelphia to Sagua La Grand, Cuba thence to Del-Breakwater Proceeded to Boston	1049 Tons coal Passage 11 days with Sugar Passage 15 days
1893	July 20th Portland to Buenos Ayres thence to Freybentos for Boston	38 Days to the Line Passage 60 Days Passage 57 days
1894	March 3 Boston to Buenos Ayres thence to Rosario for Boston	515730 ft. Lumber 31 Days to the Line Passage 63 Days Passage 50 Days

left when he took command of the *Grace Deering* only nine months earlier, had just been wrecked that past month. Sumner attended her salvage auction and purchased two brass plates bearing her name, one of which has since been donated to Yarmouth's library. These souvenirs may originally have been used as ornamental treads on the companionway ladder leading to the cabin.

January 26, 1898–March 5, 1899

The Drinkwaters' second voyage on the *Grace Deering* did not take them "around the world," as had the first. Then they had circled the globe past the Cape of Good Hope (Africa), returning by way of Cape Horn (South America). On this passage they rounded the Cape of Good Hope, both coming and going, and visited Australia, Singapore and the island of St. Helena. Each of them kept diaries during this voyage. Alice's is the more readable because she wrote short commentaries during the passage, whereas Sumner merely listed each day's events. Occasionally, however, Alice omitted information which Sumner included in his account, so that his diary provides cross reference.

Forty of Sumner's extant fifty-three diaries were manufactured by the Standard Diary Company. An innovative feature appeared in their diary of 1898; the company included a personal-statistic form, which Sumner filled in.

Left to right: James Lockie, cook, mate, James McKimnon, Sumner, Alice and Mrs. Lockie.

The *Deering* at Auckland.

FOR IDENTIFICATION

My Name is   *S P Drinkwater*

My Address is   *Yarmouth Me*

In case of accident or serious illness please notify

Watson Gray Drinkwater [his father-in-law]

Yarmouth Me

Box 73

THINGS TO BE REMEMBERED

The make of my Bicycle is

Its number is

The number on the case of my Watch is   *2002*

The number of the works is   *149875*

The number of my Bank Book is

My Weight was   *154 lbs*

On   *Dec. 25*   189   *7*

and my Height   *5*   feet   *9½*   inches

Size of my Hat   *6⅞*   Gloves   *6½*

Hosiery   *9*   Collar   *15½*

Cuffs   *11*   Shoes   *8*

Shirt   *15*   Drawers   *36 + 34*

Sumner's diary.

Since Alice's account does not begin before January 26, when they were already under way, we are dependent on Sumner's diary for events preparatory to their departure.

From the information Sumner recorded on January 26, 1898, it seems that the *Grace Deering* began her long voyage to Brisbane, Australia, with a handicap. While the tug *R. S. Clark* was towing the bark at nine o'clock in the morning, the *Grace Deering* was rammed by another tug, the *Emperor,* which came on to starboard quarter head on, striking the mizzen channels and breaking and splintering them badly. (The channels spread the rigging above where it was fastened to the vessel's side.) Although the damage delayed their departure until four o'clock that afternoon, it could not have been too critical because Sumner does not record the mate repairing the channels until over a month later. There is no further reference to the tug *R. S. Clark.* Sumner merely reports how the journey began:

Tug Emperor came off at 4 P.M. with bills of Laden and towed vessel to sea. Left us at 6.45. Pilot left us at 7.15 with letters.

Strong N. W. wind & clear. Set foresail topsails & main top gallent.

7.30 Passing Scotland Light Ship from which I take departure course S.E.S. East.

During the approximately fifteen years they had by now been married, Alice had been Sumner's companion on about half of his voyages. With that experience behind her, she prepared projects for the current trip to ease the boredom of a year-long passage in a constricted space. She and Sumner were childless; she would be free from interruption. Among the materials she packed in 1898 were photography equipment and her journal, the only one she apparently ever kept.

Her first entry introduces a woman of dignity, courage and wry Yankee humor as she focuses attention on the storm they encountered, and only obliquely mentions her state of seasickness during those four days. The "oil" she refers to was used to lessen the impact on the vessel of breaking seas. Small bags filled with oil were hung over the bows and pricked with a sail needle so the oil would drip out slowly and create a slick, a smooth area of sea flattened by the oil on its surface.

JOURNAL OF VOYAGE FROM NEW YORK
TO BRISBANE, AUSTRALIA

Feb. 10th 1898   15 Days at Sea
Lat. 32′, 45° North Long. 43° West

We left N.Y. Jan 26th and for four days had heavy N.W. gales with high seas which broke on board continualy. One found its way into the cabin by forcing open the Pilot house door. I escaped getting wet however as I was in my berth at the time where I spent most of the four days.

Oil was used more or less during the time. Jan 31st we had a heavy S.E. gale was layed too during one night oil bags over. Since then have had mostly fine weather with S. & S.W. winds and warm and nice, have spent much time on deck & have done some sewing & more reading & have practiced some with the Camera. Have finished some pictures with verrying amt. success.

Today is Hattie Johns & Lucy Princes birthday. I wonder how they are celebrating. Would like much to know how they all are at home & what is going on in the world but must wait more than 3 months longer before I can know. We have sighted one Bark & two steamers the past week.

Every voyage required an initial period of adjustment as the ship's crew and the officers tested one another's limits. Since this was Sumner's second voyage with the *Deering*, he could better anticipate how she would behave. But his officers would have to learn both the vessel's way and his. For the crew it was a time for gauging the consistency of the discipline they were to work under. The crew had never come together before, much less worked as a unit, but the storms the *Grace Deering* met as she sailed from New York gave them common purpose and a hurried initiation.

Most communities share responsibility; aboard ship all power is vested in a single man. For the span of the voyage, Sumner was not only captain but magistrate, chief of police, treasurer, purchasing agent, water commissioner, food inspector, doctor and undertaker. In addition to these roles Sumner operated the "slop chest," the merchant seaman's equivalent to a military canteen. In the following entry Sumner makes a sale to Seaman Otte. When sailors came aboard without such necessities as knives or oilskins, they could purchase them from the captain for a sizable markup—sometimes as high as 300 percent. No money was exchanged at the time; rather, the captain noted these purchases and deducted them from their pay.

We do not know why Seaman Otte was "disrated." Perhaps he had claimed to be an able-bodied seaman when he was hired and had proved unable, when ordered, to perform the work satisfactorily. Not every sailor possessed discharges rating their conduct and ability from former captains and no way other than actual trial proved a man's proficiency. A rough and ready indication of a seaman's experience was the number of tattoo marks he bore.

Sumner's reference to "old sea" describes a sea that has not subsided, although the storm which generated it has passed. It can also refer to a sea a ship encounters which has been created by a distant storm that never reaches them.

Thurs. Feb. 3, 1898 P.M. Continuous moderate S.S.E. wind & cloudy
    Old sea from South.
    L. Otte this day disrated to Ordinary Seaman. Wages reduced to $12.00 per month.
    Seaman Otte had sheath knife and belt.

Demoting the seaman occupied less space in Sumner's diary at this stage of the voyage than healing his helmsman, who had developed abscesses. A common problem during long-continued, bad weather, abscesses were caused by oilskins chafing on wrists wet with salt water. Continuous applications of linseed poultices had not slowed the swelling on one wrist, and minor surgery became necessary.

Thurs. Feb. 10, 1899 George off duty. Consider it best to lance wrist & did so from which flowed much blood and matter. Dressed with Linseed Poltice.

The minor surgery Sumner performed proved successful, and on February 17 Sumner notes: "George able to do duty." He had been incapacitated for fifteen days.
    Alice's diary continues:

Feb 27th   32 Days at Sea
Lat. 17° 01′ N. Long. 29° - 04′ W.
    We are having a long passage to the Line but yesterday we took the first of the N.E. trades & today it is fine warm weather with quite

A lamp and clock hang on mast which passes through dining area.

a good breeze. Ther. 76. We had 26 days of head wind from calm to a gale so a fair wind is quite acceptable. I have been sick for a week but am about well again & have had a walk on the Poop with Sumner. There is a nice moon & it is very pleasant on deck in the evening. We have taken several pictures both on deck & in the cabin & are getting quite expert in the business. We took two Ships at a mile distant but they proved a failure. I have been sewing on some thin dresses that I need in the tropics & tomorrow I intend to do a washing. Sumner has shaved his mustache off & looks something dreadful. I shall be glad

Sumner without mustache. Behind him hanging on the pilot house are the capstan bars. The low structure is the booby hatch.

when it grows again. He caught a Globe fish & the mate skinned & stuffed it for a curio. We have a good crew & mates but the Steward is a <u>Peach.</u>

In the following entry Alice mentions that she and Sumner had discovered some "flying fish" in their walk on deck. Not only were these fish a welcome variation to their diet but finding them was considered a lucky omen. She also mentions a few of the goodies that she had included for the journey—fresh fruit and candy. Actually, some of the meals produced by the cooks in that era were truly extraordinary, considering the lack of refrigeration. Without refrigeration, most vessels carried pens to hold livestock which traveled aboard—until they were eaten.

March 13th   46 Days at Sea
Sunday 8 P.M.
Lat. 00° - 12′ N. Long. 27° - 32′ W.

This has been a hot day & verry moderate. We are just about on the Equater at this time & have been long enough about it. Have had moderate head winds most of the time & heavy head sea making it verry uncomfortable. We have done quite a rushing business in the picture line. One day I took Sumner & the mate & they turned out verry good <u>considering.</u> Last tuesday one of the men caught a large Albacore weighing over 40 lbs. He could not hold him but the end of the line was made fast so he let him go & sung out lusterly for help. The mate put a harpoon into him when they got him along side & they got him on deck. The men began to skin him at once but when he took to kicking they had to get out of the way. It was caught at 4 P.M. but we had fried fish for supper that night & all we wanted forward & aft for the next two days. About all hands made themselves sick by eating too much. Even the Capt. had a sick spell he layed to the fish but I steered clear.

Several Flying fish came on board while S. & I were walking on deck one night so we had them for breakfast. Yesterday morning early it was nearly calm & we were in a school of Black fish as they lay asleep on top of the water. They were from 10 to 15 ft. long. They soon began to stir & make off in all directions. The mate got the iron ready but got no chance to shoot it into one of them.

Sumner's mustache is sprouting beautifuly & he begins to look quite familiar. Last sunday I cut his hair & find I am quite a barber. We saw two Barks today bound north & a few days ago there was one in company with us but we have lost her & think she is astern. Today I made some Claret lemonade. We have got one lemon & three oranges left & about a lb of candy but that is getting poor. I have done more reading than work so far but it is to hot to do much for a while. I shall make it up when it is cooler.

Alice computed the logarithms needed to navigate the voyage. When visibility was too limited for a reading, a vessel's position was calculated by D.R.—dead reckoning. This reckoning was calculated by using their previous position and estimating the distance run that day, but it was complicated by the variable influences of the wind and current.

"Run 206 miles with square yards" means that the sails were positioned at right angles to the *Grace Deering*'s keel because the wind was coming from astern. The opposite of being *squared away* is *close-hauled* when the vessel's sails are nearer to being on a parallel plane to the keel.

Alice mentions passing Tristan da Cunha, in the South Atlantic, then and now one of the most isolated communities in the world. Roughly 280 people live here, midway between Africa and South America. Their home is formed by a volcano that rises to about 6,750 feet. In 1942 an important meteorological and radio base was set up on Tristan. Then, when the long-dormant volcano erupted in 1961, the population was evacuated and eventually transported to England, where their curious nineteenth-century speech was studied by linguists. A year later the islanders, unhappy with civilization, voted overwhelmingly to return to Tristan da Cunha in 1963.

Feb. 22   Lat. 24.15 North, Long 34.42. Starboard side looking forward.

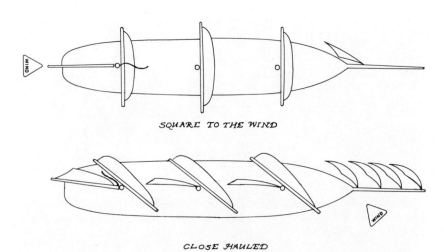

SQUARE TO THE WIND

CLOSE HAULED

April 3d   67 Days at Sea
Lat. 38°.00'S. Long. 09° - 52' East

Our position today is by D.R. as it is thick weather & no observation, but we have made a good 24 hours run 206 miles with square yards rolling heavy & shipping much water. We are having a verry good run from the Equater with fresh S.E. trades all the time. At 9 P.M. yesterday we passed the Island of "Tristan da- Cunha" about 6 miles to the southard of it. We could see it like a heavy black cloud & make out its shape pretty well as there was a moon but heavy squally clouds passing over it. In daytime it would be a grand sight being over 8000 ft. high. The clouds hung over the top so we could not see it at all. It is nearly round in shape & 6 miles wide & settled by people from Cape Colony. Ships sometimes land there for water & vegetables.

Since writing last we have been upholstering the Sofa & large chair in the after cabin. It was quite a difficult & hard job to do but look better enough to pay for the trouble. I have made slip covers for them.

At the time Sumner helped Alice upholster the lounge, he made two entries which expand upon hers.

Wed. Mar. 16, 1898   Ther = 82, Weather Fine, Fresh Trades & Passing Clouds   Wind S.E. by S.   All sail set
Tore Cabin Lounge to Peices Preparatory to reupholstering it & found a boot buttoner, several slate pencils, 2 spanish cents & various other things in the back.

May 18, 1898   Ther =82   Barometer = 29 80   Wea = Fine, Fresh Trades & Passing Clouds S.E. by S.   All sail set
Working on lounge. Got the seat fixed, retracing all the springs & recovering with matting & the Seat upholstered. crew employed on making a cover for the Large Boat [lashed to the Forward House] out of old upper Topsail condemned.

While Alice may have not thought to mention the above details of the upholstering to her private journal, she most certainly was deliberate in not confiding that they photographed the lounge after they finished.

Tues. Mar. 29, 1898   Ther = 74 Bar= 30 10   Wea= Fine
First Part Moderate Breeze N.N. East   All drawing sail set   At work shifting Sails
Took 2 Pictures of Alice on lounge & in berth
Partially nude   looked fine

The Victorian Age was outwardly prudish and it was natural that Alice didn't admit to intimacies. That Alice doesn't mention disrobing is no more surprising than that these photographs of her were not among those land and sea scapes the Drinkwaters kept. However, Sumner, less circumscribed by taboos, in recording their photo session provided us with an unexpected glimpse of their personal life. Whether Alice draped herself in the classical mode or played the coquette, it is evident that the captain and his wife had fun together behind closed doors.

In the following paragraph Alice mentions an "English ship." Many British vessels were easily identified because of a distinctive pattern of painted ports used to decorate the vessel. While other nations used the same device—it was originally an attempt to create mock gun ports to scare away pirates—the style varied with each country.

We have seen several vessels lately. A few days ago an English Ship passed north & signalled that she had on board a Naval Reserv Officer & bound from Pt. Stephens to Windsor. We could not find her name in any book we have but her signal letters were P.C.G.L. We gave our signal number J.S.G.L. where from & where bound.

The night of Mch 20th in Lat. 15 -12′ Long. 36 -31′ a small two masted Schooner came verry near us & at one time it looked as it she would run into us. She was heading S.W. & either did not see us, or thought they could cross our bow but finaly she hauled to a while then kept off our stern. She was evidently bound to some port on the S.A. coast.

The mate caught a fine Bonita weighing 6 lbs, so we have had another taste of fresh fish. He has commenced to make a full moddel of the "Grace Deering." It is about 2 ft. long & will be as near like her as possible & will make a pretty thing when completed which will not be for some time to come.

The weather is much cooler now this morning. The Ther. was 68 in the cabin—but we do not need a fire yet.

The Flying Fish have all disappeared & the southern Birds have taken their place, the "Cape Pigeon" "Cape Hen" "Molly Hawk" & "Albatross." We sunk the North Star about a month ago but can still see the Long handled Dipper late in the evening when it is clear. Sumner has been taking observations lately of the moon & some stars & working navigation by them. "Jupiter" rises at sunset & is a wonderful brilliant star & lights up as much as a small moon. With the

The ship's model aboard the *Deering*.

DEARBORN STUDIOS

long glass we imagine we can see some of the Satellites. I shall have to give up going on deck evenings now as it is so cool. Was up for a walk last night after supper but tonight the decks are soaked continualy, but there will be times when I can walk the deck crossing the Indian Ocean but it is pretty rough there all the time & plenty of seas gets on board. Sumner dreamed last night that our house was burned down but as I do not believe in dreams shall not worry about it. However in less than 2 months I shall know. I certainly hope it still stands as I want to see it again.

Sunday Evening, April 24th   88 Days at Sea
Lat. 40°, 50′ S. Long. 58°, 12′ E.

It does not seem possible that we are nearly three months at sea for the time goes so fast that I can hardly keep track of it. The days are so much alike there is nothing to distinguish them & only for the daily observations I think we should sometimes loose run of the days.

Today has been pretty nice for these disagreeable regions for it is cloudy, dull weather nearly all the time. The sun never shines only for a short time then is hidden again. We are going about 7 knots on an average today wind right aft, all fore & aft-sails furled & she does some tall rolling at times. Sat. the 9th in Lat. 38° Long. 12° - 09°, we had a heavy gale from S.W. with tremendous cross seas. It threatened all day & at 6 P.M. it burst in all its fury. The Bar. was very low 29.20. They took in sail until only lower topsails were on & there was danger of them going to pieces. We layed too all night & she rolled something terrible & shipped heavy seas constantly even with Oil bags over.

Sumner was up all night & I never turned in. Once I layed down on the berth with the weather board in but in a few minutes I was fired down against the partition, board, pillows & all. The sea that did it nearly put her on her beam ends & filled the main deck solid full of water so it took half an hour to free herself of it. The next day "Easter" Sunday was some better but the high confused sea still

running & all the forenoon shipped quantities of water. One sea broke two water casks adrift & smashed them. They were full & we are sorry to loose the water but still have a good supply as the main tank has 11 ft. in it besides some in another on deck. That is the worst gail I have experienced so far & dont care if I never see another like it. I have hardly been on deck for two weeks & shant much until we get over to the Australian coast & in better weather. I have been sewing more lately as I havn't been out & now am mending the flags as a good many of them had ragged ends. Last sunday we saw a Bark 10 miles south of us & steering east but have not seen her since although she may be within 25 miles of us & if the world was not so small we could no doubt see her.

Well it must commence to look spring-like at home now & I hope they are having a finer one than last year. I shall be verry glad to get in port & get news from home & hope it will be only good news that we shall here.

Kodak had produced a rolled film by 1888 which was nitrate-based and as stable as gunpowder, but the Drinkwaters eschewed the new-fangled invention and used the "rapid plate"—a piece of glass pre-coated with emulsion. Prior to the development of the rapid plate, photographers had used the "wet plate," which necessitated spreading an emulsion on the glass surface immediately before taking a photograph.

Alice did not print photographs in a dark room. She worked with a printing frame and printing-out paper in the sun on the deck of the *Grace Deering.* The printing frame firmly sandwiched the glass negative against the paper and was sectioned so that it could be opened, checked and closed from behind without blurring the image. When she was satisfied that the print looked dark enough, Alice would take it below and remove the photo from the frame, wash it and fix it. Quite often these slow printing papers gave the photos a brownish cast.

May 8th   102 Days at Sea

Lat. 41°, 20′ S.   Long 104°.-57′ E.

We are now within 9° of Cape Leeuwin the most S.W. part of Australia & in two days from now hope we shall have land north of us not many hundred miles distant. . . .

Friday the mate hooked a fine big Albatross that measured 10 ft. 8 in. from tip to tip. It was a handsome black & white bird verry much like a Swan in shape. He intends to skin & stuff it.

We have had no cold weather at all. The Ther. has not been below 50 & this morning it was 56. We have a fire part of the time. I have done considerable sewing & reading. I have not been able to print any pictures for some time as we havnt had enough sun for it, so I have hung up the business for a while but intend to finish a good many before we arrive as I want to send some home & some to friends in New Zealand.

Alice, like many captain's wives, was in her element entertaining in port. No matter how pragmatically their cabins had been arranged to weather the rough passage, arrival in port was a call to arms. Carpets were unrolled and laid; treasured bric-a-brac unpacked and artfully placed; paintings uncrated and hung. Overnight, utilitarian quarters were replaced by salons of Victorian effulgence.

Entering port, the *Grace Deering* automatically became one of "the fleet"—the group of sailing ships lying at anchor in the harbor. There were sure to be new friends, and more often than not, old friends as well. Local dignitaries would call, curious to have firsthand news and impressions. Inevitably a round of parties, "companies" as they were called, would begin, each family striving to outdo the other. The ship's routine would shift to accommodate a round of social calls, parties, sightseeing and excursions. If the passage seemed interminable, port, in contrast, could be a gay time.

THE CHARLESTON STUDIOS   58 HUNTER STREET
                                NEWCASTLE,
                                N.S.W.

May 22nd   116 Days at Sea

We are now 9 P.M. passing by the Hogan group of Islands at the
eastern enterance of Bass Strait. Wind N.W. moderate & raining
hard. We made Cape Otway about noon yesterday but to far off to
signal. Am sorry not to get reported as they will be looking for it at
home. I spent most of the forenoon on deck looking at the diferent
Islands as we passed. Sumner took a picture of "Rodondo" off Wilson
Promontory, over 1000 ft. high; & of two rocky Islands about 150 ft.
high. We could not see the mainland verry plain as it was hazy. All
the Islands are high & some of them entirely barren rock. On one there
are wild dogs. Most of them are uninhabited. Since I wrote last we

Sumner's private quarters.

May 19   Lat. 39° 32′   Long 135° 30.′
Port side looking aft, three hundred miles out of Australia.

have had a good deal of moderate weather & head wind & the 12th we had a heavy gale. The Bar. went down to 29.10 the lowest I ever saw it but once.

I have been doing a little house cleaning on a small scale & a number of things that I want done before arriving. Have made two ruffled cushion covers, a plush sofa pillow, head rest, crape tissue lamp shade & several important things so when we are ready for port & the carpets layed we shall look stunning. 11 months ago today we passed through Bass Strait bound to Auckland, N.Z.

Since the ships took so long to get from one port to another, the families back home, as well as the shipowners, had no way of knowing how the vessels were doing beyond the reports from other ships. Unlike steamships, which often saw one another on the more direct, heavily trafficked routes, sailing vessels followed lonely lanes. They went out of their way to benefit from favorable winds and currents, and kept far offshore in case gales blew them landward. The few ships that passed close enough to use signal flags were limited to the code-book phrases. In the following entry Alice notes that a coal steamer answering their signal in passing will be likely to report them. The steamer's captain, upon reaching Melbourne, would normally give notice of their bark and its position. That information would be relayed to the States and published within a week's time in a newspaper. Shipping news occupied many columns in the nineteenth-century press.

May 25th   119 Days at Sea

We are now 30 miles east of Newcastle N.S.W. & only 350 miles from our port of destination. Since I wrote sunday we have had wind enough & to spare. Monday morning when we were out by all the Islands in the Strait we had a violent squall from west which turned into a heavy gale with high sea & pouring rain which continued nearly two days. We made 231 miles in 24 hours under lower Topsails & reefed Foresail. The upper Topsails were badly torn in furling them.

There was plenty of water on deck & over the house. The steward was thrown out of his berth by a sea striking the forward house with great force. Today the weather is some better. The wind has abated & the sun shines between the showers. We are making 7 knots with square yards & I hope will continue as good to port. It has been bad about doing work that we intended before arriving & I think we are likely to get in before we are ready. I have 30 pictures to finish but it is too rough to undertake it. My trays would need to be 2 ft. deep for a pint of water to stay in them.

Yesterday we signalled a coal Steamer bound from Sydney to Melbourn. She answered us & will be likely to report us. She was heading right into the teeth of the gale & the seas piling over her terribly. She seemed to go right through some of them.

I expect this is the last I shall write for some time as I shall be to busy in port to keep a Journal or do anything but go ashore for it will seem verry nice to get on land again even if it is at the Antipodes [an uninhabited group of islands southeast of New Zealand].

The next entry in Alice's journal was written two and a half months later, after the *Grace Deering* had left Australia. The ship had arrived in Brisbane, discharged her cargo, and then had gone south to Newcastle for a cargo of coal. Brisbane, the capital of Queensland, sits on the Brisbane River above Moreton Bay. It primarily exports wool, meat, fruit, sugar and coal. The city was still young when the Drinkwaters visited it. Established as a penal colony in 1824, it had only been known as Brisbane for sixty-four years. Newcastle, south of Brisbane, like the famous English city it is named for, is the center of a coal-mining area.

Perhaps the most interesting comment appearing in this section of letters and diaries is in reference to the Spanish-American War. On February 15, 1898, three weeks after the *Grace Deering* had left New York harbor, the U.S. battleship *Maine* was blown up in Havana, killing 260 of her crew. The United States declared war on Spain on April 24, and an armistice was reached on August 12, 1898.

The Drinkwaters family history made them personally aware of the vulnerability of an unarmed merchant vessel. Alice's grandfather, Captain Allan Drinkwater, had been captured by a French privateer while master of the brig *Ça Ira* off Barbados in 1797. The brig, then valued at $9,000, was owned by Alice's great-grandfather Joseph Drinkwater, among others. In 1799 a vessel carrying Sumner's great-grandfather John Drinkwater, Jr. ("African John"), had been captured by a British man-of-war and he was impressed for three years. The poor man had been heading home after narrowly escaping with his life from a ship's mutiny which had left him marooned on the African coast.

From Newcastle to Singapore
Aug. 2nd   10 Days at Sea
Lat. 16°.07'S. Long. 155° - 56' E.

It is more than two months since I wrote last & just as I expected it would be. I was to busy in port to keep a journal. I could hardly spare time to write letters home. For we was going out or entertaining company or callers about all the time. We arrived at Brisbane May 28th, 121 days from New York.

We found Brisbane a beautiful city with about 65000 inhabitants. Some verry fine buildings especially the Government Bldgs, but no lofty ones at all. Only 3 or 4 stairs at most. The houses are all low wooden flat roofed cottages & large verandas around them. The Streets are broad & level with Electric [trolley] cars. The scenery mountainous & grand.

After we had been there a few days, a fine appearing man came on board & introduced himself as Mr John A Clark. He is ex Mayor of Brisbane, & cordialy invited us to his home & made us feel as if we was among our own people. He has a nice family consisting of Mrs. C. two sons & three daughters who did all possible to make us enjoy our stay there. His home was a low 7 roomed house with verandas all arround & plenty of trees in the grounds & situated close to the river & near the Vessel so we were there verry often & they on board

the Deering when we was not up there or off sightseeing together. (He & Sumner . . . attended Lodge meetings together.)

One of the girls in particular, 24 years old, was with us more than the others. She and I would go on a Bus or Electric ride or about town or go into the Gardens for an hour or two & have Tea at the Pavilion, in fact were somewhere every day & then we would go to their house to supper & a game of cards in the evening. One afternoon Mr. Clark, Addie, Sumner & myself went in a Cab about 7 miles where there was a large encampment of Soldiers mustered once every year for practice. It was a verry fine sight as there was hundreds of tents put up & it was as near like the reality as possible. We spent a delightful afternoon & went with them to dinner & for the evening.

Dinner with them is at 6 P.M. then at 9 or 10 they have their supper consisting of bread & butter several kinds of cakes, fruit, jam & Tea. It is tea all the time in Australia. Their chief occupation is tea drinking. They simply leave off long enough to make a fresh supply, then go at it again. We was not long in getting in to the habits of the country, <u>Tea drinking & all.</u> It was the same in New Zealand so was not entirely new to us.

We was surprised on arriving to learn about the Spanish-American War that had been going on for most 3 months. We had been in blissful ignorance of the danger we was in of being captured & are now for all we know unless war is over as there was prospect of its being when we sailed.

It did not seem much like winter to us in Aus. although Newcastle was much cooler than Brisbane. At B. it was to warm to need an outside garment except some evenings, and fruit, vegetables, & flowers were growing everywhere. The public gardens were beautiful, what must it be like in summer, but I don't think there is any great diference in the seasons only summer is intensly hot.

We made no acquaintances but Mr. Clarks family, & the consul Mr. Weatherell & a few friends of his. We had some invitations ashore but declined them all.

We sailed from there June 21st for Newcastle & a party went down river with us & back on the tug "Beaver". There was 8 grown people & two babies, the smallest of the party being 11 weeks old. His name was Russell Bruce Elliot Dix Esq. It was a fine pleasant day & they enjoyed the excursion much being something new to most of them.

About 4 p.m. & not long before the tug left us we had a calation on the Poop using the booby hatch for a table. It consisted of <u>Tea</u> bread & butter Cake of diferent kinds & fruit to which justice was done for about half an hour. Then good bye to them & to Brisbane. They waved hats & handkerchiefs as long as we could see them, & we dipped the flag to them & headed the Grace Deering for Cape Moreton.

Alice's entry continues unbroken through their departure from Newcastle, but I am interjecting Sumner's record of his business affairs in Australia, which she omitted. Alice, as the captain's wife, could enjoy port life more wholeheartedly than could the captain. He had bested the sea to reach port bureaucracy with its custom officials, health clearances, cargo transactions and crew matters. Anything untoward in this strange harbor could damage his reputation for efficiency.

Sixteen letters had been waiting for them when they arrived in Brisbane. Two from Captain Webster authorized Sumner to charter the *Grace Deering* to best advantage; in other words, to pick up what cargo he could. Nothing came to Sumner's attention in Brisbane after he lost out in the bidding for a cargo of guano and another cargo to San Francisco. He left Brisbane by train for Newcastle, and apparently, since rates for moving coal were too low, went on to Sydney.

Tues. June 13, 1898 Pleasant morning, threatening weather later.
Took 8.25 train to Sydney arriving at noon. Called on the U.S. Consul, Colonel Bell from whom I got much friendly advice. Got firm offers of 191 shilling coal New Castle to Frisco

161 shilling New Castle to the ports of Singapore, Macassar or Antung
Cabled offer to Capt. Webster

The search ended on the following day.

Wed. June 14, 1898 Rainy all day at Sydney waiting reply from Cable & looking up business but find nothing better. 3.30 got reply from Capt Webster preferring Singapore & thought it advisable to except as could not do better. Cabled closed & got ready to take 7 P.M. train to Brisbane.

Reaching Brisbane at midnight the next day, Sumner made preparations to move down the coast to pick up coal at Newcastle. Since the *Deering* carried a remaining cargo of only 75 tons, she would quite easily have capsized on the open sea. Sumner therefore began taking on ballast to stabilize the bark; by June 21 they had taken on 205 tons of ballast and were able to leave for Newcastle.

Mon. June 20, 1898 Pleasant
Got stores on Board & water & 25 tons more ballast
Settling accts. Cleared from custom House & ordered Tow Boat and Pilot for tomorrow.
Took tea at Mr. Clarks. Spent the eve with them at Play "Tree of Knowledge" Very good.

Tues. June 21, 1898 Pleasant
2.30 P.M. took tow & Pilot to Sea. TowBoat Beaver. Miss Clark & Company of Friends went down river with us. Left [tow] Boat outside the Bar and made sail & Proceeded to Sea with Pilot. [tow] boat left us at 4.35. 7.30 P.M. off Yule roads struck Buoy on North Edge of Yule road Bank.
10 P.M. Pilot left us off Cape Moreton. Wind S.W. Bar 29.90

Alice goes on to describe the journey from Cape Moreton to Newcastle, a distance of about 500 miles.

Had a good run that night & got about 75 miles off shore the next morning when we went into a heavy S.E. gale which continued 24 hours. During that time we were hove to & as high as she was being in ballast, the water flew over the after house pretty lively.

After that we had pretty good weather but head wind about all the time so we was 8 days in beating down & arrived June 29th. There we found the Bark "Holliswood" of N.Y. Capt. Knight formerly of Yarmouth. He had his wife with him & his son 24 years old was mate.

We was verry glad to meet them there & enjoyed ourselves together verry much. Capt. K. & his wife were some older than we being over 60 but were much younger in appearance which made us verry

well mated. Capt. K. & Sumner had Bicycles & were off together most of the time so we <u>girls</u> had to ammuse ourselves without the boys. We would go ashore every afternoon & do some shopping perhaps & take a walk. We could walk all over the town in 15 minutes. The place is verry small with only one St. with any stores, the only business being coal mining & shipping. There was about 30 Ships & Barks in port & I think the Holliswood & Deering was the only American vessel among them.

We celebrated the 4th of July by us four taking a trip to Sydney for the day. We left Newcastle at A.M. & arrived back at 10 P.M. making quite a long day. We spent 6 hours there & after having dinner at the Metropole Hotel, we made the most of our time & see as much as possible of the City. There are some magnificent buildings & verry lofty. One could almost imagine themselves in N.Y. only there is no life & rush to the people & the St. cars are dirty smoky steam cars which almost spoil the beauty of the place. We went into the gardens & through the Art Gallery which is well worth visiting & did a little "Souvenir" shopping & by that time we had to think of getting supper & starting on our way back to N. We all enjoyed the day verry much. The 80 miles ride took 4 hours but the scenery was grand about all the way & where it was not grand it was all new to us & interesting. We passed large fields of growing Pineapples from 50 to 100 achres in some of them, Orange groves & many sights that one does not see in the State of Maine. In some places we could see where the Shafts go down into the mines & the track running to them. It was verry mountainous & we thought perhaps was pretty well undermined as they have dug for coal for years under those same mountains. In some places the train would go up over quite steep hills & went nearly as slow as one walks but generaly the mountains were tunelled & we went through dozens of them. We nearly looked ourselves blind going down but comming back it was dark, only a large moon that would light up the beautiful lakes & hills making grand moonlight scenes. We tried to entertain each other by talking over what we had seen but the noise the train made was deafening so we were forced to keep quiet and save our breath.

We left Newcastle July 23d [with 956 tons of coal—the Deering's draft was 18.11 aft and 18.3 fore] & the Holliswood left about half an hour before us bound to San Francisco with nearly 1600 tons of coal. She is a nice vessel of 1080 tons built in '93. Our last evening in port Mrs. Knight & her son & the Consul Dr. Goding took supper with us. We made some nice acquaintances among the Ship people, Capt. & Mrs. Edgett of Ship "Timandra" (they are St. Johns people) also Capt. & Mrs. Smith of Ship "Annesley". We exchanged photos with the "Smiths" & "Knights." Both Ships sailed for the West Coast.

From Sumner's diary it is evident that the Spanish-American War did not affect the *Deering*'s timetable, although, after they left the trafficked lanes, he noted that he had stopped using the vessel's sidelights at night hoping to avoid enemy vessels. He was repeating a strategy that he had used in the passage from New York before they entered Australian waters. Though he'd been unaware of the declaration of war at the time, he had chosen not to use the sidelights as a matter of conservation; otherwise, the amount of kerosene they had on board might have run out before they reached Australia. Rather than risk a collision in the more heavily trafficked lanes close to the continent, Sumner ran unlit at night in the isolation of the Indian Ocean. Down-easters conceded nothing to darkness and carried all the sail the wind would allow both by day and by night.

August 28th   36 Days at Sea.
Lat. 5°, 48′ S. Long. 109°, 50′ E.

We are now in the Java Sea & only about 500 miles from Singapore having fine weather & fair Trades all the time. Have had some of the nicest sailing one could wish for.

The 16th day out we entered Torres Strait. It is over 100 miles through & filled with Islands high & low, many of them well covered with Cocoanut Palms & inhabited with natives of Papua who are

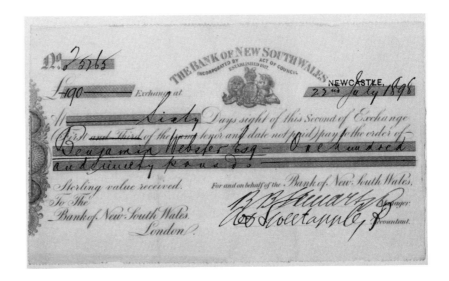

naturaly a savage race but are now friendly with white people. The Coral Reefs & sunken rocks are the chief dangers as the currents are swift & uncertain. We anchored one night near Rennel Island in 17 fathoms water as it is impossible to go along during the night with safety. I was half afraid we should have visitors from the Island but no boats came off. We got an early start the next morning & at dark passed out by "Goode Island" at the western enterance, where there is a Light house & Signal station. We showed Ship numbers J.S.G.L. [their call letters] where from & where bound & number of days out & was answered so hope in a weeks time they will see it in home papers.

Then we sailed along the north coast of Australia through the "Arafura" Sea making points of land & Islands several times. Made "New Year" Island passed to the south of "Timos" & Sandalwood Islands, & passed through Allas Strait between Sumbawa & Lombok Islands, into the Java Sea. Was nearly three days getting through a distance of only 40 miles, had but little wind with a strong current against us for 16 hours in the 24. We passed a large Ship ashore that was being stripped, also passed one ashore in Torres Strait. The Mountain scenery on both sides the Strait was grand. Lombok Peak 12000 ft. high & an extinct Volcano was a magnificent sight especialy when the clouds would fall below the top showing the peaks above them. We took a picture of it but being such a distance does not do it Justice. We then sailed along the "Java" coast to the Island of "Madura" & passed through a short Strait called Sapodre at the eastern end of the Island, having strong winds which if they continue we can be in Gaspar Strait in two days & after passing that, will be in the South China Sea with only one more Strait to pass before we are at our journeys end & I think it is quite enough Straits for one passage as they are all more or less dangerous, although making a nice variety & something besides sky & water to look at.

We have seen some strange looking craft in the Straits. The Malays use a kind of Catamaran with Lateen sail & with a corner hauled down look quite like a Baloon going along & can sail verry swift. They passed quite near us several times but did not come along side or speak us. Some were loaded with lumber & some with other things.

We have had a variety of fish since leaving Newcastle. The other day the mate speared a large Black fish that weighed between 200 & 300 lbs. We had the liver fried but could not eat the rest. Part of it was verry tough & dark colored & did not taste at all like fish. They got some oil out of it & sent the rest overboard except what the kitten wanted.

Last evening we developed some pictures & they turned out very fair.

We are having pretty hot weather which one must expect in this Lat. We shall be likely to have verry hot weather at Singapore being in only 1° -17' N. & only 77 miles from the Equater.

As we shall most likely arrive in the course of a week I am not likely to write again for a while, so this will hang up until after we leave port again.

In his description of their arrival in Singapore, Sumner refers to "Singapore Roads." The term "Roads" means the outer harbor in most ports.

Mon. Sept 5, 1898   Passing showers   Pleasent
    Comes on Calm. Breezing up from South
    2.15 P.M.   Came to anchor in Singapore Roads
    Heaving to 35 fathoms chain on Port anchor. Ashore to Consuls & reported arrival to Conseigne. No letter from home or Capt Webster. One letter from Alice's folks.
    So ends the Passage. 44 days to Anchor. 42 days to Entrance.

A month after their arrival, Sumner wrote to his mother. Happily, this letter survived to provide a basis for comparison of his and Alice's attitudes toward Singapore.

Singapore was founded by Stamford Raffles, who obtained permission from the Sultan of Johore to establish a trading post for the East India Company in 1819. Five years later, Raffles negotiated a new treaty with the Sultan and the whole island came under the control of the East Indian Company. In 1965 Singapore became an independant republic. Because it is virtually a free port, goods from all over the world can be sold at prices far lower than in many other countries. Singapore is about 450 miles from Vietnam.

Singapore 4 Oct 1898

My Dear Mother
    I am going to write this time to you in Particular although my letters have allways been to you as well as father. But Alice has written to her father which she never has done since when a little girl & I was thinking if I had ever written you. I can't remember that I ever did even when I first went to sea as I most always wrote some of the Brothers or Sisters. So I shall hardly know how to write a letter to you, but will try & write a few lines hoping it will reach home safely & find you as well as it is leaving us.

The Hot weather does not Hurt us any as I can see only that we don't grow fat. In fact I am not weighing quite so much as usual but feeling very well. It's no use for me to write of our voyage out or stay in Australian Ports or our voyage here, as that you have read of in former letters. There is much of interest here that I would like to write of but am to Poor a hand at describing or trying to Portray.

Singapore is a city very different from any I have ever seen, filled with so many different races principly Chinese but also many Japenese, Malays, Hindous, Indians, & natives of Ceylon & Borneo. Then the mode of travel in the city is so peculiar & interesting. Fancy being Hauled about in a little 2 wheeled buggy (called here Rickshaw) by a nearly naked Chinaman with only a Pair of pants with no legs to

them. In fact all the different native races wear but very little clothing so that their tailor bills are very small & most of the children up to 10 years of age wear nothing. It is quite common to see a group of little children both girls and boys playing in the street just as they came into the world.

The English part of the city is quite seperate from the other races, that is where they live and the business part too. Some streets will be entirely of Chinese shops & very peculiar & interesting & some of them have a very rank smell. There is said to be 15,000 thousand Rickshas in the city so you can imagine how thick they must be in the busiest places. At the large Iron pier where all the boats land from steamers & sailing ships there will be often as many as 200 of them waiting for

Singapore harbor.

passengers & when we land of course we are surrounded by them singing out "Have a Rick." That is about all the english they can speak.

Then there is the Harbor filled with little Boats called "Sampans" going in all directions carrying passengers back & forth from the Shipping. Then the cargo boats as all vessels discharge & load at Anchor in the Harbor. It presents a lively appearance from daylight till dark.

I have a Sampan Hired by the day to take me back & forth whenever I wish to go. He comes off in the morning & brings our fresh meat & co. & waits for me laying at the stern. They cook their food in their boats (which is mostly rice). We can look over the stern & see them eating with their "chop sticks" & it is quite amusing to watch them. Then they have a little mat of Rattan which they place like a roof over the boat & lay under it & sleep till we call them.

The streets outside the Chinese districts & a little out of the city are very beautiful of good width & smooth as a floor. Many of them for long distances are completely shaded by the large trees meeting over head and the foliage very thick & beautiful. It is quite impossible to give an Idea of the Tropical luxuriance to be found here, such lovely great Palm Trees & so many kinds that I know not the name of.

I have been taking some bicycle rides with Capt Nichols of Searsport Maine, Ship Emily Reed & we have enjoyed them very much. I have a hired wheel. He bought one. The first time we went out we rode 20 miles on beautiful level roads. It's scarcely an effort to drive a wheel. We usually go out in the afternoons from 4 to 6 P.M. it being the coolest part of the day.

I wish I could picture some of the scenes presented to us out in the country districts, immense Groves of Cookenut trees & acres of Pineapples & many fruits we do not have at home. Then the City Reservoir is a beautiful Place about 8 miles from the City square & the Public Gardens also are very fine. And then such beautiful Summer residences as we should call them of the wealthy Europeans &

Chinese aristocrates. I never have found anything so Grand or perhaps I should say so much like paridise as pictured.

Alice won't try riding, thinks it is too hot. It is difficult in the city to keep clear of the people & carriages but I am quite at home on a wheel now. I can go along very well with my arms folded or read a letter & light a cigar on my wheel very easily. The roads are so nice one can't help learning. I wish we had such roads at home.

Well I wonder shall I say something of our everyday life. We make it quite comfortable & easy. I generally get up about 6 A.M. sometimes ½ past, have a bath most every morning & shave every 2 days. That's my usual habit before breakfast. Sometimes if we are lazy or been out late we sleep till seven or Alice does. Then I look about ship & see that everything is going on all right & at 10 a.m. go ashore in my Sampan. I have tiffen [lunch] at 1 o'clock then perhaps I send

off for Alice if she has planned to come ashore & we take a rick ride. Otherwise I go out for a Bike ride.

Now I have begun loading. The days when I have cargo I stop on board all day to see that it is stowed properly & then perhaps take a boat sail in the evening. I have a larger Boat than the Russel's boat & have her all rigged up fine & enjoy a nice sail. We are planing a race now among the fleet. There are now 5 Sailing Ships in Port though only 3 have good sailing Boats.

We are going ashore this afternoon to take our pictures with the Kodak, going up to the Public Gardens in a Rick. Of course we shall dress in white, the prevailing color here. I have 8 suits of white. They are quite cheap, about $1.50 . . . in gold a suit. Of course they have to be done up & often will only do for one day, 2 at most, but Laundrying is cheap. We get our washing done for one cent & ½ a peice right

through whether starched clothes or not. I hope we shall get some good pictures but the Hot weather is rather against it.

Singapore's warm temperature made it very difficult to develop negatives. As they had no way of cooling the developing solution, the hot water would separate the emulsion from the glass plates and produce reticulation, or "frilling."

The name "Kodak," to which Sumner refers, rapidly became a synonym for camera after George Eastman's first model appeared on the market in 1888. Advertised as "simple enough for a woman to use" its operation was straightforward. According to the Kodak manual, the photographer had to:

1—Point the camera   3—Turn the key
2—Press the button   4—Pull the cord

Although Sumner and Alice refer to their camera as a Kodak, they did not in fact own one. Kodak never manufactured a model which could have utilized the Drinkwaters' glass-plate negatives. From its earliest cameras, Kodak used only "American film"—paper coated by two layers of gelatin.

Each roll of film had 100 negatives, which initially had to be sent back to the company, inside the camera. Kodak removed the film, developed the pictures and reloaded the camera before returning it to the photographer. A Kodak was not something everyone could afford. Their development service cost $10, and the camera, at $25, was priced approximately $10 higher than other models. However, the slogan for these early Kodaks, "You Press the Button. We Do the Rest," proved very inviting to many amateurs.

The Drinkwaters' 4 × 5 camera, although far bulkier than today's models, would have seemed compact compared to its predecessor, the 11 × 14. In their day, "snapshot" indicated that the camera was easily portable and might be hand-held or rested on a stable surface rather than needing a tripod. However, it was a far cry from today's automatic cameras. The Drinkwaters would have used a black cloth to block out the light while they focused on and framed their subject which would have appeared disconcertingly upside down. Due to the long exposure time required to record images on the glass negatives, a subject had to hold a position for a few seconds. This handicap made today's type of fast, candid photography impossible; nevertheless, several of the Drinkwaters' "snapshots" achieve an effect of life and motion rare for that period.

In concluding this letter, Sumner makes a rare comment about the *Deering*:

Well Mother I suppose you are thinking of us often as we are often thinking of you all at Home. It will be spring before we can see you all again. But if all goes well I hope we shall be home again next

March. That seems quite a long way off, yet how soon it will be with us. Well you won't have war & its dangers to fear for us so you must keep an easy mind for the Deering is a good vessel & I havn't a doubt but she will make many safe passages yet. She has testified well to her seaworthiness & is very easy in a heavy sea & would live when many a younger one would not.

Now I must really stop. I have written more than I thought I should yet I fear it's not of much interest. I am trying to think what I can bring you, shall bring something but it's hard to choose for others. I wish I could bring you all something nice from here but the family is so large.

With much love from your affectionate son.   love to all

Sumner

Sumner continued this letter on October 12, 1898. His cargo, as noted in his diary, consisted of rattan mats, pearl tapioca, sage flour and hides, and Gambia (gambier), which contains tannin used in dyeing.

Dear Mother   I missed mailing this letter when I intended to so will add a line more as since then I have got Yours & Fathers of Sept. 2nd & 5th & I was very glad to have a letter from you & know that you were all quite well at that time . . . I hope you will learn through Capt Webster how long we are to be here & so write again. Your letters are 32 days on the Road. Longer than to Australia. . . .

Well things are much the same with us. We have in now about 400 Tons of cargo. It comes very slowly & I guess they are going to use all the lay days [permitted by contract for] loading.

Monday I went on a long Bicycle Ride to a place called "Johare" 15 miles from Singapore. Went with Capt Nichols of Ship Emily Reed. We found beautiful roads & a pretty place. We went in the morning & returned towards night when it was cool. We rode 36 miles but after a Hot Bath & a good Sleep I felt nicely next day, although it was quite a long ride for me.

THE PREMO "B" CAMERA.

No. 6520. The Premo "B" is one of the most popular hand cameras on the market. It is strictly high grade throughout, great care having been exercised in its construction, and for a high grade camera at a moderate price it stands second to none. It is fitted with the Victor shutter having iris diaphragm with pneumatic release, and can also be released by the lever; has the new center swing back with rising and falling front thus adapting it to either snap shot or tripod work. It is furnished with either a single achromatic or Victor rapid rectilinear lens, as may be preferred. A reversible view finder is fitted to the bed for both vertical and horizontal pictures; has spring actuated ground glass screen and two tripod plates. It has room inside for three double plate holders, weighs a little over 2 lbs., and the 4x5 measures only 4⅜x5⅝x5⅝ inches when closed. It is covered with fine grained black leather; has handle for carrying. It will use glass plates, cut or rolled films, as may be desired. Price includes camera, lens, shutter and one plate holder.

PRICE.

	4x5	5x7
Price the Premo "B" with single achromatic lens	$13.60	$19.55
Price the Premo "B" with Victor rapid rectilinear lens	17.85	25.50
Extra Premo plate holder	1.05	1.28

Other extras same as quoted for Premo Sr.

Last eve we were invited with the rest of the fleet (Capt & wives) on board the Maitland Bark Strathisla. We spent a pleasant evening & had a fine supper with Ice Cream & coffee served at 10.30 & came away about Eleven o'clock.

I think I mentioned in a former letter of our having a similar Gathering on the Deering. Since then there has been a new arrival Bark E. C. Mowatt of Philadelphia, Capt Mowatt & wife. Now there are 4 ladies in the fleet. Saturday next we meet on board the Mowatt. Mrs. M. chooses that night as it is the 11th Anniversary of their marriage. Then we are talking of an Excursion around the island of Singapore which is 60 miles in circumference, going in a small steamer if not to Expensive.

Well goodbye for this time.   With lots of love   Sumner

On the nineteenth, a week after Sumner wrote this last letter, his diary shows that he attended a ship's auction with "Capts Mowatt and Forbes." When a vessel was wrecked but not completely lost, the owners—or more likely the insurance underwriters—balanced the cost of repairing her enough to bring her home against the profit to be realized by selling her salvaged gear & fittings at the nearest port. Salvage from the ship *Earl of Hopetoun*—built only six years earlier in Glasgow—had been assembled in Singapore for auction. Many captains besides Sumner took advantage of such functions to buy secondhand chandlery, even though what was purchased might not be to the exact size of their vessel.

Wed. Oct. 19,1898   Ther. 84   Barometer 29.80   Wea. Pleasant light S.W. wind

Rec'd on Board 626 Bags Pearl Tapioca

Marks ⟨a⟩   [presumably the different bag markings]
     m∨p   315
     s c
     ⟨a⟩   311
     m∨p   626

P.M. to Aution of Salvaged Goods & wreckage from Ship Earl of Hopetoun lost in —— Strait

Boat	15.00
Jib	15.00
Water casks	20.00
Blocks	3.25
Deck Iron	1.50
	39.75

44 days in Port

The bark *E. C. Mowatt.*

Sumner, in his letter to his parents, and Alice, in her journal entry, were understandably more interested in describing exotic Singapore than shipboard routine. But from Sumner's diary we learn that he had hired a diver in this port to check and patch the copper on the bottom of the *Deering*'s hull. Wooden sailing vessels of this era were plated with thin copper or other nonferrous composition metal to protect them from a borer, the teredo worm, and also to inhibit marine growth which would cut their speed. This sheathing needed to be replaced every four years.

Hiring and firing crew members continued to occupy Sumner. He paid off two men that he had shipped at Newcastle: Thomas Smith earned $14.92 for the forty-four-day passage, and Peter Callahan $13. While in port in Australia, he had had several cooks on trial but paid off the one hired for the passage as soon as the bark reached Singapore. He again searched for a good cook, but a Mexican-Chinese, Charley Song, "on trial at $1.50 per day," also proved unsatisfactory. Just before leaving on November 7, 1898, Sumner hired a new cook for the passage to New York.

Sumner's earlier letter to his parents, by implication, depicts Alice as fairly inactive in Singapore. He describes her as staying aboard ship in the morning, occasionally joining him for a rick ride, although they do stay out late some nights. The following description of Singapore from her diary presents quite a different Alice. She seems to have pursued activities apart from her husband.

FROM SINGAPORE TO NEW YORK
Sunday, November 13th 1898
6 Days at Sea
Passing through Banka [or Bangka] Strait.

We arrived at Singapore Sept 5th after a verry good passage of 44 days, passed 62 days in port & sailed the 7th of this month for N.Y. with a cargo of Gambia & general merchandise. We found Singapore to be a large City there being a population of nearly 1,000,000 the greater part being Chinese & Malay, but every other Nation on the Globe both civilized & uncivilized are represented there.

We met a few Americans. A Methodist minister & family by the name of Morgan who are from Maine & went there only 4 years ago. Capt. Sherman & family of the Ships "Lucille" & "Fannie Skolfield." He has given up the Sea & gone into business in that <u>Heathern Chinie</u> place. Also Mr. Blake & wife of St. Louis. There was three American Vessels in port, the Ship Emily Reed, Capt Nichols, the E.C. Mowatt, of Phil. also the Barkentine John Baizley of Phila. but owned by parties out here in the East.

The Bark "Strathisla" of Maitland N.S. Capt. Urquhart with his wife & two children, the Ship "J.V. Troop" English Capt. Beveridge & wife. She came in there in distress having struck a rock in Banka Strait [in the Java Sea] bound from Hongkong to Liverpool with hemp. The cost for repairs was 18,000 in Singapore money [then about $9,000]. She had to be disq. [discharged] damages repaired & recoppered.

I would like to discribe Singapore as it realy is but that is quite an impossibility. It is on an Island which is but 60 miles in circumference & so is verry much crowded.

Some of the Sts. are verry pretty quite wide & smooth & fairly clean. The Esplanade running along the water front is by far the nicest. It is verry wide with beautiful trees on both sides (of which the whole city is well supplied). It is crowded most of the time with Rickshas drawn by almost naked Chinamen who cannot speak or understand hardly a word of English but will haul you arround all day at a good speed too for 20 cts an hour which is realy less than 10 cts as Singapore money is worth but 48 cts to the dollar. They are small men but verry tough for they will take two people in a Rick & go miles with them & as fast as many horses travel & do not seem tired or out of breath but the sweat will run down their naked back in small streams.

At first I did not like going with them by myself, but after getting some used to them I did not mind at all & often went anywhere I wanted to on my own responsibility, & as I could not tell them where I wanted to go I just gave them a little poke with my umbrella & pointed where to stop or where to turn a corner. I used to think it would be verry handy to have reins fastened to them & steer them in that way. There was always plenty waiting at the boat landing & one could step in to them & the fellow would at once start off like a machine.

There was not many places to go except to the Gardens which were verry nice & not much to be seen any where but a crowd of natives swarming the Sts. dressed in all sorts of gear & plenty of the small children had no gear at all unless it was bracelets arround their ankles & arms. The Malays wore bright plaid "Sarongs" or skirts that was made of a piece about 2 yards long & 1 yd. wide then sewed up & was put arround them & twisted in a tight knot in front but was always getting loose & they were twisting them up as they walked. They usualy wore a loose white sack. The Indians dressed in verry much the same way.

The Chinese wore loose trousers & a loose Jacket, without any hat at all & their queue sometimes pugged up & sometimes hanging with red or blue cord braided with it to make it longer & would sometimes hang about down to the ground. I saw Arabs dressed in white muslin skirts & jackets & a large piece twisted in a turban arround the head.

Late in the afternoon the wealthy Europeans would come out in their fine carriages in all their glory. The Coachman & footman in Livery, the footman standing on a little step at the back & hanging to a strap. Some of the turn outs were quite grand & with beautiful Australian horses.

Almost every afternoon without fail I went ashore either in our own Sampan or with Capt. & Mrs. Urquhart in their Ship boat. There we would meet the other ladies of the fleet & all take a walk perhaps & a Rick or "Gharry" ride & do a little shopping at the Native stores

& sometimes have tea or ice cream & go back on board by 6 in time for supper. Then unless we went on board the Strathisla or E. C. Mowatt we spent the evening on deck under the awning, one of us in the hammock & the other in a Rattan long chair. That is the way we passed the 62 days combined with fighting mosquitoes & swinging a palm leaf fan for the Ther. was always between 85 & 90 & the nights not much cooler. We generaly felt a breeze in the evening but it did not cool the cabin any. We sometimes had callers & twice we entertained about a doz. to supper & had the table spread on deck & used Jap. lanterns hung up arround the awning & on the Spanker boom making it verry nice & <u>Oriental.</u>

All the Native Shops & houses are small wooden buildings not much better than huts, & on High St. they are painted bright blue, nearly all of them, & being so small they look like toy houses. The counters in the shops are against the walls & the clerks stand up on them to reach down whatever you ask for, then sit down on them with their feet under them & wait until you make your selections.

The houses where the Europeans live are verry good & large & are in the nicest part of the town & on high land. The houses are but one story, have plenty of windows but no glass in them. There are inside blinds, & wood shutters to close & keep out the rain. They live in great style with plenty of servants, all Chinese or Malay.

We had dinner once at a house & twice at the Hotel De Europe. At the house there was two who waited on the table & another to see to the small children at another table & a chinaman to swing the "Punker." In fact there was more servants than food. At the Hotel there was 10 or 12 courses & all served verry nicely.

I would like to discribe the Dressmaker I had while in port. He was a fat old Arab named "Askar" with curls about 4 inches long all over his head & was dressed in clouds of white muslin from top to toe, the pants comming below the long skirt. He came on board to take my measure & get the goods but afterwards I went to his establishment. It was a crazy old shed with uneven brick floor & on one side a bench

or table about 15 ft. by 10 ft. covered with matting, & 5 or 6 men was squatting down on that sewing. On the other side was two of the verry oldest fashioned sewing machines, & accrost the room was lines to hang the dresses up out of the dirt. The old fellow was chewing the Betel leaf. <u>All</u> <u>over</u> <u>his</u> <u>face,</u> it looks worse than tobacco if possible, being blood red. I expected the white skirts he was making would come back with that <u>Trade</u> <u>Mark</u> all over them but they were returned all right however.

One afternoon a party of us visited a "Mahomet" temple where they was preparing to worship. They had incense burning in two dishes & flowers all arround. The walls were all covered with gold & silver paper ornaments & small mirrors & glass beads & with the daylight shut out & lamps lit it looked verry pretty. They gave each of us a tiny red rose.

The Chinese have celebrations about every evening. They collect in Thousands on some street so one cannot pass through hardly, & have all sorts of noises possible with tin drums & horns & think they are frightening away the Devil. The din is terrible, they would soon frighten away a civilized person. We went through a St. in a Rick one evening when they was having a Jamboree just to see what it was like. Our Rick fellow kept singing out to them to let him pass & I think we were the only white people on the St. They stared at us in wonder & I was glad to get through alive.

We left port in company with the Ship "Emily Reed" & comming through Rhio [or Riouw] Strait we was near enough to talk with Capt. Nichols. Then he gained on us & at dark was one mile ahead, but next morning we was ahead of him & kept gaining until 2 P.M. The 3rd day we sunk him [lost sight of him] below the horizon astern. [Racing added interest to a passage. Thirty-seven years later Sumner noted in his diary with evident satisfaction that he had beaten Captain Daniel Nichols of Searsport, Maine, to New York in 1899 by six days.] We came up with & passed the French bark "Alexandre" of Rouen & bound there from Saigon with salt. Saturday morning early we was

Sumner, mate and helmsman.

quite near her. She set her Ensign then asked where we was bound. We carried on quite a conversation through the Code. She was then 11 days out. She is now astern nearly out of sight.

We have had verry moderate weather since leaving & are now only 400 miles from Singapore. We intend to stop at Anjer [short for Anjer Lor, on the western tip of Java] for some vegetables & fruit & to mail letters.

Indian Ocean, Dec. 11th   34 Days at Sea
Lat. 23°, 53′ S.   Long. 68°, 56′ E.

It is sunday & as perfect a day as one could wish for but more wind would be acceptable. We are going 5 knots & quite smooth sea except a long sea running with us. We have had 4 verry moderate days making but 75 miles each day, but 10 days ago we made over 200 miles for several days in succession, with strong S.E. trades & tremendous rough sea. We passed Anjer Nov. 20th 13 days from Singapore. We got potatoes, yams, onions, pumpkins & bananas from boats that came off so we did not lay too at all. We also sent letters by one of the boats for one shilling each.

. . . We passed within 6 or 8 miles of the Island of "Krakatoa" this side of Sunda Strait. We could see it verry plain as it is verry high, 2000 ft. In 1883 there was a fearful eruption occurred there which sunk over ½ the Island which was 13 square miles & now is but 6, & killed thousands of people in the Island & surrounding country at a great distance. The old town of Anjer 25 miles distant was entirely distroyed & about all the inhabitants killed. It throwed up a high Island in the middle of the Strait that they have named Thwart-the-Way. It sent ashes & pumice stone all the way to Manila & Hongkong a distance of 2000 miles, & even to Western Australia. The sea all arround was so covered with pumice that it looked like land to a Ship sailing through it. It floats there now after 15 years & we got some pieces in a bucket. The erruption caused a tidal wave that was traced around the world, & at Sourbaya on the east end of Java, Ships were driven ashore & wrecked. For years after the erruption it continued to smoke & a deep rumbling noise could be heard by passing Ships. I was quite disappointed to find it was all quiet now. People have built houses & are living arround the foot of the great mountain again waiting to be blown up again.

We passed Thanksgiving day in Lat. 7°, 54′ S. Long. 104°, 14′ E. & had a verry nice dinner even if we had no company. We had Turkey although it had ceased to <u>gobble</u> some time previous, tomato soup, sweet potatoes, etc. & dark pudding with hard sauce. That was the first good day since we passed Anjer. Sunday the day we passed was fine but verry hot with light fair wind, but the next day was miserable with head wind & heavy head sea & continued so up to thursday night when we got the wind south which finaly worked in the S.E. trades & during one week we made 1250 miles. We have not seen a vessel since leaving the land. We made Cocos Islands about 600 miles from Java head & the gulls came arround us in swarms before we made the Islands. They sailed over the vessel quite near us as if to see what we were, & at dark all started together & went back to their Island home where there is no human being to disturb them.

Yesterday was J. M. Bucknams 37th birthday, & I shall soon be there.

Alice was referring to James Monroe Bucknam Jr., who had married Sumner's sister Lucy in 1885. James must have been warmly remembered by Alice, for he had accompanied Sumner in his courting days. The boys, out for an evening stroll together, sometimes encountered the Drinkwater sisters and would see them home. Since Sumner was pursuing Hattie initially, James obligingly entertained Alice. Unfortunately, James's own marriage to Lucy, his first cousin, had heartbreaking consequences. Of their six children, five died before maturity: Lena, their second child, at six months; Carrol, their third, at three months; Elden, their fourth, at twenty-four years; Muriel, their fifth—a pretty, dark-haired girl who spent most of her life in a wheelchair—at twenty years; and Eldina, their sixth, at two months. In addition to these children, Sumner recorded one stillborn child, "made of stone."

Alice's description of Christmas dinner in the following entry shows little correlation to the typical ship's diet. Here she refers to "dinner," which, in Maine, is traditionally served at noon. "Supper" is the evening meal.

Christmas in the Indian Ocean   48 Days at Sea
Lat. 30°, 20′ S.   Long. 37°, 20′ E.
     Sunday.

This is the warmest & finest Xmas day I have ever experienced so far. This morning the Ther. was at 78°. Just perfect, only rather moderate. We have made but 90 miles during the last 24 hours.

We have had Xmas presents even if we are at Sea. Sumner gave me a pair of Japanese vases, & a Jewelery box made of Japan wood. I made him a house jacket, & gave him a cegar stand which is quite a novelty. We also had a nice Xmas dinner consisting of roast chickens, frigasee, tomato-soup, string beans, sweet potatoes & pudding. The Chickens were real ones only being <u>Chinese</u> instead of <u>Yankee</u> ones.

For supper we had fried Dolphin that the mate harpooned, chicken frigasee, baked sweet potatoes, bread, butter, cake & jam tarts. We have got a verry nice Chinaman steward shipped in Singapore. "Sung Gee" by name, he wears his queue in a pug instead of hanging down his back & I am glad as it cannot be dipping into things while he is cooking. As we did not go to Church we took a few pictures on deck this afternoon.

We are now within a few days sail of Cape of Good Hope. We passed 125 miles south of Madagascar Island, have had generaly light winds & fine weather with verry rough sea most of the time. We have not seen a vessel since leaving the land but may see some at the Cape. We are likely to make the land there.

This is a great contrast to what the day must be at home. It is now 8.40 P.M. with us & 1.30 P.M. at home. I know it is cold there & wonder if there is snow on the ground. It is hard to realize the diference. We have worn thin clothes all day & they are wearing furs & sitting by the stoves.

We have the same large moon though, & our nights are so short that it is light most of the time. We have been on deck until it got too damp so came below for the night, & later on we shall have our usual cup of tea & lunch & turn in. So ends Xmas day.

A few days following Christmas a total eclipse of the moon occurred. Sumner noted:

Wed. Dec. 28, 1898   Ther = 80 Bar = 30.04 Wea = Pleasant   Comes in Calm
     Total Eclipse of Moon [the] Middle or Total being at 1^h-53′
     [′ is the navigational symbol for minute, not feet.] A.M.
     Moon left Shadow at 3.50 A.M.
     Latitude by obv. 31°-39′ Long. by obv. 31°-59′-30 distance 63
     miles   True course W. by S. ½ S. Compass course various
     variation 26° westerly
     ALICE'S BIRTHDAY

The Drinkwaters have different dates for the eclipse of the moon, which occurred after midnight of December 27, 1898. Sumner recorded the phenomenon as taking place on December 28, the morning of Alice's thirty-sixth birthday. Alice dates it in the following paragraph as occurring overnight, the twenty-seventh. Sumner limited his notation to basic statistics, while Alice's description reveals the camaraderie between herself and her husband.

In this entry, Alice describes their visit to St. Helena, an island in the South Atlantic 1,200 miles west of Africa. St. Helena is best known as Napoleon's place of exile. He was sent there in 1815 and

B. GRANT

Jamestown, January 18, 1899.

died at Longwood near the capital, Jamestown, in 1821. His home has been maintained as a memorial.

Alice uses several nautical expressions which would have mystified other ladies of her time. "Stood off" and "stood in" mean that the *Deering* didn't anchor off the island but rather sailed away and returned. "Hull down" means that the lower part of the vessel, the hull, has disappeared from view below the horizon as a result of the curvature of the earth and that only her sails can be seen. To be that removed from the *Deering* must have made the Drinkwaters feel a bit uneasy. "Filled away" refers to the boat gathering headway as the sails fill. This was the only unscheduled stop that the Drinkwaters made on the voyage. Was Sumner's business really so pressing or was the temptation to visit Napoleon's island too strong?

Sunday Jan. 29th   83 Days at Sea
Lat. 5°, 40′ south   Long. 24°, 42′ West

Over a month has passed since I wrote last & we have been making some progress towards home. Dec. 27th we witnessed a total eclipse of the moon. It came on at about midnight & passed off at 4 A.M. next morning. It was a remarkably clear night & we had a grand chance to see it. Sumner was up all night watching & spying it. I layed on the sofa & slept & he waked me several times to go on deck to see it. It came on early in the evening at home so they had a chance to see it all & then go to bed.

The 31st we passed Cape Recife at the entrance of Port Elizabeth. We was about 10 miles off & a tug thinking we was bound in there came off to us. Her name was "Garth." The Capt. said he would report us. Between there & the Cape of Good Hope which we passed Jan. 6 we had three heavy blows from W. & S.W. The one Jan. 4th was the heaviest & while the men was up on the yards reefing [Shortening Sail], Sumner took a picture of the Vessel, which has finished up verry well.

When we was off the Cape [of Good Hope] a Bark came up with us, going about 2 miles to us one, & it prooved to be the "Strathisla,"

Capt. Urquhart, which left Singapore 17 days after we did bound for Boston, & had gained on us all that time. It was about sunset when she got abeam but we exchanged signals. The next morning she was out of sight.

While off the Cape they speared two large Porpoises, so we had curried porpois for breakfast & fried porpois steak for dinner & hamburg steak for supper for several days. We was nearly 12 days from Good Hope to St. Helena, made the Island at daylight on the 18th & hove too near it at 8 A.M. Two boats came alongside & as Sumner needed to go on shore I went with him. We went in one of the boats which was a whale boat & a fine able craft or we should have been swamped for we got some smart squalls in under the mountains that caused the boat to take in water several times. She carried no ballast at all. When we went up from the shore we crossed a moat, the first one I ever see or crossed. The little town "Jamestown" is a queer little place situated in a Valley between two mountains & not over ¼ of a mile wide & the one street they call "Napoleon" St. runs up quite a hill. We walked the length of the town which is perhaps a mile & we could see the width of it all the time. A dark skinned Native, "Thorp" by name went with us. He was verry nice & has been about the world a little.

I took the camera ashore & got 6 snapshots of which 4 prooved verry good. The American Consul heard we was ashore & sent for us to call at the <u>Consulate</u> a verry pressing invitation. We did so & found the office boy Just rigging the <u>stars</u> & <u>stripes</u> out the window in our honor. The Consul said so few Am. Ships called there so the Capts. came ashore that he did not fly the flag all the time, he was economizing to help the U.S. pay her big war debt. He was a fine old gentleman not far from 70 years of age with white hair & beard. He lived in a verry good house (in fact they said it was the best in the place,) close to the office & he quite forced us to call at his home. He locked up his office & went with us & we stayed nearly an hour [with] his family. There are only his wife & one daughter but he has 10 more children scattered over the world. He was born on St. Helena but has lived a good many years in America & Africa. They gave us some quite late N.Y. Heralds not more than 40 days old (quite late news) but we found plenty of things in them that was new to us. About the terrible snow storm at home the last of Nov. & the great amount of damage done. & we saw that the "C.J. Willard" was among the Vessels ashore, & as John was in her earlier in the season we think no doubt he was in her then, but cannot know any particulars for some time. They also gave us a fine bunch of flowers & now after 11 days they are quite fresh looking.

We bought pictures & ornaments as Souvenirs of the place.

Off Cape Good Hope, January 4, heavy S.W. blow.

B. GRANT

Flight of 700 Steps.

We would have liked verry much to go to Napoleons house & Tomb, but they are four miles from the town over a rough mountainous road & even if we could have taken the time, there was not a conveyance of any kind to be had. It seems to me a more desolate place could not have been found on the face of the earth to banish a man than that barren mountainous pile of rocks 2300 ft. high. It was indeed a Sea girt Prison & as far back as 1820 there was not many people on the Island besides soldiers. Government is now building Barracks there & doing a good deal of work, & the Soldiers quarters are on the flat top of a mountain to the right of the town & a flight of 700 wooden steps leads up to it.

We was gone from the Vessel 5 hours & a Native pilot stayed on board during the time. After we left the Bark they stood off & when we got in shore she was hull down & looked a long way off. At noon they stood in again & we got back on board by 2 P.M. & at 2.30 filled away on our course again.

We made the Island of Ascension early in the morning of the 24th passed about 2 or 3 miles to the south of it & signalled. I took a Snapshot & it looks quite like it. It is nearly as large as St. Helena but some higher being over 3000 ft. at the highest peak, about the same kind of an Island but more varied in hight. There is not much of a town about all the settlement being Soldiers Barracks. The signal Station is on the top of a very peaked mountain near the coast & just back of "Georgetown."

When we was passing the south east end of the Island we saw what I thought was the town, but it prooved to be vast amounts of Lava rocks that covered a mile or two between the shore, & mountains. Today I have thrown a bottle over board with a note in it giving name of Ship our position where from & destination Etc. I also sent one adrift the 12th. I intend to put one over quite often & possibly some of them may be heard from in time.

We are beginning to loose the southern stars, the far famed "Southern Cross" only shown late at night. We can see the Long

Handle Dipper towards morning & I hope in a week we can see the familiar "North Star." It has been most 11 months since we lost sight of it & it will seem as if we was nearing home to see it again.

I almost forgot to say that while on St. Helena, our guide took us in to a little Church that was open. It was the "Church of England" denomination & the first I had ever seen inside, so was quite a curiosity to me with its little pulpits on all sides. We also went into their Park which was about the size of a <u>door yard.</u> The walks were stony & rough & hardly any green grass or flowers. Quite a number of Banyan trees were growing about & some of them verry large.

Another curiosity was the little pack mules not much larger than a sheep. They was comming & going all the time carrying loads of fire wood & grass & packages of all discriptions hung over their backs. People from all over the Island come into town with things to market loaded on them. Perhaps one woman or man would be driving a dozen of them with only a stick, no harness or halter on them at all.

We met two or three shopping parties consisting of a couple of women & perhaps 5 or 6 children. Their mule was loaded with packages tied on any how with strings & a child on the top of that, & all were verry much dressed up in bright colors & all bare footed. How ever they walked over the stony streets I don't know for it hurt my feet with heavy soles on my shoes. They use but verry few carts as the mountains are too steep & rough for them, but the mules can climb like Goats & carry quite a load.

Alice didn't record either her birthday on the day of the eclipse or Sumner's birthday, which followed soon after, on January 11. He mentioned them both and he also notes that a year earlier, in 1898, his cousins Clarence and Jenny Bucknam had had a boy born to them on *his* birthday whom they christened Sumner Bucknam. An earlier child of theirs, of that name, had died.

Wed. Jan. 11, 1899   Ther = 72   Bar = 30-00   Wea = Cloudy   Moderate S.W. winds
MY BIRTHDAY   40 Years Life is fleeting
Smoked cigar given me by Clarence as Treat in Honor of a New Baby Boy. Have kept it a year.
65 days at sea.

Though Alice doesn't discuss it in her earlier entries, she and Sumner had started treating a young sailor for venereal disease the day after Thanksgiving. Even now that his condition has become critical, she is vague, unspecific and genteel. Fortunately, his crisis passed and he returned to duty on January 20. Her Victorian sensibility about this matter contrasts sharply with the graphic detail she provides about another seaman.

She refers to "eight bells," which means the end of a watch and the start of a new one. Sea time was/is divided into periods of four hours, beginning at 12, 4 and 8 o'clock, although the four hours between 4 P.M. and 8 P.M. were broken up into two watches of two hours each. These last were dubbed "the dogwatches." "Dogwatch" is still used occasionally in Maine to mean suppertime or the cocktail hour—the ship's workday had tapered off by this time.

"Turning up Jack" means simply that Sumner is working about the cabin in preparation for port. It was the family's reference to Alice's brother Jack, a skilled carpenter. He had an excellent reputation for doing "finish" carpentry, specializing in fussy work like china cabinets, staircases and hardwood floors. Jack had earlier been employed primarily in the Boston area, but at this time in his life he was back home courting Nellie Groves. Following their marriage in 1899, he worked only locally—around Portland and Yarmouth.

Sunday Feb. 12th 1899   97 Days at Sea
Lat. 9° .02′ N. Long. 48° .08′ W.
Thursday, several exciting things took place. We saw a Barkentine astern heading north, caught a Dolphin, & one of the crew, a young fellow who has been running down for two months, gave up

work because he could not stand at the wheel any longer. We have doctored him all the time as best we knew, & if he dont improve soon I am afraid he will never see N.Y. At eight bells that night when the man at the wheel was going forward, in stepping down from the house on to the top step he put his foot on a sharp tin dipper & being barefooted cut a piece completely off his heel about the size of a dollar which bled terribly. Sumner put the piece in place again & wrapped his foot up, so we are two men short. I hope no more will give out. One day south of the Line & near "Fernando Noronha" we sighted 4 vessels bound south. We passed the Island Feb. 3d (on brother Jacks birthday) & near enough to get a Snapshot which looks quite nice but small.

It is a mountainous Island like all in the South Atlantic & is used for a Penal station only so of course is not verry thickly settled. There is one rock 1000 ft. high. It looks Just like a church steeple & is called the Pinacle. We made the Island last voyage on our way home from the Horn but it was evening & we could not see much of it.

I have been growing Sweet Potatoes ever since we passed Anjer. I put one that has started to sprout in a large tumbler of water & put it in the skylight & in a week it grows a full foot high & is a bright green & pretty star shaped leaves. They get to be about 20 inches then wont grow any more but last a long time & look verry pretty.

Sumner is turning up Jack here in the Cabin, is painting all the white work over new, but it will look pretty fine after it is finished &

Using a long glass.

A passing barkentine.

we shall look pretty well to go into port. She has been painted & decks scraped & oiled & even the Lazarette & fore peak scraped & varnished. I had to go down in the Lazarette one day to pass my Judgment on it, but I have not visited the fore peak [a triangular storage space in the very bow of the ship]. I have been in the vessel most two years & have only been on the Forecastle deck once, & that was in port with some callers who wanted to go up there. [Alice is referring to the deck at the front of the ship. Of course, the forecastle area was the crew's territory and Alice would have respected their boundaries.]

Last evening we actualy saw the North Star. We was far enough north to see it the night before only it was cloudy. We had not seen it for most a year & I was the first to find it between the clouds.

There are some Crickets in the hold & every night we can here them singing as we walk past the Booby Hatch. It sounds quite like home to here them.

Wednesday March 1st 1899   114 Days at Sea

We are nearer home than we have been for some time. Cape May bears N. ½ W. 60 miles, but it is verry moderate today & thick weather & terribly cold it feels to us all. The Ther. was 34 this morning. We only needed a fire in the Cabin since tuesday night when we came out of the Gulf Stream. All day tuesday we had a heavy blow about N.W. & was layed too during the night. A Bark in Company bound north. Today we are quite near a three masted Sch'r the "Nantasket" loaded with hard pine. A four master is in sight some distance to the westward & also a fishing Sch'r. We are 22 days from the Line & had strong N.E. trades. In 8 days we made 1703 miles then it commenced to fall off but we are doing pretty well if we have a run to N.Y. by Sat. & dont get any heavy blows or storms.

We are pretty well through with the painting & other improvements for port. Sumner finished some varnishing today which is the last I believe, & when a Tug gets hold of us we will lay the carpets &

put the finishing touch to things then take our Carpet bag & strike out for Yarmouth.

We feel quite anxious to here from home & know how they all are.

In this last entry in her journal, Alice reports their triumphant arrival in New York. By "we had a good chance up to anchor" she means that the prevailing weather conditions were so favorable that they sailed to their anchorage without the assistance of a tugboat.

Even sadder news awaited them at the end of this voyage than on their arrival a year ago when they learned that the *Mattie B. Russell* had been wrecked. The steamship *Portland* had been lost with no survivors on its run to Portland from Boston during the 1898 Thanksgiving holidays. The tragedy was not realized immediately because those expecting her in Portland thought she was waiting out the storm in Boston, while those in Boston assumed she had made it to Maine. Her master, Captain Blanchard, some of the crew and many passengers were from Yarmouth.

March 5th

At anchor off Staten Island at Upper Quarrantine. We arrived early yesterday morning 116 days from Singapore.

24 [days] from the Line & 5 from Cape Hatteras. We layed nearly two days within 10 miles of Barnegat [Barnegate Light] becalmed or light wind ahead. Friday night at sunset the wind breezed up about east & we had a good chance up to anchor, had no need of a Tug & nearly missed a Pilot, but finaly one came along side & it happened to be the same one who took us up last Voyage.

As soon as the Doctor had made his call on board, Sumner went on shore & entered. He got back at 6 P.M. & brought the news & several letters which we was glad to get & know they are all right at home, for we had had no news from home for nearly five months & that is time enough for many things to happen. And many terrible things have taken place in that time. The loss of the "Portland" seems fully as bad to us as the loss of the "Maine" or even more so as there was some on her who we knew.

We consider ourselves fortunate to get on the coast & into N.Y. with so little bad weather in this stormy month. It is foggy & raining ever since we anchored & seems terrible cold after spending nearly eight months in hot weather.

This morning the 2nd mate & 5 men went on shore for good & when they was ready to get into the boat, they gave three cheers for the "Grace Deering," three for the Capt. & three for the Mrs. as they all called me, quite a loud celebration in our honor.

This voyage of over 13 months is ended & now I will close this Able Effort although I am almost sorry to do so.

Evidently Alice decided that two years at sea was enough. She did not accompany Sumner on his third voyage with the *Grace Deering* when he again set sail for Dunedin, seven weeks after they got home. Her absence may have proved Sumner's loss and our gain, for not only two of his diaries but also several of the most beautiful letters in this collection survived from that voyage.

Because Sumner's route to New Zealand took him via the Cape of Good Hope and back past Cape Horn, this passage was his second and final circuit of the world.

April 30, 1899– February 15, 1900

Sun. April 30, 1899   Weather= Mild & Pleasant
   Preparing for Church when recd [a] Telegram from Capt. Webster to go on to N. York at once as the Deering was to finish loading Tomorrow. Made a few hurried calls to Mother & the sisters & Brothers & went to Portland on 1.30 Electrics [trolley]. Edith, Alfred & Hattie Gould [a close personal friend to Hattie John] riding in with Alice & I. Called on Captain Webster. Took P.M. Train to Boston, spent the Eve

with Hattie [Alice's sister, Harriet] & took the 11 oclock Express to N.Y.

Sumner notes in the following entry that the *Grace Deering* had been repaired and has passed inspection by the American Shipmasters Association. This society, currently known as the American Bureau of Shipping, published the *American Record,* a listing of insured ocean-going vessels. The *Deering* was granted the highest rating, which assured the underwriters that they were insuring cargo in a seaworthy vessel. The *Bureau Veritas* was the French equivalent of the *American Record.*

The *Grace Deering* was showing her age. A brand-new vessel would be certified for a ten- to fifteen-year period. Since she was twenty-two, the American inspectors were keeping an eye on her by only classifying her for three years at a time.

Monday, May 1, 1899   Weather= Warm & Pleasant   light variable winds
   Arrived in New York at 6.30 am. On board the Deering at 8.30. Found her loaded. Begin duty this day. Ship has been reclassed in the Amer= Record with the Class ✠ A 1 for 3 years from April 1899. Also in the Bureau Veritas with the Class ✠ 3/3 L 1 1 four years from December 1898. Calked from Garboard [by keel] to Deck, newly metaled [on hull] & various iron work & repairs about Deck. 2 water casks, 1 Kedge Anchor [a small anchor used to move the vessel by setting the anchor ahead and taking in the attached line], New Spanker [lower sail on the mizzenmast], & aft hawse pipe taken out and etc. [an iron pipe through which the anchor cable passes]. Allso had new Rudder & Allso Main deck under Poop deck recalked.

Sumner is evading another bit of bureaucracy, however. The United States government had passed the Act of December 21, 1898, which required masters of sailing vessels over 700 tons to meet federal government standards. Formerly, the only necessary licensing for sea captains was that done by the American Shipmasters Association. Sumner is taking advantage of the act's grace period to leave for New Zealand, postponing the examination for as long as possible.

Sumner writes Alice that the vessel's draft is different from their last voyage. The vessel's draft affected her handling, and moreover, a few inches' variation between bow and stern could markedly affect the sailing abilities of a three-masted bark.

Much earlier in maritime history, in the Middle Ages, sailing technique was not so subtle. Speed was not a factor. Vessels were military weapons—fortresses that floated out to meet the enemy. Their tactics were limited to ramming the opposing ship and pelting it with fire pots and boiling oil. The ship with the taller castles had the advantage; her defenders could throw downwards. Each ship could accommodate two castles, the "forecastle" and the "aftercastle," wooden towers located at either end. With the use of gunpowder, these castles became more a target than a protection. Gradually they were cut down until only the name forecastle, pronounced fo'c's'le, remained to designate the crew's quarters.

Sailors' quarters, over the last three or four centuries, had no resemblance whatsoever to the grandeur of a castle. It seems to have occurred to no one that giving deepwater seamen decent living quarters, reasonable hours, good food and a fair share of the profits might prove sensible in the long run. Sumner, like most captains of his time, credited the school of hard knocks for his own character development. He therefore resisted improving the working conditions of his crew on the premise that anybody who remained a common sailor had only himself to blame. This attitude was very much the mentality of the time, and somehow it doesn't jibe with the softer side Sumner shows in his letters to Alice.

With the steamships draining the supply of good seamen, Sumner and the other sailing captains were often dependent on "crimps," or boardinghouse keepers, to round up sailors. The keepers would put aboard any human body they could find. In most instances they brought the men aboard after the vessel had pulled away from the wharf and was anchored in the harbor. The sailors were usually too drunk to reveal their own inadequacies or raise any objections to being shipped. Sumner's remark "Had to pay $22.00 for sailors" refers to the crimp's fee. Captains called it "blood money."

The "library" he mentions was probably furnished by the American Seaman's Friend Society. The system worked so that books could be exchanged for a new collection at any American port. Most of the rather dull books that were provided were printed in English. There were few in other languages, despite the fact that many seamen did not read English. The library also contained many Bibles, to be given to those crew members who wanted them.

Captain Meach is master of the *Grace Deering*'s "sister" ship, the *Onaway,* a 932-ton bark built in Yarmouth in 1883. No doubt he and Sumner compared notes on their employer, Captain Benjamin Webster.

Rather than renting a bicycle for excursions in foreign ports, Sumner was economizing by bringing his own on this trip.

The other "Captains" to whom Sumner refers in this letter are friends. Captain Nicholas and Sumner had bicycled together in Singapore and Sumner was delighted to beat him and the *Emily Reed* to New York by six days. Captain Beverage's ship, *J. V. Troop,* had entered Singapore harbor "in distress" for extensive repairs and Sumner and Alice had helped celebrate Captain Mowatt's eleventh wedding anniversary in Singapore.

Arnold Cheney is the merchant shipping the cargo, the employer of the vessel. By "folks" Sumner means Arnold Cheney's firm.

New York   Monday eve May 1st 99
Dear Alice
I wrote you a note last eve just before leaving Boston. I got here safe this morning. Have cleared from Customs & shipped crew today & the Deering is loaded & will tow to stream tomorrow noon. I expect it will only take a short time to get the Bike if John sends it.

The vessel is drawing just 18 ft aft & 17 ft 3½ inches forward making a mean draft of 17 ft 6¼ inches. Last voyage the mean draft was 17-10 so that she is a few inches lighter but a little more by the stern. I shall write a line by the Pilot later.

10.30 a.m. Tuesday   I left this last night quite sudden & will write a little more now. The Bicycle has just come all right, $1.00 charge on it. . . . Took Tea on board the Onaway. I like Capt Meach & wife very much. Mrs. Meach hoped to meet you & was very much disappointed not to meet us at Singapore. She is going to stay home this voyage so we, Capt M & self, can sympathize with each other.

Our sails from Boston have not arrived & it will detain us untill tomorrow. Otherwise we are all ready. I had a very pleasent call on Mr. Bradford [a friend who lived in Brooklyn] & they had a package of Books for me. Also I have a library.

Have seen Capt. Nichols. He is loading for Hong Kong. Capt Beverage arrived safe at Liverpool March 20th. Had a long passage from St. Helena. The Samar arrived here yesterday & is down below. Capt. Mowatt went to Calcutta.

I have your letter & also one from Capt Webster. I told you I had money [an advance] of him $300.00 dollars. He thinks I should only [be allowed] $25.00 a month till that is paid by wages earned. So if you can get along with that untill I get out, had better do as he wishes.

I think Nellie [Alice's new sister-in-law] ought to sell her wheel quite reasonable & if so it would please Edith [Sumner's niece] about as well as a new one . . . I expect you will have a bike soon & hope you will enjoy it & you & Nellie will take lots of rides together. If you get her old one for Edith you will make quite a team. Don't get hurt on your wheel.

I felt very badly coming on but have no time to here. Expect I shall be awful lonesome. I shall take good care of myself & hope you will. Arnold Cheney's folks tell me they will wire you when they get news of my arrival at Dunedin as they get a cable from there every Monday. I left them your address. Don't write letters to Dunedin later than the middle of August & to Auckland—you can think I may be there as late as the middle of Nov=   If Arnold Cheney telegraphs you my arrival, it would be well to acknowelege it by a few words of thanks.

I think I shall like Mr. Dodge the mate very well. He impresses me quite favorably . . . I like the appearance of the cook. He was in the Johnson when we were there and he remembers us from the last voyage. Had to pay $22.00 for sailors. A new law is out with a whole mess of stuff in. Got to give sailors Butter & Pickels & vegetables & co. & co. I expect bye & bye they'll have spring Beds & Ice Cream & an extra cook to wait on them.

Have got my Postum & a pot to make it in. Shall have to go without either an organ or Typewriter. [Sumner had hoped to learn to "operate" one of these on this voyage.] It may be just as well. I have had my Sextant fixed & got what I need for charts of Dunedin & a new one from Cape Cod to Cape Hatteres. I have only about $2.   50 cts. left. . . . Barker, Carver & Morrell [merchants from whom he bought supplies & tobacco] made me a present of a fine Pocket Knife so I'll have something to whittle with. . . . I wish you would make mother a present during the summer of something to wear . . . & call down often to see them.

Write long letters & all the news. Tell Hattie Poole [Alice's girlhood friend who had sailed with them on the schooner *Bramhall* in 1889] I was sorry not to say good bye. Shall expect a letter from her with your permission. Of course she will ask that & perhaps want you to read it. . . .

I hear the Samar is to be sold. I wish John could get her. She is a nice vessel. . . . I do hope John will get something for business soon. I thought he felt quite Bad when I came away & I pitied him. Wish I could help him. If he has to buy in to anything of a vessel, perhaps if it should be later on you could do so to a small extent.

Well good bye for now. Shall send back word by the Pilot. I rather dread the outward passage but it will soon pass, I hope.

With much love   Your own
love to all   Sumner

excuse the great ink blot

The Drinkwaters' passage from Singapore had brought them home in time to attend the marriage of Nellie Groves to Alice's brother, Jack, on April 15—a few weeks earlier than the following letter. The newlyweds provide an example of how complicated Drinkwater family ties could be. Nellie, the bride, was the daughter of Hattie John's elder sister, and, therefore, John's niece by marriage. Thus, Alice was the sister of the groom, and Sumner was related distantly through his brother John to the bride. After their marriage Jack and Nellie made their home in Alice's family homestead, where Sumner and Alice had been living for sixteen and a half years. Eventually Jack would inherit the property.

The chair Sumner refers to in this letter was of rattan and had been purchased in Singapore. Sumner and Alice wanted to give it to the newlyweds as a wedding present, but customs officers were about when he had a chance to send it ashore. The "table" he mentions was

a plant stand he had made for Alice during the voyage home from Singapore. The customs officials would evidently not object to his handmade table.

6 a.m.   May 5th 99
Dear Alice
We are towing out. Clear nearly calm since midnight. At present a light air N.N.E. & Hayzy. Tide Ebb so hope to drift off clear for a breeze later on. . . .

I thought the 3rd we would have a good chance to go to sea, but the wind shifted S.E. fresh. No loss without some gain. The crew were most of them full when they came on board so they had a chance to sober up. . . .

I wanted awfully to send the Chair for Jack & Nellie but did not dare to as a officer had been aboard to see if they were still in the Cabin. I was afraid they would see it [leaving] & seize it so will have to take it on the voyage. I slipped the Table on the truck when we had Paints & Oil delivered from the Portland Boat & they took it back to the Boat. There will be 25 cts [freight] to pay on the Table.

Well good bye again. I don't like sleeping in our Berth without you but will have to get used to it.

Take good care of yourself. With lots of love.
Sumner

The "canned goods"—actually in jars—that Sumner mentions were probably purchased in New York. The ship's stores were provided for the crew by the shipowner, but the captain, according to his personal taste and digestion, often purchased additional food for his table at his own expense. The steward would add these provisions to the simple fare sent from the galley. Most captains treated themselves well; many ship-chandlery lists with every delicacy imaginable survive from this time.

Back home in Yarmouth, home-canned produce from family gardens was far more commonly consumed than commercially processed food. Although Sumner hadn't been home to garden in the last few years, the family might have contributed some conserves to his private larder.

The farmer/sailor tradition in the State of Maine meant that men were not entirely dependent on seafaring or shipbuilding and could spend their slack time farming. In the eighteenth century the farmer built his own vessel near growing timber on his own property, and during the long Maine winter he went to sea. Captain Benjamin Webster's grandfather, John Webster, built a vessel in the dooryard of his Freeport home, just north of Yarmouth, and with oxen, hauled it on sleds over the fields to Cousins River, where it was launched. He put his nineteen-year-old son, Benjamin's father, in command, took on a cargo and sailed as passenger to his home in Cold Kirby, England, which he had left with one guinea to his name some thirty years before.

At Sea Sunday May 14/99   Lat 31°—32'
Long = 53°—57'

P.M.
My Dear Alice

It is two weeks this afternoon since I bid you adieu at Union Station, two weeks that I look back on as months. As I have been thinking much of that day & my rather hurried departure & my thoughts being with you, I thought I would see if writing a few lines would take up my mind & in a measure drive away the lonely feelings which seem to trouble me more today than any previous ones, although they have all, since leaving New York, been quite lonesome enough. I don't know as you can quite realize my feelings, yet I have no doubt you too have felt lonesome. Still I can hardly think it equals mine. I suppose I'll get used to it by & by, but next winter looks a long way off just now. I must think of things more cheerful—that as I write this you may be taking a ride on a new bike perhaps down to Mothers & cheering her up a bit. I think she feels my going away on these long voyages more & more, she & Father too, & quite naturally so, for they know their years in life are growing less. I hope you will go down often to see them.

Well shall I write something of the past 9 days since I sent you a letter by the Capt that towed us out which I hope you got all right? We had light Easterly & Southerly winds for 3 days & got a head but little. We lost Barnegat Light about 3 a.m. from aloft Sat. morning. Since then we have had 2 days of N.W. & Northerly, 1 of calm, & the rest S.W. to westerly fresh. Today has been lovely with westerly wind up to the present.

This forenoon, I have shaved as usual, had a Bath & Put on summer underclothes. We got the carpets up & aired & Beat them. I have Busied myself much of the past week in arranging the Cabin as I thought you would want it. I stowed away the canned goods, put up the library & stowed our wicker chairs away . . . Most of which I stowed covered up in the Berth of the Port room. My Bike I cleaned thoroughly & covered with a Slop room Blanket [the slop room is where he stored merchandise to sell to his crew] & keep it back of the Lounge in our room. I found the Plants in rather a wilted condition, but have brought them back to life. The large one in the forward sky light has 2 Blossoms on it & 3 buds. Do you know I hunted everwhere for the old coverings for the lounge & chair & could not find them Untill today in looking over the trunk for under clothes & my Blue Trimed house Jacket I found them? I forgot you carried them home to wash so I'll change them tomorrow. I have put Hattie's sofa Pillow on the lounge in our room & have not had a nap on it yet. Evening I'll write a line more.

I think on the whole I have a pretty good crew. I like the Mate very well so far & being a down Easter & knowing many coasters & people that I know, it's more pleasant than having a dutchman. The 2nd Mate is not up to Johnson but a well meaning fellow & wants to please me & so of the cook. . . . The steward is a colored fellow Belongs at Demerara. Very good natured and obliging.

There is a new law in force now in regard to sailors & a new scale of Provisions which gives them lots of dainties such as Butter, dried fruit, Pickles & co but I have fed them much as usual. Yesterday I called them all aft & asked them if they were satisfied with their Grub as they had it or if they wanted it weighed out to them as per scale. They all were quite satisfied as they had it (a plenty & no waste) & I made a writting of it & had them all sign it & the Mates witness it.

Tonight I have my first patient so I have had to get the Doctor Books out again. Well I'll smoke a little cigar & turn in but it's awfully lonesome sleeping alone. It's past 10 & you are soundly sleeping I hope. With a Kiss Good night   S—

As Sumner could not post his letter until he reached Australia, he simply continued it three weeks later.

A vessel carried two sets of sails. The old ones were used during the good weather of the tropics in the middle of this voyage, while the stronger ones which they had begun with were stored away for the storms at the end.

Sumner included a long list of the clothes that he washed in which uniforms are notably lacking. No one wore a uniform or gold braid, nor was there any saluting on board these ships. The sailors, in fact, might have been taken for farmhands in their blue jeans, and the mates could have passed for factory foremen. But no sailor addressing an officer omitted "sir." And another formality which was observed was that the officer on watch, when not supervising work elsewhere, took his post on the windward side of the poop deck. He yielded this position to the captain, moving to the lee side of the deck, if the captain came up from his cabin. The windward side of the poop deck, or quarterdeck, was the captain's exclusive domain.

Sunday   June 4th/99   Calm   Lat 3° north
                                             Long = 27° 30′ west

3 weeks, Dear, since my last writing & passed quite quickly, yet I havn't got at all reconciled to this voyage without you yet.

The 2 Sundays interveening I have comenced letters, one to Father & Mother & to some of the many sisters & nieces. . . . I'll mention right here that I miss you everyday when I come to look up Logarithms. I am using Beverly Tables [his preferred logarithmic tables] all together this voyage.

Now to return to the 14th May, my last writing & bring the incidents of the voyage up to the present. On the 16th we made a sail on our starboard bow which proved a Bark out-ward bound. We passed her before night to far to windward to signal. During that week we bent all the old sails & commenced over-hauling the Best ones.

On the . . . 28th we caught our first fish a fine Bonita. . . . May 30th (up to which from the 23d we had steady Trades & fine weather) it died away at noon & from 2 till 4 o'clock P.M. we had as heavy a shower as one could wish for & about calm. We scrubbed the after house clean & filled up everything with nice fresh water. (I don't know if I mentioned Capt. Crickett got 2 Water Casks & Kedge Anchor.) May 31st I did a big wash. 2 sheets 3 Pillow slips 3 Towels 4 HKer-cheifs 3 suits of under clothes 3 outside shirts 2 House Jackets Lounge & Chair coverings Port Room Berth Curtains 5 Pr. Stockings 1 Blan-kett & 2 Pair Pants. I all so had all my old Pants Coats & vests washed out by the Boys. They plugged the Scuppers [overboard drain holes] in the main deck & had 2 or 3 feet of water & Mates & all had a general scrubing of old clothes. On June 1st 8-30 a.m. we were up with another Bark, which on signaling we found to be the Charles S. Rice (Yarmouth Built) from Halifax N.S. for Buenous Ayres 31 days out, our 27th. I found her reported at Boston April 1st but she must have gone down there to load, or had been in there. She was quite light loaded, but we out sailed her. I think the Deering sails better than she has heretofore & perhaps its being 3 or 4 inches more by the stern. That afternoon I Ironed my wash & done a good Job too.

Today we have a ship in sight to the S.E. of us, in fact has been in sight since Yesterday Morning. We lost the Rice the next day after signaling her. We were quite near her at one time & I took a snap shot of her but have not developed it yet. . . . You see from the above we have had some little variations along the way & of course it's gratifying to Pass everything you fall in with. I don't know how it will be with the ship [that they were then racing]. Will tell you later, when we get a Breeze. Now I'll take a rest. It's so warm. Ther. 86 in the cool.

I wish you was here. If you were I suppose you would be having your after noon nap. That is if I would let you, which I think very doubtful, especially if you came aboard now, for I should be awfully glad to see you. I can scarcely bare to think of it, & such a long time to look ahead. Now Bye bye for a while. If you are reading this letter to your mother you can do as you like about omitting the above, with lots of love your longing Sumner-

Evening a gentle breeze from E.N.E. about 4 knots & overcast & a little cooler

Good night.

Sumner includes some of his poems in this section of his ongoing letter to Alice. Poetry was very much in vogue during the Victorian era and writing it was not considered "unmanly" at all. Autograph books were circulated among friends, and people would vie with one another to create highly stylized poems. Because a great many of these poems centered on death and the "here-after," some of these autographs books are depressing when read today. Despite the charm of yesteryear, people were very aware of the shadow of death—and for good cause.

Sumner had a penchant for language from his early childhood. It is still remembered that when he was only four the family would proudly set him on the kitchen table to give a recitation of "David and Goliath."

Sunday June 11th/99   Lat=1° 38' north
Long=29.53 west
2 P.M. 38 days out

My Dear Alice Another week gone by & just look at our Position. 180 miles S.W. of where we were last Sunday. That Gentle

Easterly Breeze that I mentioned in retireing last Sunday night died out just after midnight & there has been scarcely any wind since. Some days calm the entire 24 hours & others little puffs for an hour or so from all about & we have done little but drift to the westward. Today finds us 40 miles N.W. of St. Pauls Rocks & I don't see how we are going to fetch by St Roke unless we get very favorable trades. . . .A moderate breeze S.E. set in last night. We head up about S.W. by S. I think we have the Trades & am very thankful. It's been a long week & of course I have fretted about loosing a good run to the Equator as last sunday I thought I should do it in 33 days sure. But if we only fetch clear of the South American Coast I shan't complain.

I have busied my self this past week in cleaning scraping & varnishing the Bath Room & it looks fine. I don't use the salt water Bath much but have had a fresh water one about every day this week. It's pretty warm nights & a Bath is quite refreshing & cooling.

I have written quite a lot during the past week. I thought as I had no Organ to learn music & no Typewriter to Practice on I would turn my spare time & talents into new channels of acquirements & amusement & take to Poetry. And when this Letter you receive

  I hope t'will set Your mind at ease
  Will fill your heart with Joy & Peace
  And all your doubts & fears will cease.
  Will bring to You a sweet content
  That over half the voyage is spent
  That ere Thus 4 months from its receipt
  If God so wills again we'll meet.
  Then let the meetings fond Embrace
  These (Lonely hours) thy Love Erase.
  And thus embracing heart to heart
  A richer deeper love impart.

I call to mind while my thoughts are all aglow with this little effort, what Capt Nichols said to me when I told him you were not going

this voyage. Perhaps it was more in fun than ernest yet I have often
thought of it. He said in answer, "I am glad of it. You'll know how
to appreciate a wife after making a long voyage alone, which we are
not apt to do as we should when they are with us all the time." He
ended his consolation by saying, "It will do you lots of good Drinkwater. I've had lots of experience & know something about it." I
think there is much truth in what he said. Now Dear I'll lay this
aside for a time but not my thoughts. I'll accompany them on deck
with a cigar & see if we are gaining on our neighbors any.

Bye bye with love

Sumner did not continue his letter to Alice until later that evening.
Neither did he remain sedately on deck but "ascended to the Mizzen-
top"—went aloft on the mast closest to the back of the vessel.
Sumner was now forty years old.

Evening. . . .

I took my long glass on going on deck after my P.M. writing &
ascended to the Mizzen-top [see page 57] & focussed it on our new
neighbor & straight-way concluded it was the Chas-S Rice which had
crawled up in sight again during the Calm. . . .

I want to add a few more lines relating to the past week. On
Tuesday the 6th the German Steamer Larinia Passed north close to,
so that I hailed the Bridge & found she was bound to Philadelphia &
would report us. She had lots of Passengers who waved their kerchiefs
especially the Ladies & the sight of them (the Ladies I mean) "so near
& Yet so far" was good for sore eyes. We heard voices wishing us a
pleasant passage & I was so taken up with looking shouting & waving
that I forgot my Kodak & so lost an opportunity of getting a picture.
Too bad wasn't it? That's all that's occured of consequence during the
week. The rest has been gazing on a Glassy Sea & trying to occupy my
mind. . . .

Now I want to tell you what a thrifty, Industrous, little plant we
have. The same old plant, as Eldon says of the moon, but renewing Its

Port side, looking forward.

Edith's high school picture.

life. Today it is arrayed in all its Glory having no less than 20 lovely Blossoms on it & 7 Buds yet to Bloom. Ain't it a wonder? But I have tended it with Zelous care & thus has it rewarded me. I am very Proud of it. The little one in the after skylight seems frail & I fear for its future. I mean to have some New Zealand Plants coming home.

But I musn't devote to much time to wee wifie for she might tink I was in love & that would be awful at my time of life. So I'll say good night for it's late & I have been writing more Poetry.

Lovingly yours (Summie)

You'll think my spirits quite Bouyant this eve & they are for its such a welcome change. A nice cool Breeze of 5 or 6 knots heading S.S.W. & a new moon that <u>you</u> see.

Sumner's letter to Alice continued unbroken throughout the voyage to Australia, but because it was written at about this time, I am inserting a letter to "Cousin Eva," who was staying with his brother John's family at their Yarmouth village home during the school term 1898– 1899. I have not been able to identify Eva. She was sixteen, the age of John and Hattie's daughter, Edith. But none of the Drinkwater descendants remember an Eva. There may not have been any kinship; Sumner could have used the title "Cousin" as a courtesy. In any case, he was quite gallant to both young ladies and they had given him notes to open after he was on the high seas. Eva, just turning sixteen, had included her photograph in her letter, but both the girls' letters and Eva's photograph have been lost.

It is a pity that none of Sumner's letters to his niece Edith have survived because judging from this letter he wrote to Eva, they must have been gems. Edith was his surrogate daughter, the person he loved best in the world next to Alice and they corresponded during all of his voyages. Edith was about five foot four, had auburn hair, grayish-blue eyes and a sweet, obliging disposition. According to her grateful cousin Winifred Glover Blanchard, Edith ran an errand when Winifred was born in 1898, the year prior to Sumner's present voyage. Winifred's mother had come off Cousins Island to stay at the home of her sister, Hattie John, because it was in the village where she could be sure of a doctor for her time of confinement. Edith was dispatched hurriedly across the street to fetch a set of scales from the grocer to weigh the newborn baby.

Lattitude = 34° 30'N.
Longitude = 60° 00'W.

On Board the
Bark Grace Deering, at Sea, Friday Eve May 12/99

Though swiftly sailing o'er the Sea,
My thoughts tonight are all with thee.

My Dear Cousin Eva,   More particularly as I have just got a nice letter from you. Perhaps you would be quite surprised to know that one sometimes gets letters even when far off on the Ocean. Yet it is even so for . . . this morning some winged messenger of Love, flew to me with such a dainty little morsel of good cheer. I oppened it wondering who could be its author, yet I half guessed for I knew the address was familiar. [Eva was living at his niece Edith's home and initially Sumner supposed the note to be from Edith.] I had not guessed quite right (how similar are your Handwritings or did one of you address both).

Well I wish to thank you for a very pleasant little surprise. It's most as nice as having a May-Basket. How sorry I am that I missed that little "Plan" you had in view. Just imagine an <u>Old</u> <u>Fellow</u> like me running after "<u>Sweet</u> <u>Sixteen.</u>" Yet I fancy you would have been quite surprised to find how fast I could go & I feel quite sure you would in the end become a laughing captive & paid dearly for your fun, for I should no doubt have been a very exacting master.

And so this little letter tells me You are Sweet Sixteen & You, Cousin Eva, do not realize what it means. The Happiest time of Life, the Halcyon days of Youth & Innocense, a maytime of Blossoms. May it remain thus to You for many many years. Try to realize that these are Precious hours & profit by them all you can. Yet not to take from youth all . . . inocent & healthful pleasure, the memory of which will be pleasnt to recall in maturer years. Gain useful knowledge as well as those essential lessons of duty, Patience, faith, & love, which point to the highest attainment of pure womanhood.

Did you ever think that those who have passed that stage of life often look back to it with a longing to live it over once again . . . for its sweetness & others still, that he or she might live it differently, perhaps to blot out some error of Youth for all of us have an inner life of which the world knows nothing, to say nothing of the outside of which it is so fond of knowing all. I sincerely hope & Trust yours will pass so Pure & happily that to recall it in later years will be a pleasure. In a great measure Dear Cousin it lays with you to make it so, choosing only those associations in life that are good & True thus laying the foundation upon which to build a good & useful Life.

It is my intention to answer every part of this little letter which you choose to call nonsense so . . . it will be quite lengthy. Quite likely you will not try to get through it all but throw it in to the waste basket or the fire. But if either (the fire please) for it is written only to you & an answer to that Birthday letter. I should feel very badly if I thought others read it (say that maiden Lady I met at your home) for I don't wish to amuse the Public, even though I have lots of spare time.

But now I am going to retire as the hour is late & I imagine that you are in the arms of Morpheus Dreaming of Sweet Sixteen. I hope the day has been a pleasant one to you. I wish I had known it was so near. I should [have] left some little remembrance of it for your. Good night.

June 16th- 99 9 P.M.   Lat = 05° -49'South
                                                 Long = 31° -49'West

[Cousin Eva had promised Sumner that she would arrive mid-Ocean in Fairy form on this date.]

Dear Cousin, To Calm my disappointed mind this eve, (after a day elated . . . by the expected pleasure of a Fairy visitor, which "Alas" came not), I'll Pen a few thoughts to you. Shall I scold you for disappointing me so or shall I think that

> As Twice two thousand miles divide
> My little Bark from home and Thee,
> I fear some ill would sure betide
> A flight so far across the sea.

Yes I guess that is the best way to think about it but I have Been on the watch all day expecting to see some enchanting vision of lovelyness appear in the heavens & coming directly towards us. But all in vain, & to think how I had prepared all the choicest delicacies the ship afforded, such as roast chicken & vegetables, Lobster salad & cranberry sauce, Strawberry Pie, & Jam tarts, & roly poly pudding. Besides I had Oranges & Bananas & a lot of J.C. Morton's English Pepermint drops & three kinds of Sugar, & I had to eat it all alone. What a shame & what a job to, but I let the mate help me a little.

I've thought about it so much that I have even wrote Poetry about it or comenced some verses but may not send them. If I do you are hereby strictly admonished & forbidden to allow them to be seen by curious eyes. I mean by those who would criticise & make fun. Of course, you can laugh all you wish to over them & show them to Edith, as I am writing her some which she will show you. Her letter I oppened on the 25th & comenced an answer that night.

I wonder if tonight you are all collected in "Paradise Alley" on the doorstep & if it is as lovely a night as with me. I hope, if so, you are enjoying it & . . . feeling rather glad that you will now have a nice long vacation. Mine is over for a long time just as the fine weather was coming & spring just buding in lovelyness. I can imagine now that dear old Yarmouth is clothed in her fairest garments. The Trees full leaved & blossoming, the fields green & flowers fragrant, & the streets alive & Picturesque with the variagated costumes of the many Bicy-

clists who doubtless are now enjoying that new Bicycle road that was voted for them.

Isn't it just awful one has to be imprisoned on the Ocean for months & loose all these pleasures of life on shore. Don't you Pity me? I wonder if you will go to Brunswick [a nearby town in Maine] this year & see the Fatty-Man? But you musn't flirt with him, Young Misses of Sweet Sixteen should not flirt but be real good & mind their Aunties, & study the Organ, for I shall expect you to Play & sing to me next winter lots of nice peices. You must learn "Paradise Alley." I shall think of you often as one of the group on the doorstep & . . . I wonder if you will have a thought for me in your merry making. I think you will & yet not realize as I do how far from Yarmouth I am tonight & what a vast Ocean rolls between me & "Paradise Alley." It makes me quite lonely to think of it & the many thousand miles I must sail before I can return to it.

. . . Day after day the Sun rises a golden Ball out of the Ocean flooding sea & sky with unbounded light & Glory, & when it has traversed its daily Hemicircle through the heavens sinks again beneath the Oceans western Horizon only to repeat it, an endless round of monotony. Yet the days at Sea are not tiresome or lonely if one is disposed to be occupied as I am. Generally, there is allways plenty to do. But the evenings, . . . those are the most lonely hours to contend with & thought & mind have then full play. Even the generally soothing influence of a fragrant manila [cigar] is not always an antidote for lonesomeness. Especially the beautiful moon-light ones, (so different it seems to me than at home). The full moon presenting to the eye a perfect globe of soft light floating in the pure ether, not as a simple disc against the sky. Then too it is the one thing alone the lonely mariner can most nearly associate with home, knowing that those he thinks of while he looks at it may at the same moment be gazing at its mellow light with thoughts of him.

You never have been on the Ocean. Perhaps you are not interested in it. Yet possibly you would like to know something about it & what it is like. . . . For the past few weeks we have been passing over its best side, through the Tropic, sailing day after day over a peaceful Ocean ever grand & solemn, yet calm & beautiful . . . Tonight is a lovely eve, with a growing moon shedding her soft light upon the ocean, & the stars which seem double their ordinary size as seen in our northern clime, shining so brillantly, seem to drop like myriad Lamps from the blue vault of heaven, which is shaded here & there by light fleecy clouds sailing over its surface. The gentle breeze rippling the surface of the sea causes it to glint & sparkle in the moonlight. This would greet the eye on deck, while to the ear as I sit in silence comes the gentle splashing of the water along the side as the vessel glides through it, & I feel just a gentle rise & fall or heaving motion to which one becomes so accustomed as to scarcely feel it or take any notice of it. From the Deck comes scarcely any sounds, perhaps the foot-falls of the officer of the deck as he paces to & fro & a sort of chirping of the Blocks aloft. Everything else is still. . . . But storms & boisterous Seas & Gales must be encountered later on, so that the Ocean like the Sea of life is not all sunshine.

You said you knew I should be delighted on receiving your little letter, & though you seemed to write in Jest, yet never-the-less I was very much pleased to have it to open at sea. I shall allways keep it as a pleasant remembrance, & look upon it as the first bright Sun beam to greet me after the last lingering look at the receeding shores of my native land which was just six weeks ago tonight, & is now 4000 miles away. Oh! Dear!

You spoke of my departure as sudden & you were not prepared to say good bye in a real tragical manner, not having at hand the necessary requisite for the occasion. Now I am real sorry it happened so, I'll try next time to give you notice so you can be prepared. Yet let me assure you that I have a greater power of decernment that you may be aware of, & a face is to me quite often as an open Book. So although you were in fun & in fact are, so often so, it is difficult to pick out the ernest moments, yet I fain would believe that I saw real

manifestations of regret, & shall think that the reference to "the quiet of the evening" was in Ernest.

I don't know why but I do know it is pleasant to feel one is missed. I hope I shall get a nice long letter from you when I reach those distant shores, but I expect your summer vacation will be filled with so many pleasures that I shall get but few thoughts. I hope you will sacrifice an hour or so of the season's gayeties to your distant yet mindful cousin. How clearly does the Eye of faith discern the fair vision that is wont to enrich the beauties & delights of Paradise Alley & 3 times every day too. I don't think you intended that I should forget my Black-Eyed Cousin, neither shall I, more especially as I have a beautiful likeness of her arranged on the wall over my secretary [desk]. As it greets my vision each time I enter my state-room, you can easily imagine how many times you will be brought before the eye of faith. (3 times 3 times 3 times 3=81 everyday.)

> **But now Goodnight May Angels Keep**
> **Bright Vigils o'er thy slumbers deep**

> Coz-Sumner

This is the poem Sumner wrote in response to Cousin Eva's fantasy of paying him a call on her last day of school (June 16). "Auntie" refers to Hattie John:

> Tis eve, all through the long bright day
> I've thought of thee & visions fair.
>
> My thoughts are all with Thee today.
> With Thee and fairy visions fair.
> Which wings to Thee their airy way.
> And feels that I your thoughts will share.
>
> Me-thinks I see a fairy form
> In dotted muslin soft arrayed
> With Gauzy wings and golden horn.
> Fit emblem for a fairy maid

For wrote you not in Happy mood
That on this sixteenth day of June
You in a Beauteous Vision would
A sylph-like fairy form assume

That on this day from school tasks free
With-out a ray of doubt or fear
Would wing thy way in Joy to me
The long & lonely hours to cheer

And thus I thought and Hoped and feared
The Fore-Top watched with wistful eye
Yet to my gaze no form appeared
No vision fair could I decry

Nights shadows now obscure my view
As Sea and Sky together blend
And fears my saddened thoughts persue
And Hopes in disappointment end

Ill look no more t'would useless be
The passing hours no gladness brings
Perhaps she dared not cross the Sea
Perhaps her Auntie clipped her wings

Sumner continued his ongoing letter to Alice mentioning that they have "crossed the Line." Traditionally, seamen crossing the equator organized a ceremony. Those in the crew who could prove they had passed it previously were deemed "shell backs" and they masqueraded as King Neptune, his Queen and retinue to initiate the inexperienced members of the crew." The antics ranged from practical jokes to near atrocities and the ceremony sometimes was not permitted by the captain. Neither Sumner nor Alice ever recorded its occurrence, which means that either Sumner didn't allow it or the crew hadn't organized it.

It is interesting to read in this section how much Sumner enjoyed going "visiting on the Ocean." One of the reasons must have been that with another captain—as with Alice—he was able to be himself rather than an authority figure. During the passage he was forced to isolate himself from his men or risk a challenge to his authority which might, in an emergency, endanger the ship and their lives. Sumner's letters reveal so much of his gentler nature that it is easy to overlook the fact that a sea captain's success depended on his ability to command obedience. Sumner was mild-mannered, not given to violence or profanity and he rarely raised his voice, but—he never lost a ship.

Sunday June 25th/99   Lat 20-24   Long+36-11   51 days at sea

2 weeks have passed my Dear since my last issue & I think fortnightly reports will be often enough. If I make them to often it will more than fill an ordinary envelope.

I feel some more contented as the weeks go by but still feel awfully lonesome at times & now the evenings are lengthning & become more lonesome. The sun sets at 5.30 now. . . .

Now I'll make a brief report of the past 2 weeks. There was not much occured of moment up to last night. We have been in Company with several sails during the time but we pass everything we fell in with. . . .

We crossed the Line about 4 a.m. that morning 13th. 39 days out in Long=30° 15′. Up to the 16th the Trades were very favorable & we passed St. Rouke about 100 miles off. That day a bark passed north in Ballast.

That eve, it being the day schools closed, I wrote some Both to Eva & Edith & some nonsensical verses which will do to laugh over. In fact I havn't finished them yet. . . .

Yesterday morning we discried a Barkentine to windward steering S.S.W. & as we were steering S.S.E. we gradually drew together & the mate said it was Emita, Capt Pray, & sure enough it was. That evening we were close together & we altered our courses & kept to-

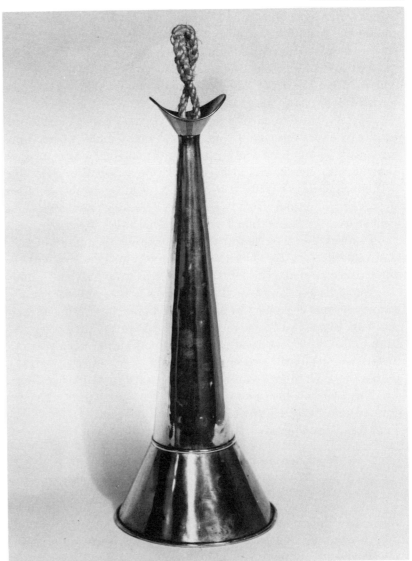

Sumner's speaking trumpet.

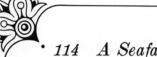

gether for an hour or more. As the wind was light, only 2 knot breeze, we put the small dingy over & went aboard & staid half an hour. I wrote you a few lines & so did Mr. D to his wife. As I think he ought to be a Bahia Blanca in 10 days you ought to get it by the first of Aug=   I hope he won't forget it & won't you be surprised & tickled. I wish I could have one from you tonight.

Wasn't it fun to go visiting on the Ocean. I carried him a maritime register & a few cigars & he gave me some matches as our supply was small. Young Capt Pray is in her, the one that was mate of the Deering with Meech. His father is sick. He sailed from N.Y. April 26th & was 59 days out to our 50. Wasn't it odd we should meet under so peculiar conditions. He says he is awfully lonesome & that he thinks I must be & I assured him I was. It seems twice as lonesome after going on board & then Seperating. At 10 oclock he was out of sight.

Yesterday was the Queen's Birthday but we didn't celebrate & I don't think we shall. The 4th I hope we will be to Tristan Decunha.

Now I'll close for a time. I wish I knew how you all were at home & how you were enjoying yourself & if you have your teeth out & how you look. I hope you'll send me a picture. [Alice was having her front teeth pulled, which seems odd as she was only thirty-seven years old. Teeth were regularly extracted as a cure for toothache, but some people chose dentures because they were terrified of the dentist.]

I wonder how the new couple get on. Finely I expect & loving as doves. Quite likely Hattie John is over to [Cousins] Island. I hope John has a vessel or some employment.

& now adieu no more I'll write
So bye bye Dear with fond good night. S—

The prevailing winds in the *Deering*'s position were north and when they shifted south or southwest as in the following instance, they became a "Southerly Buster," so called because the shift is always violent and sudden. Sumner was not caught entirely unaware, since the day had been squally on and off. He had reduced sail, but

even so, he was expecting the storm to come from astern when it suddenly swept in from the side. His crew had no time to take in sail. "I had to let the upper Topsails go by the run," he explained. In order to spill the wind from these sails he let go the lines (halyards), holding them in their hoisted position. When this was done, the halyards went "by the run" through the blocks, the yards dropped, and the sails flapped in the wind until the sailors could get up to furl them. Since he had not yet exchanged the poorer set of sails he had used in the tropics for the stronger ones, some of them flapped to ribbons before the men could get aloft.

Sumner reminisces about a "real old fashioned sailing Party . . . that Mr. Hamilton took us on" years before. His host, Joseph Hamilton, was Hattie John's father. The sailboat, the forty-foot *Bertha,* was only used around the islands and for trips to Portland.

Joseph Hamilton had died in 1894 walking across the ice bridge connecting Cousins Island to the Yarmouth mainland in the winter. He had been going to fetch his daughter Lizzie, Hattie John's younger sister, who taught at the "modern" schoolhouse which had replaced the old Ledge school. Lizzie boarded in Yarmouth all week and spent the weekends with her parents on Cousins Island.

On that winter day, Lizzie waited on the Foreside shore, watching her father come toward her, pulling a sled behind him for her bag. Suddenly he broke through the ice and disappeared from view. By the time help arrived, Joseph Hamilton was dead. Family legend has it that he did not drown but suffocated between two layers of ice, for after his death, no water was found in his lungs. Lizzie could never forget that day; she sobered afterward. Although she met and married John Glover the following year, the incident was rearely discussed in front of their daughters Doris and Winifred.

Independence Day   July 4th 1899   Lat=29-13S.
                                                         Long=28-48 W.

I know mid the Joys of this Glorious Day
Your thoughts will be with me though far far away.
As mine in bright fancies so often will Roam

Back to My Alice and the loved ones at home.
How much I'd enjoy being with you at Mess
To share in the Goodies of Dear Mother S.
But I have a Dish of which you'll not partake
I'm dining today on fresh Turtle Steak.
But I'll not write much if I try to compose
So turning from rhymes I'll continue in Prose.

Although My Dear I had intended not to write more than once in two weeks Yet as this was an exception 4th July I thought I would just write a few lines as you doubtless have me much in mind today (unless you have found a handsomer & more accomplished man. But if you have got all your front teeth out I don't beleive you have).

It has been a calm & therefore rather lonesome 4th today. You see how little I have done since my last writing. We are having lots of calm weather & are 60 days out & today noon was just 35 miles W. by S. ½ S. from where we were last voyage when 60 days out, so you see we are getting on very slow. Have only made 660 miles since I wrote last or in 10 days. Last wed= night we got a real Southerly Buster lasting 3 hours & blowing a gale. It shifted suddenly from north to S.W. & we had not shifted the old sails. Though it had been squally & I had all the light sails in & furled I didn't think of such a shift. How it took us aback. In fact I had the degallantsails [topgallant sails, see page 57] clewed up as I expected a squall from astern. But taking us on the starboard beam I had to let the upper Topsails go by the run & the old mainsail (you know how Poor it was) went all to peices & the old fore upper. But they were both ⁹⁄₁₀ worn out so it's not a great loss. We have all our best sails bent now & well prepaired for the eastern.

Yesterday P.M. I saw a turtle floating (it was calm) on the surface & put the dingy over. I took 2 men with me & rowing up close to him we scooped him in. I rigged a sort of slip-net of a large barren Hoop & a pole to it & clapped it right over him. He weighed 17½ lbs. alive. He made a nice 4th of July dinner for all hands & was fine, much like chicken. I am going to keep the shell or sack to Bring home. You see you are losing all the exciting times. I expect we'll get a gale next. I hope you are all well & enjoying the day on a picnic or sail.

I should like a real old fashioned sailing Party such as we used to have years ago. I remember one that Mr. Hamilton took us on to Harpswell. What a fine time we had & many others, all pleasant memories of long ago. As I let my thoughts go back to that one to Harpswell which must have been upwards of 25 years ago, I think how many of that happy company on the 4th of July have gone over the River, the other side of which is seen only by the eye of faith. At the foreside there is Capt= Soule & Sarah, both of Capt Cleaves sisters, Aunt Jane D., Lizzie Merril & her father, Chas Pendy & Mrs. Royal & Aunt Abbie B. & Fanny & John B. & Grace. Of those from Cousins Island I can only recall two, Ed Thompson & our Good Pilot Mr. Hamilton. All have departed hence to that "Land from whose bourne no traveler returns."

So again Good night
S.—

Sumner's notes for interpreting weather conditions based on barometer changes were written on the flyleaf of his 1891 diary:

a Rapid Rise = unsettled weather
a Gradual Rise = settled—
a rise with dry increased cold in summer [look for] wind from north if rain has fallen [look for] better weather
a rise with moist air & low temperature = wind and rain from north
a rise with South wind = fine weather
Steady Barometer, dry air & temperature = a temperate weather
a rapid fall = stormy weather
a rapid fall with westerly wind = stormy weather from north
a fall, wind north = storm, rain hard in summer, snow in winter
fall with increased heat & moisture = Southerly wind & rain

fall after any calm warmer weather indicates squally weather and rain

Barometer rises for north from northwest to east for Dry weather or less wet weather, less wind & sometimes rain, hail & snow from north, not strong wind

Bar. falls, wind from S from South East to west [look] for wet weather & stronger wind except sometimes when moderate wind North with rain or snow

falling Bar. with South wind=rain

sudden fall, wind west indicates violent storm from north or northwest

steady fall and East indicates wind to go South unless rain or snow falls at once

Falling Bar. wind north=worst kind of weather

if after storm Barometer is steady, severe weather follows but on its rise wind will change

This letter is illuminated by Sumner's sweet openness in expressing his love for Alice. In the letter, he first describes to Alice how he had exchanged signals with the British bark *Ravenswood.* Because he was not sure of her longitude, since her last sail (spanker) obscured his view, he asked Alice to check it in the newspaper report she would have seen by the time she wrote. By his record the vessels were about ten miles apart—"17-29 W=, ours 17-38"—when passing. Vessels ran up signal flags usually four at a time on a halyard located near the spanker. By referring to the International Code, the captains could interpret their meaning, even at a considerable distance apart. The first set of signals run off always gave the call letters of the ship. The diagram (page 57), the model (page 73) and the painting on the book jacket all show the *Grace Deering* flying her call letters, J.S.G.L.

In this letter Sumner mentions the fact that the barometer is low. He will be checking it constantly because a falling barometer signaled stormy weather, and the fact that "the sea is not bad" could rapidly change.

Sumner's brother John loved to tell a story about a voyage he made in the Caribbean when his barometer dropped so low and so fast he couldn't believe it. So he spoke a vessel alongside, "How does your barometer read, Cap'n?"

The captain answered, "Hell, my head's my barometer!"

The next morning this captain floated by him on a raft with just his long johns on and nothing left of the ship.

Sunday July 23d/99 Lat 38-56 Long=18°-48′   East=

79 days at sea

20 more days have gone by Dear, since my last writing & we are only off Good Hope, 4 days behind our last voyage & 13 behind the first so that we have got to make some big runs to be any where this voyage. On July 10th we exchanged signals with the British Bark Ravenswood.

We have had a great deal of moderate weather & no heavy gales so far although it is blowing heavy to night about North. . . . The sea is not bad but a low Barometer 29=44. We have had no cold weather yet, hav'nt had a mitten out & it's the dead of winter here. But one thing I greatly appreciate is John's Reefer [short warm jacket] or I should say yours, more especially, your persistance in my having it. It demonstrates the fact that a man needs the Love & care of woman to lookout for him & is rather a helpless Biped without her. So the appreciation of it fully expresses my thanks for your thoughtfulness.

We have seen nothing since the Bark referred to above & only have the company of the Cape Pigeons & hens. There has been very few Albatross about but no molly-hawks.

We are now having our shortest days & long nights, but are blest at present with a Glorious full moon. Tonight it is peeping out at intervals through the rifts & chinks of the cloud swept sky. Its bright beams dancing & shimmering o'er the crests of the foam capped billows & lighting for miles around the surface of the wind swept Ocean. I am glad to have it here off the Cape where I imagine the weather &

sea is more boisterous & capricious than farther East. I can't expect now to reach Dunedin before Sept. 10th which will be near the first Quarter of that moon. But the Days will have lengthened some 2°-30' as that would correspond to March at home.

One Year ago today we sailed from the busy Harbor of New Castle for the East Indias & the Hot Equatorial clime of Singapore. What a lovely voyage that was through those tranquil Coral Seas, the beautiful Tropical weather & gentle winds & the solem yet captivating Grandeur of those mountain peaks & rugged cliffs that met our wondering gaze. For many days with gentle balmy breeze & sunny weather, we sailed o'er the smooth bosom of the peaceful Java Sea. Today finds me again sailing o'er Ocean's trackless waste, yet how different! Just entering the turbulent restless waters of the Indian Ocean which stretches away two thousand Five hundred Leagues to the distant shores of my destination, no pleasant companionship of my bosom's partner to cheer its lonely passage, no summer skys & gentle winds & sea, no coral Isles, or mountain scenery to gaze upon with raptured eyes. Instead a tumultuous waste of troubled Ocean, broken only by the circling tireless flight of the spotted Cape Pigeon & majestic white winged Albatross.

But I have settled now into a sort of calm content & feel quite resigned. If I knew you were well & enjoying a pleasant summer & not sparing what means you have to make it so, I should feel more so. I think you needed the change of a stay at home. I hope you will enjoy it fully & be benefitted by it & I shall find you thus on my return—Fat & rosy & grown younger by the Benefits & pleasures of a year of home life & rest & as glad to extend to me a wifely welcome as I shall be to do so & receive it. I try to feel easy in mind about you when thinking of you out riding but sometimes I get to imagining you trying some hill not very steep but still enough so to be dangerous & then I imagine all sorts of things happening. But I know you are naturally cautious & so hope & trust you will not meet with any accident.

I hope you got a new suit & a good one for I should wish you to look as nice as the best & hope you have a good wheel. But no more tonight. It's getting rough & so not comfortable writing. I shan't write much during the eastern amid the rolling 40ties so bye bye again. Your loving S.

Sumner refers to "during the eastern amid the rolling 40ties" in his last sentence. Once sailing ships bound for Australia or New Zealand from Europe or the United States rounded the Cape of Good Hope, they were said to be "running their easting down." The 40° to 50° latitudes of the Southern Hemisphere were respectfully called the "roaring forties" because without a substantial land mass, the wind and seas could build incredible velocity as they moved around the world. Perhaps Sumner's substitutions—"the eastern" and "rolling 40ties"—are colloquialisms.

"Goose winged main topsail" which follows in the next section of Sumner's letter means that he ordered the weather half of the sail furled in order to form a triangular piece with the lee side of the sail. This measure greatly reduces the amount of sail the wind exposes to the wind.

In this section Sumner complains of his lack of toning solution. Photographers use toning as a final step in the printing process for changing the color of the image as well as lengthening the life of the print. Gold toning of albumen prints on printing out papers ("P.O.P.") such as Sumner and Alice used was common and produced a brown tone on the finished print. The first step in toning the print was to bleach out the print until the image became faint or disappeared. Then Sumner would submerge the bleached print in the toner. As he watched carefully the image would reappear and he would remove it when it had reached the shade of brown that he wanted. The process made use of a gold solution which he mentions. Photographs from Sumner's era, printed on fiber-based paper, may well outlast those of today. Contemporary pictures are predominantly color rather than black-and-white, and they are printed on plastic-based (resin-coated) paper which has a relatively short life span. Fiber-based paper is an endangered species because manufacturers cater to the amateur dark-room photographer who prefers the simplicity of using resin-coated paper.

Aug 27th   Lat 38°-38′ Long=111-35   114 days out

It is over a month since I wrote last but as I have no more of this paper, I thought I would write a little & copy it off when I get to Dunedin & get some thin. I will make a few notes from July 23d & continue East to the present with a few remarks as you know quite well what the Eastern is like. . . .

On the 27th with nearly calm weather followed by a light Easterly breeze we fell in just after night fall with the Bath Ship Charles E. Moody standing north while we were heading to South. We come so near Each other that I had to keep off for him & hauled close under his lea & spoke him. He was bound to Honolulu & had lost his steering Gear off Cape Horn & had to bear up for Mauritus. He reported the Ship John R Kelly (same owners) of Bath also wrecked on the Falkland Islands. I asked him to report me & hope you may see it & so find we are making a long passage.

We have had several days of calm & light winds between the Cape & St. Pauls which we made on the morning of Aug 16, a fine day. I passed it to the northward about 2½ miles dist= & took two Snapshots of it on different Bearings one S.S.E., the other S.W. by S. I hope they will be quite good but I have no toning Solution. That I had, has gone bad & refused to tone. The Gold has deposited itself in the Bottom so can not fix them up till I get new. The hollow in the Island abreast of pinical rock is a crater of volcanic origin. It is quite Barren & desolate appearing.

On Aug 21st we encountered a fearful gale from South & was obliged to heave to for 12 hours & the last 5 or 6 it was a Hurricane. We were under storm topsail & Goose winged main topsail & the sea was terrific, worse than any storm I have ever encountered. We rode it out safely but done some fearful pitching & rolling about. It died out like a flash when it give up & falling into the trough of the Sea I thought for awhile we should be dismasted but a light breeze soon sprang up & we got her before the sea & was all right. Since when we have had very strong westerlies & are doing fine now. I hope in 10 days more to reach Dunedin & shall be quite Glad to get on shore again for a short time.

I shall not write again till I arrive & shall hope & trust to find Good news awaiting me & lots of letters. So bye bye till such time. S.

The port city of Dunedin is located on the southeast side of South Island, New Zealand, at the head of Otago harbor.

Dunedin Sept 14

My Dear Alice   I am much pleased & thankful to write a few lines tonight in Dunedin & have at hand so many pleasant letters of Good news from home & know that to the date of your last writing all was as usual at home & life going smoothly on, which I hope is still the case. Tonight I have 3 nice long letters from you telling of the summers doings & all about Yarmouth also one from father & one from Edith. Not so many as I expected but all the news & family remembrances. I shall not write but little in answer to your letters but take them up leisurely on the way up to Auckland.

We arrived off the Entrance on the night of the 11th & towed in to the River on the 12. We were 129 days or 130 counting the 12. Towed to Dock yesterday & got entered & commenced discharging this morning. I hope Arnold Cheneys Agents cabled home so you can hear soon. They only Telegreph Auckland from here but say that the Auckland Agents allways cable & I think they do.

I had a great surprise to night. Just at dusk a Gentleman & Lady came down & enquired for Capt Drinkwater & going up who should I find but Mr. & Mrs. Alfred Bailey who have moved down here from Auckland over a year ago. I hardly knew them at first as Mr. B. has

a Beard & Mrs. B. was veiled but I knew her voice first. I was very pleased to see them. He has taken a Government Job in the Iron works. I am invited up to tea tomorrow night. It seems like meeting old Friends & will be very pleasant for me. While here they expressed much surprize & regret at not finding you with me. Little Rita is quite unwell. She has the Asthma very badly & I fear they will lose her. The little Boy is fat & rosy & is dressed in Boy's clothes with long curls & looks very cunning. They say I must come up to their house every night. They were Burned out at Auckland & nearly all the household goods were burned. That was some 18 months ago or more.

I am glad you have your teeth out. You are getting on so nicely or was of course. I imagine now your mouth is all right & lovely & allso glad you have a new Bike & suit or part of one. I wish you had got a whole affair. I am sorry you are rather close for funds. I shall write Capt Webster to increase the Amt=. By the way I have got no letter

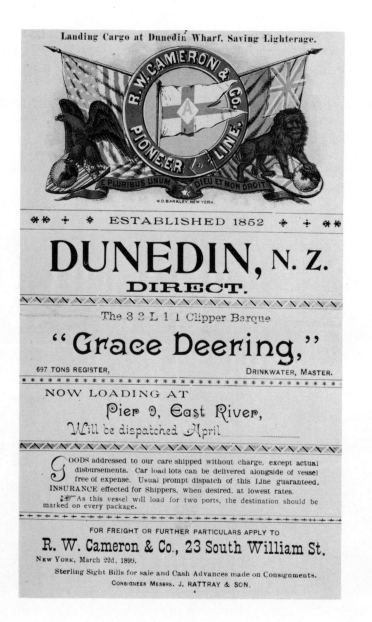

from him, a little singular. Well no more tonight. No mail going for 2 weeks so no use to Hurry & will write more Later   S.

Sunday 17th   Just a few lines tonight. I shall be nearly leaving by another Sabeth. I am enjoying Dunedin thouroughly & making many pleasant aquaintances. I have had several invitations out & of course you quite well know I have not refused them. In fact I have been somewhere every eve since arriving.

Mrs. Bailey wishes me to have a company as there is a number of her freinds who wish to come to see me & eat on board an American Boat as they call it & she says she will take your place & be hostess. So I think I will have a little Company one night this week as I have a good Cook & shan't be ashamed to have them.

Mr. & Mrs. B. have been down to tea twice, spent the eve once & the other we spent at a theatre. It was a Minstrel Co= Colored from America. They called themselves the unbleached Americans. Was very good.

They have a Girl so can leave the children at Home. I have come to the conclusion little Rita is in Consumption. The Doctor tells her the climate here isn't agreeing with her & she is talking of taking the children home to Auckland for a visit & go up with me. I wonder if she should, what you would think of that? Of course when she asked me if I would take her I said yes & last night she said she was going to really, that the doctor said it would be the best thing he could reccomend for her.

I can't tell you much of Dunedin only that it's a lovely place. The people that I meet are full of kindly feeling & hospitality & makes one thoroughly at home. I have been about quite a good bit but have not rode my wheel any to speak of. Today (Mr & Mrs B & self) we have been on a cable car ride among the Hills & out to the Gardens & enjoyed the day. Have lots of plans for the coming week. Now Good night. with lots of Love from Your Sumner

Some vessels, like the *Grace Deering* were designed with a "twen Deck" high in the hold, about six feet below the weather deck. Since he has discharged cargo for Dunedin, Sumner must lower the weight he is carrying to stabilize the *Deering* by shifting the "twen deck" cargo down into the lower hold.

Sunday eve Sept 24
Dear Alice
How I wish you were with me to enjoy the stay here, though short. We are now discharging but will not get away before tuesday 26th. The two cargos were much mixed up & it has been lots of work keeping them seperated & now all the twen Deck cargo has got to be put below to stiffen the ship & will take a day at least.

I have spent a very pleasant week, or the evenings of it. Been to 4 suppers & have given one myself & all expressed much pleasure. . . . Well Mrs. Bailey & children are really going up to Auckland with me & I hope they will enjoy it & that it will do the little girl good. But I mustn't write much more. This letter will be so bulky. I have 3 letters from you & hope there will be as many more at Auckland.

And now My Dear, I'll close for this time, hoping & trusting that this will find My Alice well as it leaves me & enjoying a pleasant summer at home. With abundance of Love & Good wish to all & especially to the new made Happy Pair & a kiss for Mother & lots for Yourself   I am as ever Your own

Sumner

Sunday Oct 7th 99
off East Cape New Zealand North Island
My Dear Alice
As it is a lovely day & Mrs. Bailey is writing her man, I will follow suit & begin you a letter. We left Dunedin dock in tow on thursday noon sept 28th but as all my crew were drunk so much so that it required 3 Policemen to get them on board, I therefore in consequence

Clare Bailey with her children, Rita and Melville, on pilot house.

came to anchor below Port Chelmers to let them sober up as the wind was strong at north & a rough sea outside. This continued till Sat 30th when it died away & we came out but it Blowed on again a N.E. lasting 2 days. My Passengers were quite disturbed internally so much so that they all kept their Berths & I of course ministered to their wants & comforts after which the wind veering to S.W. & the sea smoothing they revived & have since been well & hearty & are enjoying the trip greatly. Little Rita is improving wonderfully & has a good appetite.

I have read your letters again today & must try & answer some of the many subjects spoken of. First to congratulate you on your new teeth & I hope by this they are all right & Have no doubt made you feel & look very much better. I hope they will not trouble you but I

fear you have not paid enough to have real good ones, but hope they will prove so.

I don't think I shall try to write much of Dunedin. It's a beautifully situated city surrounded or nearly so by lofty Hills & mountains farther back, many of them covered with snow. I found the people very Pleasant to meet & enjoyed the stay much & Mr. & Mrs. Bailey done everything to make it Pleasant for me. I am enjoying their company up to Auckland & the children make it especially pleasant & lively. I took a view of Mrs. B & children on the house today & hope it will be good of them, also one of towing out of Dunedin which is quite good. I hope I shall find time to fix them up to send one. I have several negatives of different views but have not toned any yet.

I don't think I shall try to go all through your nice long letter to answer all the many things you wrote about. I shall just say how glad I was to get so many & so much news & so much about yourself & how you have been passing the season & enjoying what you can of life & not forgetting that you miss your absent partner. But I hope it has not been any drawback to your full enjoyment of the summer at home. How I wish I could have a whole summer home. I feel I could throughly enjoy it & hope I shall one of these days. . . .

Godbye for now
Sumner—

Auckland, Sumner's next port of call is on North Island, New Zealand. Volcanic cones are located around the city.

Sumner and Alice, as he indicates here, numbered their letters for each trip to keep track of whether or not they were getting them all.

Sunday Oct 21st 99

My Dear Alice
We have been in Auckland over a week & I must write a little to night. I have 2 more nice letters from you, no 4 & 5, & glad indeed to

learn of your good health up to the last writing. I hope again to hear good news this coming week as a mail is due wed= 25th. I have been invited to as much as a dozen places now & I don't expect to be here more than this week. We are all discharged & have in the Ballast 70 tons & comenced loading yesterday. I have not heard from Capt Webster or Capt Crickett as yet. Suppose they haven't anything to write.

I am not doing much riding on the Bike. I haven't the time & then it's to Hilly for real enjoyment. I have had no good offer yet for it & no time to look up a buyer but hope to sell it for something more than it cost me. I have a new washerwoman, a young miss & very pretty to & she does the washing well. . . .

You remember the Glassblower, Mr. Cook? I met his oldest son at Dunedin & he wished me to have some ferns & plants to take home and said he was going to write his intended, a Miss Read, to procure me some. Behold . . . 2 ladies, Miss Read & a Mrs Clark whose husband is a photographer, came down last Sunday with a letter of introduction & I found them very nice. They Dined with me & I went up to his studio with them & he took my Picture & has sent me down 2 nice ones & has one in his show room. They are fine, done in Black & white & I have ordered a few as I wish to give away 3 or 4.

They have been very kind & Pleasent. I have been to their home twice & stayed all night once. They live in Ponsonby. Miss Read lives with them & is to be married to Mr. Cook next winter. She is awfully in love with him & asked me many questions about him. She has given me his & her own Photo= & I gave her one of mine. Mr. Cook's father & part of the family have moved to Christ Church. She is all so having some thing made for you & Mrs. Clark (who by the way is American) is allso prepairing you a present. They have also given me lots of views about Auckland.

Then I have been up to Mrs. Bailey's Mothers where she is visiting several times & met several of her Sisters. I had them one evening on board. Have not been to Mr. Hays yet. They called down one P.M. & want me to come up. Phemia has a young man who is on one of the

Ferry Boats. She got your letter & has told me all about her Party which she wrote you of & she has a lovely great Picture of herself in her Birthday dress of white.

This afternoon I went to Northcote with Mrs. Clark & Miss Read to see about the ferns at friends of theirs & this eve have been to church with Mrs. Bailey. So you see I am having a fine time with Auckland ladies. There is a fine play at the opera house this week & I am going to ask Mrs. Bailey to go with me one night. You won't be jealous, will you? Well it's late & I'll retire. With lots of love

Sumner

"Most of my crew have deserted," Sumner writes his wife from Auckland. Deserters were common as the quality of the seamen deteriorated and the conditions under which they worked were not improved by the captain or owner. Additionally, the crews were often encouraged to desert because by doing so, they forfeited the wages they had coming to them. Furthermore, they would not earn money for sitting idle while the vessel was in port discharging and loading cargo.

Sumner and his brother John apparently helped each other throughout their careers whenever possible. If Sumner needed work and John could hire him on as mate, he would, and vice versa. Before Sumner left on this voyage he had asked Alice to help John buy into a command if one became available. John's lack of employment has contined to weigh on Sumner's mind during the voyage—as well it might have. Besides his fraternal loyalty, he and his brother were committed to a profession which, it was clear, no longer had a future. Sumner here suggests possible employment on the Electrics, the streetcars, which had only opened between Yarmouth and Portland the previous year, but John was never interested in that type of work. He was the eldest son in a long line of mariners and he found work where he could: on coasters, barges, etc. John retired a few years prior to World War I and then worked through the war on steamboats, serving as a mate, before his final retirement from the sea.

My Dear Alice

Sunday Oct 29th

I am all Loaded & in the streams but most of my crew have deserted & will delay me a day or so. A mail leaves tomorrow so I must finish my letters today. We are drawing 17 ft 9 aft, 17 ft 5 for= I have had a lot of trouble with drunken sailors but 4 have deserted, 3 here & one at Dunedin. The Mate has had a spree for 4 days & I thought had left all together as I saw nothing of him from last wed=morning till this morning I found him on board very shamefaced. I had a mate all ready if he did not show up. It has been very annoying to me but no doubt we'll get away all right in due time. The wind is Easterly so at present we are loosing nothing. . . .

We had a mail last wed= & I got 4 (making 9 in all) nice loving letters from you with all the news. Glad to find that for the most part it was pleasant news & that you were all quite well & enjoying yourselves as I have been doing here. I was sorry indeed to learn of the fears for the safety of Capt Hamilton. It will be sad if nothing is ever heard of him. I am sorry John has no better employment. Why don't he try to get on the Electrics?

I am going to send a few cards even though they will be a little early for xmas. Now my darling will you forgive a short letter this time as I have so many to finish up. In fact I shall have to leave some unanswered. I fear I have devoted to many evenings to pleasure & the days are to busy for writing. I have asked Capt Webster to increase your allotment to $40 [an ample amount, as they only paid $5 a month for the upstairs apartment in her parents' home]. If he will do so I hope you will have enough for the winter requirements. Get you all the nice warm clothes you need & don't deny yourself anything you want so long as you have the means to get them.

I have had a lovely time the past week, in fact all the time here. Have been out every eve since in Port except those I have entertained on board.

I have not sold my wheel or chairs [probably those rattan chairs from Singapore]. There doesn't seem to be anyone that wants to pay much & then they say they have to pay duty or take the chance of having it taken away if found out.

I have a letter from Hattie Poole, May [his eldest sister], Edith, Merian [his niece] & Stella Fuller, father & mother & Capt Crickett also Capt Webster to write or add to so I'll be pretty busy today. I shall add a line to yours in the morning before mailing.

Be real carfull of your self as I will be & live & grow fat on the Happy expectancy of my return as I shall do after leaving here & the first lonely feeling wears off. I have been so overwhelmed with kindness here that I should be hard hearted indeed if I could leave with no regrets or no lonely thoughts & feelings for awhile. But it will soon turn to the happy realization that I am again speeding toward those who are nearest & dearest—to my own loved home & my darling Alice.

So be of good cheer & do not worry for I feel that I will again be permitted to hold you to my heart & know that I am blessed with a love I hardly desearve. Forgive so short a letter & know & believe that this long voyage is teaching me that I love you more than I have known before. With love & a sweet kiss
(much love to all)

your own Sumner

Sumner had achieved his life's goal when he took command of the *Grace Deering* in 1897. However, in this letter he seems to be desperate not to have Alice along.

The examination to which Sumner refers is the one he put off taking before this voyage, so he has the next few months to worry about it.

Auckland Nov 6th 99
Dear Alice
I am sailing today at noon. I have been awfully anoyed for the past week trying to get a crew. I begun to think I was not going to get any at all & I have freted so much over the delay that I am half sick. You know how I fret when things go wrong & just think of laying her over a week for a crew. I don't know what Capt Webster will say.

I don't think there is a mail for some time but I leave several letters for the next & when you get this I hope we shall be round Cape horn. I cannot write only a few lines for I am hurrying to get away. So I can only wish you one & all a Mery Xmas & Happy New Year & send lots of love to my Dear Alice. I shall hope to have a safe passage & be with you again by the middle of feb= Have a letter waiting me in N.Y. & if you don't want to go on these long voyages let me know for I shall not go alone. But I may not be able to pass the examination & so not be able to go in any case but have to return to coasting again.
Now goodbye with lots of love & Kisses from
your loving
Sumner

Sumner was ill ("feeling some better but very hoarse") as he left New Zealand behind. Never before this occasion had he been lonesome while *homeward* bound. There is no real evidence that Sumner was ever untrue to Alice, but, from his letters, it is obvious that he noticed and admired women. In particular, it sounds as if he may have been attracted to Clare Bailey. They attended church and the theater together, and although one or more members of her family were quite often in the company, it was unusual for Sumner to see a woman—any woman—eighteen times during twenty-six days in port.

No extant correspondence covers the voyage home. Perhaps he did not write because he would be home before the mail could be posted. Instead, here are some diary entries:

Thurs. Nov. 9, 1899   very light airs Easterly
Very lonesome. Thinking of those at races today. [Evidently his friends in Auckland were going to the track.] Would like very much to be there. Am I forgotten? Oh no! 2 days out

Fri. Nov. 10, 1899   Fine Pleasant weather   Moderate westerly winds . . . New Zealand faded from sight . . . Awfully lonesome. Shall I ever see it again? I hope so.

3 days out

Rounding the Horn, one of the more desolate areas in the world, was not as strenuous in the eastward direction Sumner was sailing, but it was still a grim trial. The sea and weather conditions off Cape Horn wore men out.

Sat. Nov. 18, 1899   All this day passes with strong Gale, South by E. & high Sea. [The *Deering*] layed to as yesterday. Lat. by D.R. 43-03   Long. by D.R. 160-02 distance 48 miles N. by E. true drift Slowly rising Barometer [sign the storm is abating]. Very lonesome. Long days with Ship rolling about & no comfort anywhere.

12 days out

Tues. Nov. 21, 1899   Cloudy Wind moderate S.W. rough Sea irregular 4 a.m. set Top gallants   8 a.m. set flying jib & main sail. Noon set all drawing sail. Moderate veering W.S.W.
Lat by obv = 44-14   Long by obv 151-46 distance 153 miles
Course E by S ¼ S.
Our Aniversary. 16 Years of Married Life & where has it fled too? I wonder what Alice is doing to night but she is fast asleep ere this as it is past midnight at home.

15 days at sea

Thurs. Nov. 30, 1899   Pleasent   Passing Clouds   Wind Fresh Gale West
Expect Mrs. Bailey is home at Dunedin or on the way.

24 days at sea

Wed. Dec. 13, 1899   10 a.m. made Cape Horn ahead kept away
Lat by obv 56-06 Long by obv 67-29
find chronometer very nearly correct. 2 sails ahead. distance 207 miles
Took a snap shot of Cape Horn with Kodak at 1.30
5 to 6 miles distant. A high Rocky Clift, 1378 feet, devoid of vegetation. [Unfortunately, Sumner's photograph did not survive.]

37 days out.

Thurs. Dec. 21, 1899   Cloudy weather   light rain showers
All drawing sail set at noon. Crew picking over and sprouting potatoes.
P.M.   passed through long streaks of discolored water of a Blood Color sometimes called whale food.

45 days out Half way Home

Thurs. Dec. 28, 1899   Fresh gale N.W.   Squally   rough irregular sea
This is Alice's Birthday. Hope she is enjoying it and thinking of Me.
Pumps, light & lookout attended

52 days out

Sun. Dec. 31, 1899   Ther. 74   Barometer 30.01   Cloudy weather
Wind moderate & variable from S.E. to N.E.
All sail set   distance 138 miles
Lat by obv. 24-38   Long by obv 33-55
P.M.   nearly calm
6 P.M.   moderate breeze E.S.E. appearing much like the trade winds
evening fine & Pleasant though quite Hot
So ends this day & Year month & century

55 days at sea

After a month and a half more at sea, Sumner arrived at Fire Island, off the coast of Long Island in New York.

Wed. February 14, 1900   Ther 40   Clear weather
   Begins with strong gale N.W. by W. to N.W. Ship under
   lower Topsails reefed foresail & Main upper fore & Mizzen
   stay sails
   Noon obv Lat=40-14 dist 85 miles N.E. ¼ N.
   Long=72-58   variation 8 west
   1:30 P.M.   Fire Island light ship   bore East True 2½ miles
   distant took sights & find Chro= 1′-04″ Slow
   3 P.M. Tacked ship 6 miles W.S.W. West of Fire Island light
   Fleet of coasters passing East   100 days out

Thursday, February 15, 1900 5 P.M.   Came to anchor off Bedloes
   Island. Discharged Pilot. Veering to 35 fathoms chain on
   Starboard Anchor Got all Sail but Topsails & Topgalants
   fore staysail & Jibs unbent & stowed below in dry condition
   Day ends with fresh westerly
               Anchor, Lights & Lookout attended
                    So ends this voyage   101 days out

   In the following letter to Alice, Sumner refers to a mason of his
York Rite Chapter "Brother True" on whom he "confered the Mark
degree." Sumner was the only one of Nicholas Drinkwater's sons to
become a Mason, though Nicholas had been the Master Mason, head
of Casco Lodge for nine terms. Sumner served in the same capacity
once in 1912.
   As Masons, Nicholas and Sumner were expected to be moral,
chaste and obedient to the law of the land. Active community service
was expected from Masons of higher orders. The requirements for
entry into the Masons are that the candidate be male and that he
believe in a Higher Being. However, Freemasonry has traditionally
been associated with anti-Catholicism because of the persecutions
experienced by the French Huguenots and other Protestant groups.
   Freemasonry is a secret, fraternal society formally established
in Britain in the early eighteenth century, but its roots are found in
medieval English and Scottish fraternities of stonemasons. There is
also some evidence that the idea dates back to antiquity, with Masonic texts identifying the roots of the fellowship with the building
of King Solomon's temple. The first American Masonic lodge was
founded in Philadelphia in 1730. One of its members was Benjamin
Franklin. John Hancock, Paul Revere and George Washington were
also Masons. Had Major John André also been a Freemason, that
might account for Washington's refusal to see him before hanging
him as the spy who had plotted with Benedict Arnold to secure West
Point for the British. According to the laws of Freemasonry, one
brother could not refuse another's request. The Masons are believed
to have had an incredible influence on history; reputedly, kings began
or ended wars through their alliance to this group. No one has yet
revealed the true extent of Freemasonry's former power as, of course,
its members are sworn to secrecy.

New York Harbor   Feb 15/1900
Evening
My Dear Alice
   I hope ere this you have learned of our arrival through Capt
Webster & know that I am once again in my own country. We had a
lovely day to arrive & sailed right up to the Liberty Statue. But too
late for me to go ashore to get letters which I am anxious to get. I hope
& trust when I do that I shall get good news. I am to sleepy to write
much & I have lots of things to get ready for going on shore in the
morning. We have had quite a good comfortable passage 101 days &
arrived safe with no loss or damage to ship or sails. We have been 5
days north of Hatteras with rainy foggy weather till yesterday. Have
got most of the sails unbent.
   I wonder how you all are & if you have had a cold winter. In N.
York it has been quite mild & no snow. But I am too sleepy to write
so good night & more tomorrow. I hope you won't think it strange not
getting a telegram from me. Should have sent one if I had got ashore.
                                                  S.

Friday 2.30 P.M.   have Entered ship & have a boat engaged to dock at 4 P.M. Will add a line to mail so you can get it tomorrow P.M.

I found on getting ashore this morning that Winchester hadn't telegraphed Capt Webster so I did so at once & you to. I have your letters & one from father & Edith. Awfully glad to learn that you were all well. That is the Best news one can hear after so long a time on the Ocean. I am sorry to learn of the loss of so many of our Yarmouth People—Of Edgar & Mrs. Winslow, both seem very sad & Brother True. That seems sad to me when I recall the evening that I confered the Mark degree upon him & How I studied to have it perfect.

But I can't write but little now so I'll close with lots & lots of love to all. Congratulations & love to Eunice [his sister, who was married to Will Doyle]. Glad she has a boy.

No letter from Capt Webster. Funny isn't it?

Write me Sunday. Can't tell when I'll get home yet.

Your own Sumner

Sumner reached home on February 21. His note concerning his homecoming is interesting because he calls Alice "Mrs. D." for the first time in his diary, thereafter alternating the two. Had a formality entered their relationship or was it a result of an aging in his own self-image?

Wednesday, February 21, 1900   Pleasant weather   On the way home

Took 12.30 Train for Portland arriving at 4.30 & Meeting Mrs. D. at Union Station.

Got home at 6.30 P.M. finding all well & a pleasent welcome.

1900, The Last Year with the *Grace Deering*

Compared to 1898–1899, the documentation for the Drinkwaters' last year with the *Deering* is meager. Alice accompanied Sumner, as he had hoped, but she kept no journal and only two letters to her intimates have survived. None of Sumner's letters are extant and he further obscured the record by avoiding his diary for months at a time.

He did record, however, that on March 2, 1900, he entered his application for a federal license with the United States Local Inspector of Engineers and was told to report on March 6 for an oral examination. There were no set guidelines for his examiners as to the nautical information he was expected to know. However, the statute provided that the board review his "habits of life," his ability to perform the duties of his station, and his past experience. Sumner was expected to explain how he would react to certain contingencies. Letters of recommendation from past and present employers were accepted and, certainly, a letter from Captain Benjamin Webster would be carefully considered. Sumner was certified a Master of Sailing Vessels of all Classes on any Ocean in the World. He would not have to return to coasting; he was still a deepwater man, though his license would have to be renewed in five years.

Of the two voyages they made this year, one was from New York in ballast to Bonaire, in the West Indies, for a cargo of salt to Portland, Maine. The second was circular: to Rio de Janeiro with lumber and over to Bonaire for salt back to Portland. One of my favorite pictures of all those that Sumner and Alice took is this one from their visit to Bonaire. Because so much of the ship routine has been included in their previous papers, only a few pertinent entries from Sumner's diary are included here:

Tuesday, March 27, 1900   Clearing weather

9.30   Joined ship at Crane's Dock ——Basin, Brooklyn N.Y. Found ship with ½ (half) the required Ballast in. Sails bent today. No officers except cook & 4 men engaged.

Unable to Find Mate who has certificate which is required by Customs to clear ship. Which ridiculous nonsense is Brought about by the insane desire of our Republican Congress to ape our Cousins, the English, & slowly Bring about that which they are striving at so hard, nobility & Trusts. A democratic administration is needed to bring our Country back to a Broader view of life & right.

Saturday, March 31, 1900   Bar. 29-84   8 a.m.   Ther 40

This day begins with light Northerly breeze & cloudy weather. At 7 A.M. Tug Fred Dallzell came along side with Pilot. Got anchor & Proceeded to Sea 10 a.m. Crossed the Bar discharging Pilot & Tow Boat, having made sail.

Noon Sandy Hook Light Ship bore E.N.E. 4 miles distant from which I take departure course S.E. by S. All drawing sail set. Bark Lattie Moore in company astern.

Took obv= & found Chro= correct within one mile of Position by cross bearing of Scotland & Sandy Hook light ships. [The chronometer had proved wildly inaccurate on occasion during the preceding voyage. Doubtless Alice is working the logarithms.]

Saturday, April 7, 1900   Bar. 29.28   Ther. 62

Begins with Fresh gale westerly with heavy squalls. Barometer slowly rising [they had been having gales and bad weather for the past few days] strong gale W.N.W. & high rough sea. Running under Lower Topsails. Rolling heavily. Find ship has blowed water through air streaks on top of Ballast & will not come to Pumps making very bad work in lower hold.

Lat 34 29 Long 61 45   7 days out

The Drinkwaters arrived at Bonaire, one of the Netherlands Antilles, only eleven square miles in size.

Wednesday, April 18, 1900   Bar 30.00   Ther 79

all sail set

noon obv 12-41 Lat 67-34 Long

2 P.M.   made Bonaire Bearing S.W. 20 to 25 miles dist.

5.30 P.M.   Took Pilot off Southern Point light house bearing West 2½ miles dist=

Pilot got ship bows on Beach in coming to Anchor. Layed [on the beach] 3 hours & came off. Swing to anchor with hawser ashore but some distance Below Proper Anchorage.

Friday, April 20, 1900   Bar 30   Ther 80

4 a.m.   with 12 men from shore got lines up to stone posts using 300 fathom line & comenced to heave ship up to anchorage leaving Port Anchor & Paying away chain.

Bonaire, April 1900.

2 P.M. vessel in 20 fathoms. Greater part of Port chain out & hawser and other line ashore. Let go deep water anchor & commenced discharging Ballast. Thus employed

rest of this day.   2 days at anchor
12 men ¾ day in moving ship
12 men ¼ "   " discharging Ballast   2 days in Port

Friday, April 27, 1900   Bar 29-96   Ther 82
Part of crew painting ship outside, Black.
Recd= cargo in Main Hatch
   "   on Board   1682 Bbls [barrels] salt
Previous recd   2411
                                   4093 Total Bbls
                                     3½
                                   12279
                                   2046½
                                   14.325 Total Bushel
                                              9 Days in Port

Had diver under Bow [to check on the damage to the *Deering* when she ran aground on April 18]. Reports very little injury to metal about 4 sheets on fore foot Broken & roughed up.

Sunday, April 29, 1900   Bar 29 98   Ther 82
Passing squalls   Clouds Fr. Cu.   Scale 4
                                              11 days in Port

P.M. took walk with Alice to light House. Took a few snapshots. [Of all the photographs, none is more curious than the one Sumner took on this date at the lighthouse. Sightseers routinely pose at landmarks, but Alice & Co. stand with, not at, the lighthouse. Here the Drinkwaters deliberately use the camera playfully as a mode of expression and an art form to achieve an image that seems to be without precedent in their time.]

Three days after the preceding entry, the ship left Bonaire. It arrived in Portland, Maine, on May 23. The *Deering* lay in Portland for over a month, discharging the salt from Bonaire and taking on cargo bound for Rio de Janeiro. It included: 491,046 feet of lumber, 150 tons of ballast, and the Drinkwaters' two bicycles. Alice and Sumner went home to Yarmouth, but business as well as their family and friends' eagerness to tour the *Deering* brought one or both of them back to Portland quite regularly.

While Sumner's sporadic diary entries record only half of the six-month voyage, two of Alice's letters—one to Hattie Poole and another to her brother's wife, Nellie—survive.

When Hattie Poole discovered one of these letters in 1943, she wrote the family: "On Sunday I found I still had one of Alice's letters and so I am sending it to you. . . . It gives you such a true picture of the 'old days' when 'sailing vessels' were the thing instead of 'steam.' . . . We were the real old-fashioned friends—the kind that don't forget. . . . You get from this letter quite an inside view of Alice as she really was—a very loyal friend to her friends and a very understanding person, and a great help to Sumner. . . . Alice & I were childhood friends, but I think that trip [in the schooner *Bramhall* from Gardiner, Maine, to New York in 1889] sealed the friendship. So long together in such close quarters and *not one thing* unpleasant between us *or afterward* . . . I can not think of any break in our friendship—Alice's & mine. . . . I am an old, old lady now, but I can't realize it."

When Hattie and Alice were girls together, Hattie was the belle of Yarmouth. She never married, although she had at least one "understanding." Evidently her admirer was not in Yarmouth for some period of time and Hattie corresponded with him while flirting ("outrageously," her sister thought) with the rest of Yarmouth's eligible males. In fact, Hattie's sister disapproved of her behavior to such an extent that she felt obliged to inform the absent beau, who, subsequently, never proposed.

Alice's friendship with Hattie was never ruptured. Their relationship is noteworthy because most of Alice's intimates were drawn from her family ties—sisters-in-law, etc. It is revealing to read

Alice's list of the letters she wrote on this voyage. Only one other girlhood friend, Addie Clark, is on it.

The trip Hattie mentions in her letter had taken place in August of 1889 when the Drinkwaters invited her to join them on Sumner's first command, the schooner *Bramhall,* to New York. One of the highlights of her visit to New York must have been the Statue of Liberty, which the Drinkwaters and she toured on August 29, 1889, almost three years after its dedication.

Hattie became eccentric in her old age, and her family and old friends despaired of her living conditions. She kept chickens in her house and they often roosted on the headboard of her bed. The years had taken their toll of the girl who was once Yarmouth's belle.

At Sea August 20th 1900

Dear Hattie,

We are in Lat=3° South Long 27° West and are having a verry long passage out. We have had nothing but head winds & calms for 40 days. We left Portland with a good wind & held it several days, but after getting into the N.E. trades we did not have them at all favorable. Then we were just in time to meet the S.W. moonsoons & that was a hard beat of two weeks to get through them. Now we are getting the S.E. trades & are doing much better. They will last us about down to Rio, I hope.

We have had the roughest passage to the Equater that we ever had & then the vessel being lumber loaded & rather crank [top-heavy and leans too easily] it has seemed worse. Do you know I think there are many ways of earning a living that are worse than farming [Hattie was living on the family farm], & going to sea is one of them.

I have not been on deck but verry little, the weather has been so disagreeable, so have done quite a lot of sewing & reading. I read "Life on the Mississippi" some time ago & found it to be a verry good history of "Mark Twains" life. If you have not allready read it, I will lend it to you sometime. It was verry good of you to give it to me, but those books are quite expensive generaly & I realy don't think you ought to give me so many things.

The "Seamens Mission" at Portland put a library on board the Bark & among the books are some verry good ones, especially "Thadeus of Warsaw" & The "Protestant Queen" a story of the French Revolution which took place more than four hundred years ago. I have read dozens in all but mostly simple little yarns that I never remember or want to. Read them merely to pass the time away.

For sewing I have made a pink gingham nightdress & it is quite elaborate too. I cut & made a house jacket for Sumner & stitched all the facings by hand with red silk. It is verry pretty, but after I finished it, as Sumner had several & did not need it, I gave it to the Mate. He seemed quite pleased & it looked well on him. They are verry good to put on at meal time & evenings. Sumner has had on nothing else since we left except those. Sundays he wears white suits.

I finished up the three Dimity wrappers & did a little to several shirtwaists. Did a verry little fancy work & that is about the whole. I washed three times but for a month it has been too rough to try to wash. But I want to once more if possible & not have so many to hire done at Rio.

We play checkers quite a lot evenings when Sumner is not on deck chinning with the mate which he does a considerable of. We enjoy having him verry much. It seems nice to have a mate we can talk with, but the crew are a puzzle. Hardly one who can speak a word of English. They consist of three Portuguese niggers, one Spaniard and two white men, foreigners of course. The 2nd Mate is a Norwegian & a verry good fellow. The steward is a married man who has a family in Bath, Me. & happens to be an American. He is a verry good cook, indeed, I am pleased to say.

Well, I wonder what you are all doing. Not packing up for Vermont I hope. I don't have any faith to believe your father would go. Of course haying is over with for this year & I don't expect there was a verry large crop, but I hope there will be plenty of apples & things.

We have still a few oranges & lemons in good condition & a glass quart jar of candy.

I have been writing several letters to finish up ready to send off when we arrive. I don't much expect to get one from you this time as you wrote twice to Bonaire. I thought it quite time I was answering the one I recieved & would begin in season. . . .

Em Bedford, Alice and steward.

Alice continued her letter to Hattie Poole after their arrival in Rio de Janeiro, but another letter, because it was written at about this time, is inserted here. This letter, sent to her sister-in-law Nellie Drinkwater, is one of my favorites from Alice's material because of its warm tone and homely detail.

The shampoo recipe that she included is interesting because Alice was noted for taking care of her hair. She used curling tongs, which she heated in the chimney of a kerosene lamp. Except for the mornings when she appeared in kid curlers, she was considered quite a dramatic-looking woman. Her hair, now white, contrasted dramatically with her dark snapping eyes.

Alice mentions "surplus roosters" because Nellie's moneymaking project which began after she and Jack were first married, was poultry farming. Her husband helped her with the books and built the hen houses for her; Nellie did the rest.

Nellie was content in her marriage and it did a lot to erase the scars of her troubled childhood. Her parents, Jacob Groves and Hattie John's older sister, Janette Hamilton, were both from Cousins Island. Their marriage had been unsuccessful and they separated while Nellie was still young. Janette died prematurely, leaving her daughter to be reared by her parents and the Groves family. Nellie had a generous nature. She was conscientious and hospitable, but because of her background, she was extremely sensitive and her family and friends learned to watch what they said around her.

south
Lat = 16-44   west
Sunday Aug = 26-1900   Long = 33-42
My Dear Sister,
    It is your turn for a letter today.
    I wrote Mother a few days ago & since that time we have been going along verry well. For two days now we have had it more moderate & with less sea. It has seemed quite a treat to be able to get along without having to hold on & brace ourselves to keep anywhere.

Yesterday was so nice I did a good big wash, but not more than one half what I had dirty. Sumner hung them all out as fast as I rinced them. I blued them & have some naptha soap yet & they were white & nice.

Today we have been doing all sorts of things. This morning with Sumner's help I had a shampoo. I had one in Portland the day I left home [two months earlier] but the weather being so hot & damp, it was as dirty as ever. I did it verry well & it is as clean as possible. I got some ideas about shampooing while I was in the place that day in Portland & will give you my reciept. I took a piece of tar soap & sliced it a little up & put it into a bottle with a cup of water & a few drops of ammonia & rum, & let it dissolve. Then Sumner turned it on my head a little at a time & I only used my fingers to rub it into the hair. It made the scalp white & clean & very quickly too. I think it far better than using a brush. I gave Sumner one, so we both have clean heads.

Tomorrow if nothing happens I shall do some house cleaning & begin to straighten things up for port which won't be a verry difficult job. We shall be so glad to get in & get letters. I do hope to hear a good report from you, & when we get home again to see a decided change for the better. You must do your best to bring about such a change. I suppose you will soon think about getting rid of some of your surplus roosters & reducing the number for winter storage. Just think of it being almost fall again.

Sumner has just toned the pictures today that he took of Em & I in Portland. [Miss Emily Bedford was a doctor from Lynn, Massachusetts, whom Alice's sister, Hattie, had brought home to meet her family. "Em" came aboard in Portland harbor on June 28 and stayed several nights. She also accompanied them when the Deering was towed out, and returned to Portland on the tugboat.] I will send one if they turn out any good. I wonder where Jack is working & if you & Em got morning [bicycle] rides after we came away. I hope you did. I hope she thought of everything to tell you & I guess she would. How Captain Webster dipped his flag to us as we towed out. He was at his

Portland harbor, c. 1900.

cottage on the point of Cushions Island [Cushings Island, in Portland harbor] & we could spy them verry plain around the cottage. We waved to Em as long as we could see the tug, then I went below & made things snug for sea. It was pretty lonesome after she left. Before noon we had sunk the old Cape [passed Cape Elizabeth] & have never seen any land since. We have sailed up to noon today 5924 miles. We have each day's work & today I was adding it up. The longest day was 180 miles & the shortest 24.

I wonder if Em got her nightdresses & shirtwaists & corset waists made before going back. I hope you cut the corset waist pattern as it was what I need for mine. I have worn the green Dimity wrapper once or twice sunday, but they are all clean & fresh for port.

I suppose Edith took her trip to Phil= with the Goulds. Now I imagine Hattie & John over at the cottage [on Cousins Island], Hattie working for boarders & John sauntering back & forth between the cottage & Mrs. Hamilton's [Hattie John's mother]. I suppose there are plenty of berries now. I wonder how many barrels of strawberries you put up?

I got me some embroidery hoops in Portland but it is needless to say I have not commenced the Doilies. I may possibly out there or on the way home. We have given our wheels one thorough cleaning & oiling & they are all right but we shall soon rig them up now. I shall try hard to sell mine.

I have begun letters to Addie Clark, Em, sister Hat, Hattie Poole, Mother & you. I intend to write Hattie John & that will be about the last.

[They arrived in Rio de Janeiro on September 3.]
Sept= 4th evening

Dear Nellie, I will add a few lines to this & send them along in the morning. I was much pleased with the letters from home, especially the "private epistle" from you. I assure you I feel much better in my mind since hearing, for I couldn't help thinking about you & was some anxious of course. I believe your doctoring that way has saved your

life, but you must be careful for a long time & not do unreasonable things. Now don't forget it, will you?

I think your plans for a Xmas tree will be lots of fun & I hope we shall get home but there is a doubt as we will be some time here, & making such a long passage out. What a visit Em made. She must have enjoyed her self pretty well I think.

Sumner did not see a Bicycle ashore. He thinks they are not used here. We are going to take ours ashore & introduce them. I want to sell mine if possible. But I must not write too long for I have others to finish & a list of things to write for Sumner to get ashore in the morning.

Mother S., Nellie, Sister Hattie, Alice.

I am glad Jack has plenty of work [as a carpenter] in Yarmouth & hope it will continue. With much love to you both & the <u>children</u>. [As Nellie & Jack didn't have a child until 1904, possibly Alice is referring to household pets or farm livestock.]

I am your loving sister Al

Alice concluded her letter to Hattie Poole three days later. She avoids repeating herself in these two letters, since she knows her friends may share them.

Rio Janeiro Harbor

Well you see we have succeeded in getting here at last. There is nothing like perseverence, you know. We arrived the 3d. Was 65 days on the passage & thought that the longest ever made, but an English Bark here was 69 from Portland. It is the wrong time of year to make quick passages from north. Hope we will do better going home. We are likely to be a long time here as they have so many holidays. It will be slow discharging & we shan't begin before monday which is a week since we arrived. There was a mail left the day after we arrived but I could only finish a few letters then as I was verry busy. We lay in the stream all the time here.

I wish I could discribe the scenery. It is wonderful. The harbor is verry large being about 10×15 miles & a good many Islands in it. But it looks to be surrounded by mountains & some of them upwards of 3000 ft. & almost perpendicular on one side & rise directly from the beach. Some are covered with fine trees & plenty of cocoa palms while others are entirely bare & look a solid ledge. On one that goes up like a Pyramid to almost a needle point, to the height of 2300 ft. [Mount Corcovada] there is a summer house & an arrangement to take people up to it by cogwheel power. Halfway down is a hotel where one generaly gets dinner. We intend to take the trip some day and a Capt= who

we have met here will go with us. I have not been on shore yet but may go tomorrow to the Botanical Gardens which they tell us are very fine. It is very cool here in the harbor, too much so in the afternoon to sit on deck. Of course it is winter here. Only in this Latitude 23° South we expected to find it warmer. There is some sickness ashore. Bubolic Plague & Smallpox but nothing alarming people say.

Our Steward has been pretty sick for a few days but with neither of the diseases I have mentioned. [It would have offended Hattie's sensibilities had Alice described the Steward's symptoms, which included "inflamed bowels and a stoppage of urine." Hattie, after all, was a spinster.] He has had a Dr. but instead of sending him to a Hospital he will stop on board unless he grows much worse. The 2nd Mate & I have catered for two days & tonight Sumner brought a cook from shore for a while.

We got several letters, & verry glad to here good news from home. They wrote about Charles' [Hattie's brother's] <u>son</u>. I suppose they are pleased with a boy this time. I hope Mabel is all right & over her <u>time</u>.

They are celebrating the anniversary of their independence day here today, & all day the Ships have been covered with Bunting. There are several Men of War here & this evening they have been illumined beautifully, & morning, noon, & night, they fired a tremendous salute.

The City looks lovly from the harbor. It had a population of nearly one million & is built all among the mountains & way to the top of some lower ones.

I think I am the only woman in the port on board a vessel so that is not so pleasant. I must have my good times with the <u>men.</u> Isn't that tough?

I shan't do much shopping here especialy as everything is verry dear, & there is hardly anyone who speaks English & that makes it bad. But I must close as this is quite enough for once, you will find.

With much love to you all. I am as ever, your friend, Alice Drinkwater

Sumner sends his love also.

It seemed as though Rio had several jokes to play at the Drink-waters' expense. Alice had been unduly optimistic in expecting that the *Deering* would begin discharging cargo on the tenth, one week after they arrived in port. The conseigne kept Sumner dangling for more than three weeks before issuing a discharge permit on the twenty-seventh. In addition, there was no cargo available in Rio, which meant that the *Grace Deering* would have to sail in ballast to Bonaire for salt. The day after they began discharging, Sumner discovered that a member of his crew had removed and sold the brass pump to the main water tank as well as a coil of rope. Then they lost their anchor after moving alongside the wharf on October 10. Sumner noted glumly that it had been "nearly up" when "the starboard chain parted." Finding the cost of a diver who would locate and raise their anchor to be prohibitive, he purchased one second-hand. They left Rio on October 13.

Most of the passage to Bonaire, which they reached on November 13, was taken up by cleaning the hold preparatory to taking on salt. Both sexes were employed as stevedores by the saltworks in Bonaire, but suddenly, nine days after the *Deering*'s arrival, most of the men quit and shifted the burden of loading the vessel almost entirely onto the women. In any case, only a partial cargo was available at this port, and Sumner requested authorization from Captain Webster to move to Red Pan at the southern end of the island for the balance. Captain Webster still hadn't replied to the cable when Sumner left for Red Pan on November 25.

There were three salt pans, or ponds, on Bonaire, each with a characteristic color—red, blue and yellow. They were formed by the pumping of salt seawater into a series of fresh-water inland ponds. As salt water progressed through the ponds, the fresh water evaporated in the sun, leaving a pan containing a small amount of water with a high saline content and a distinctive color. An obelisk which matched the color of the pan was erected over it as a marker for sea captains, indicating where they should moor to take on salt.

It was November 29, 1900, before they loaded the balance of the cargo and on that day Sumner made what was to be his last entry as Master of the *Deering*.

His single-minded pursuit of a career as a mariner had culminated in his command of the *Grace Deering* at the age of thirty-eight. But the sailing ships which had offered so much promise in Sumner's boyhood were entering the twilight of obsolescence. Freight earnings had dropped as the cost of operations rose. Cargoes were increasingly hard to find. The steamers and the railroads were vanquishing this once proud industry. On January 2, 1901, Sumner Pierce Drinkwater saw his world collapse; he lost command of the *Grace Deering* and was caught in the vicissitudes of his era.

Wednesday, January 2, 1901   Ther= 7° above zero   Wea= clear & cold
> Took the 7.40 Electric to the city. Called on Capt Webster & settled accts. for the voyage recently ended from Rio Janeiro via Bonaire with Cargo of Salt to Lord Bros of this city.
> Capt Crickett an old captain in the employ & part owner of the Bark Grace Deering is [coming out of retirement] to take command of the above vessel of which I have had charge for the past 4 years. Dined with Capt Webster managing owner & returned home at night.

Friday, January 4, 1901   Ther. 8 above Zero, Continued fine cold wea=
> Alice & self to Portland to get my Effects from the <u>Deering</u>. Found her discharged of her cargo of salt with an over run of 1971 Bush=
> Got all my things home safely. Brother Josh going with a team to fetch them. Thus ends nearly 4 years service in the employ of Capt B. Webster

Sumner's forty-second birthday was a week later.

Friday, January 11, 1901   Overcast   falling Bar 30.05   Moderate N.N.E. wind   Snow fall of yesterday very light.
> Hattie John spent the after noon & eve with us. P.M.   went to villiage & to Foreside. Called at Mrs. C. L. Bucknam's to

celebrate Summie's Birth day [little Sumner Bucknam was three years old] & my own. Took him a little present & had a cup of tea & a bit of his Birthday Cake. Brought Edith back with me from the villiage. Day ends with quite a snow-fall. Barometer falling. Hattie John & Edith will stay all night with us. Thus ends 42 years of my Existance. Has it been lived rightly? I fear not.

Usually, by forty-two, a man's life and career are fixed, but Sumner had become an anachronism. His best years in the down-easters were behind him, and although many of his contemporaries were "leaving the sea and going into steam," he himself had no affinity for steamships.

In addition, even if he had not been usurped by Captain Crickett, Captain Webster was already an octogenarian, and when he died, the *Deering* management would change. Sumner's diary shows that he continued to call occasionally on Captain Webster, so presumably they remained on good terms. Indeed, a 1908 letter from Alice also speaks of Captain Crickett in a friendly way.

Clearly, Captain Webster had been forced by the other's seniority and holdings in the *Deering* into the decision to replace Sumner. It might have been easier for Sumner to accept his dismissal if he had been at fault or if he had been unable to understand the owners' position. As it stood, he had to repress his anger. Times were bad; there was no one to blame. He, a man of action, was without appeal.

Though he no longer walked the decks of the *Grace Deering,* Sumner never severed the bond between himself and the vessel. She is implicitly included in the globe of the world which stands on his grave. Tucked in his diaries are clippings about her, and his notations over the years follow her arrivals, departures, and the duration of voyage.

Friday, February 1, 1901   Ther=20   Wea= Fine   Bar= 29 78
    Calm
    Went to Portland
    Deering Sailed this A.M.   Capt Crickett

If 1901 was a year of reckoning for Sumner, 1902 was its equivalent for his old ship. She was in the Caribbean, only one hundred miles away from the Mount Pelée eruption on May 8. Her master for that voyage, Captain William H. Gooding, a Yarmouth man, bottled the volcanic dust coating her decks and mailed it off to his friends, Sumner among them.

These ashes from Mt. Pelée Eruption (May 8, 1902) were collected on the deck of the Bark *Grace Deering*, Capt. Wm. H. Gooding while laying in Barbadoes, 100 miles from Martinique.

Compliments of
William H. Gooding

Just about the time of the eruption, the *Deering*'s Class A-1 rating expired. She had apparently deteriorated greatly. The American Bureau of Shipping records show that she had to be substantially rebuilt that spring in order to meet the shipping underwriter's standards. The bark had no sooner recovered her classification than, in July 1902, her eighty-eight-year-old managing owner, Captain Benjamin Webster, died. The *Deering* was sold to Thomas Norton & Co. of New York to be used in the coffee trade between Rio de Janeiro and Baltimore. Any fantasies Sumner might have harbored of regaining his command vanished.

On February 28, 1906, the *Grace Deering* sailed from the port of New York for the last time. She was bound for Charleston, South Carolina, but encountered bad weather and was forced to put into Philadelphia for extensive repairs. She remained there all summer while her owners, Thomas Norton & Co., decided what to do with her. At length, in order to squeeze a few more remunerative years from her, they converted her to a barge—not an uncommon fate for a tired wooden vessel. Scores of the Maine square-riggers were made into East Coast tow barges at this time.

The *Deering* left Philadelphia for Havana, Cuba, on October 10 but was allegedly abandoned by the steamer *El Presidente,* which had her in tow, when a rough sea parted their connecting hawser. The tug *Admiral Dewey* found her and her irate master, Captain Muirhead, adrift off Mayport, Florida, and took them into Jacksonville. The *Grace Deering* must have been inadequately repaired because she sank off Miami on November 3, 1906, after leaving Jacksonville in tow of the steamer *Nicaragua* for Havana. She went down gently, taking no one's life. Sumner's deepwater lady did not live long as a barge.

Down-Easterners are a sturdy stock, and if Sumner's fantasies were checked in one direction, they flourished in another, as his poetry still shows. There was a trolley stop on the Yarmouth–Portland line not far from the Drinkwaters' home that was called "Rubber Neck Station"—because there was such a curve in the track, people leaned out to see where the trolley was going. "Miss Ada" Seabury was Edith's lifelong best friend.

CAPT. BENJAMIN WEBSTER.

Capt. Benjamin Webster, one of Portland's best known sea captains, died at his home, 296 Spring street, yesterday noon from Bright's disease, after an illness extending over a period of about three months.

Capt. Webster was the son of Benjamin Webster, and was born in Freeport in February, 1814. At an early age he began his career on the sea and followed that calling for a space of about 40 years.

At the age of 19 he commanded his first vessel and sailed his own ships up to the time he retired from the sea in 1863; his last boat was the ship Helots.

Among the vessels that he has built and sailed are the ships Pumbustick and J. Baker; besides these he has sailed barks and ships and has owned in all as many as 15 barks, two of which, the Grace Deering and the Ordway, he owned at the time of his death.

In 1863 he retired from the sea and moved to Portland, from which port he had always sailed and settled down to a life on shore. During the earlier part of his active sea career he was engaged in the Atlantic coast trade, but in the latter part of the 50's and early 60's he took up the China trade in the pursuit of which he had travelled all over the world.

In 1844, Capt. Webster married Eunice Pratt with whom he lived in happy union until her death about five years ago. One adopted daughter, Mrs. L. L. Hight, survives.

In looking over his own interests and aiding the poor, the captain spent his time ashore and was engaged in these pursuits until about three months ago when his health failed. About four weeks ago he was compelled to stay in the house and had not since left it.

Monday, January 14, 1901 Ther=22 Bar=30-12 Light airs all about

Mrs. D. went to P.[ortland]
at 1 P.M. & home to T.
While I to the villiage
Thence Proceedeth
& took on a sleigh Ride
Miss Ada & Edith
When after 3 hours of Sweet Probation
hastened back to Rubber Neck Station
Over took Mrs. A. upon the Road
Who's Many bundles made quite a Load
Who rested beside me in the Sleigh
brightened the Joys of this winter day.
At Rubber Neck oh! what a pity
found Mrs. D. Just from the City
& Now the sleigh is filled & more
with Packages, Bundles & Women galore
Left Mrs. A. at her sweet abode
then home in thoughtful silence rode.

The identity of "Mrs. A." is a mystery, because although Sumner's later letters show that he very much admired a Mrs. Adams, she and her husband didn't take up residency in Yarmouth until 1903. This poem was written in his diary of 1901.

Boston, Feb 5—The Portland bark Grace Deering, now at Mystic wharf, has been sold to Thomas Norton & Co, of New York for about $4000. She will be used in the coffee trade between Rio Janeiro and Baltimore, with Capt Green, formerly of the bark Xenia, as master.

The *Grace Deering*, c. 1903.

THE INTERIM

1901-1904

*"There's nothing surer in the
world than disappointments."*

1901

Turn-of-the-century technology did not include home insulation. The elements ordered Sumner and Alice's lives. When it rained, roads turned to mud; if danger threatened, people ran and their horses galloped; cold froze and heat was hot. There was nothing complex about the Drinkwaters' relationship to their environment. Sumner noted the prevailing weather conditions daily and never forgot to mention them in his letters. Because these entries appear so regularly, they become invisible, to be dismissed as routine. Yet Sumner never took the weather and the sea for granted. Rather, he personified them as characters in their own right. Alive to the world around him, Sumner stepped in gentle accord through the seasons.

During the winter of 1901 after he had left the *Deering,* he ice-skated for the first time in four years, went sleighing and iceboating, put up the double windows in the dining room and secured a ton of coal. By February 5 he had a bad cold and a sore throat. He shook off his own illness lightly, but some did not. Another in his family succumbed to the winter cold.

Thursday, March 28, 1901   Wea-cloudy with snow squalls
A.M.   Called at Mother's & [my sister] Lucy's [husband] James [Monroe Bucknam] sick. Threatened with pneumonia. Doctor there.

Friday, March 29, 1901 Wea=   strong norther, cold & blustering
Down to Lucy's. James very sick with Pneumonia.

Saturday, March 30, 1901   Ther=26   Wea-Squally
A.M.   down to Lucy's   James very sick
P.M.   over to Mr. Pooles taking tea with them & spending the eve
Later went down to Lucy's to watch with James
Found him very sick, wandering at intervals with much fever & profuse sweating & high pulse 98

Sunday March 31, 1901   Cloudy
With Lucy till noon   Doctor there
rest of this day rainy
Home getting sleep

Monday, April 1, 1901   Cloudy   light southerly winds
a.m.   a little sunshine. Brother James died very suddenly last night at Midnight from Palsies of the heart.
a.m.   down to Lucy's also in the afternoon with her a few hours. Eve to lodge meeting of red men [James was a member, hence Brother]
after meeting went down to Lucy's to stay with her.

Thursday, April 4, 1901   Rainy   Easterly winds
A.M.   to villiage engaged team for P.M. went to Barber's
P.M.   Attended Brother James funeral. Age 39 years 3 months 13 days. Order of Red Men attended in a Body. Stopped at Brother John's after funeral.

The last words of James Monroe Bucknam, Jr., were: "I don't want to die yet." He was survived by Lucy, then thirty-six, their first-born child, Howard, and by Elden and Muriel. Howard, the only one of their six children who would reach old age, had just turned

ICE-BOAT REGATTA.

fifteen. He immediately became the head of the family, dropped out of school and left the town of Yarmouth looking for work. After apprenticing in a foundry, he took a correspondence course, and eventually became foreman of a shop with sixty men under him.

Despite Lucy's pitiably tragic life, she is recalled as being the merriest of Sumner's siblings. She was shy with strangers but a practical joker with her intimates. At one point in her life Lucy, who never remarried, was housekeeper for the Pullen family in Yarmouth. Joe Pullen at eighty-three still recalls the setdown she gave his older brother Will one day.

Everyone in the family knew, though they never dared to say anything, that Will would not catch even a chub the day he announced that he was off to Sebago Lake. Will rarely, if ever, caught a fish. Lucy watched for his return and when she saw him, she grabbed a skillet and marched out of the kitchen to greet him. Poking the skillet toward him, she said, "Now Will, you just put them fish right here." Will, empty-handed, was nonplused.

Sumner has recorded his attempts to find a new ship, but by spring he had had no word. He was highly respected in Yarmouth, as deepwater sea captains always were. Sailing was seasonal, and periods of unemployment were expected, especially in these last days of the down-easters. Thus there was no stigma attached to a captain taking odd jobs or accepting payment from neighbors and relatives. Sumner worked with his employers, not *for* them. He helped Jack to clapboard Nellie's new hen house, and then he agreed to contract out with him as a carpenter, although Sumner was nowhere near as skilled as Jack.

Alice's brother, Jack, was a medium-set man, leaning toward the chubby side with a good sense of humor. To boost the income from his carpentry and Nellie"s poultry farming, Jack kept a fleet of about thirty rowboats for summer visitors to rent. Prince's Point and Drinkwater Inn on Yarmouth's Foreside drew many summer visitors at that time. In fact, Jack and Sumner were part of a group building the new casino for their cousin Ella's Drinkwater Inn. The casino

was a long-needed recreational facility where the inn's guests could play cards and cribbage or just sit and socialize.

Wednesday, May 1, 1901   Ther=Mild   Bar=30 00   Wea=Fair
    light s. winds
    Worked all day [on the casino]
    Total 12¼ days [or] 12 days 2 hours
    Alice and Nellie down to walk home with us.
    Picked May flowers along the Road side.

The work at Drinkwater Inn left time enough for planting, so Sumner's garden was sprouting even while the "May flowers" bloomed. His garden plot was more exotic than those of his neighbors. Watermelon seeds from Bonaire kept company with the standard Yankee fare.

Spring turned to summer, but Sumner was still a journeyman. In his spare time he powdered the potato plants with Bug Death, staked his tomatoes and watched for a household auction where he and Alice purchased a carpet, grindstone and a what-not to hold their curios. Under pressure to finish the casino, Jack and Sumner worked nine hours on the Fourth of July, but stopped for a picnic dinner that Nell and Alice packed down to eat in the grove. By the end of the month the raspberries invited picking, the nights were nice for walking with Alice, and the schooner *Lizzie Chadwick* needed a skipper. Sumner, certified as a Master of Sailing Vessels of all Classes on any Ocean in the World, returned to coasting.

Monday, July 29, 1901   Mild   Barometer 30.12   Cloudy
    Noon time team from Russels came for me to see what was wanted at Telephone. Found what was wanted. To take charge of Schooner Lizzie Chadwick for a trip to Brunswick, Georgia for Hard Pine. Wages $75.00 Per Month. To Come right on. Left on the 6 P.M. train from Union Station [without Alice].

He was able to sign four men and a boatswain the day after his arrival in New York, and they left at 5 A.M. on August 1. They made Brunswick, Georgia, in twenty-one days. There Sumner hurt his hand while supervising the loading, paid off the second mate and bailed three members of his crew out of jail by paying their fines. None of these troublesome details kept him from watching for, and recording, the comings and goings of his old love.

Thurs Sept. 5, 1901 Grace Deering sailed for Montivideo from N. York

Friday Sept. 6, 1901 Ther 74 Bar 30.20 Fair Wind light N.E.
No cargo. Employed Painting & Tarring etc
8 a.m. comenced to be showery
Called on skippers & reminded them that ship was on demurrage [a fine required when the time to load or discharge exceeds charter contract] from 8.30 of this date.
rec'd letter from Alice & Father
President McKinley Assasinated [shot by an anarchist] at Buffalow, N.Y. at 4 P.M.

15 days in Port

Saturday, September 14, 1901 Ther 80 Bar. 30 17 Fair light westerly wind [in port]
wrote Alice
Sad news of the Presidents death occuring at 2.30 this a.m. has reached us this morning. Flags set at ½ mast throughout the Port & on shore. The Nation Mourns a great Loss.

President McKinley was not the only dignitary to have encountered death this year. Nine months earlier Sumner had recorded that Britain's monarch had passed away.

Tuesday, January 22, 1901 Ther=18 above Bar=30-20 Wea=Slightly overcast
2.30 P.M. News came by cable of the passing away of Her Majesty Queen Victoria after a long and unparralled reign of 63 years, 6 months & 23 days at the age of 81 years and 8 months. Nations Mourn her loss.

These two entries are very typical of Sumner's diaries because he often mingled events of world-wide interest with his personal itinerary. Like his father, Nicholas, before him, Sumner was fascinated by history.

Sumner noted in an entry of September 6, 1901, that the *Lizzie Chadwick* had not been loaded within the time her contract specified. Therefore, he collected $500 in demurrage before leaving on October 3 for New York City, where he discharged the deck cargo. The schooner was then towed to Piermont, a little town on the western bank of the Hudson, twenty-six miles above New York. Sumner had brought along a stevedore's crew from the city to unload the schooner. Rafts transported the lumber from the *Lizzie Chadwick* to shore.

Sunday October 27, 1901 Overcast to Fair light N.E. wind
On board all day. Had an avalanche of Callers on Board. Old & young Male & Female. Some very pretty Girls in this place & some would stop a clock.
3 rafts taken from ship 2 left along side
Stevedore's crew went to town last night

10 days in Port

Shipowners expected coasting captains to move the cargoes along as well as they sailed the ships. By the next day Sumner, already unimpressed by the stevedore's crew, was utterly disgusted by the haphazard progress they had made in unloading. These workers that he had imported to Piermont were behaving as though they were sailors fresh off the ship in a foreign port. The *Lizzie Chadwick* was making so little progress in discharging that although Sumner had not worked as a stevedore since 1886 on the *Grace Cushing*, he and the cook volunteered to help.

Monday, October 28, 1901   Ther=44   Bar=30.50   Wea=overcast
9.15 . . . discharging with 3 men in stevedore's gang & cook. Terrible work going on. The very worst I have ever seen in all my Experience.
11.15 Went to work for Stevedore as he couldn't get men & some of them Drunk.
Forgot to mail letter to Alice. Wrote a few lines in the Eve. Worked 5 hours for Stevedore.   11 days in Port

When the stevedore's men had recovered enough to return to work, Sumner left the schooner and bicycled along the Hudson to nearby Nyack. He first saw the Hudson River Valley in the fall of 1879. The young sailor had been impressed enough to pen a rare

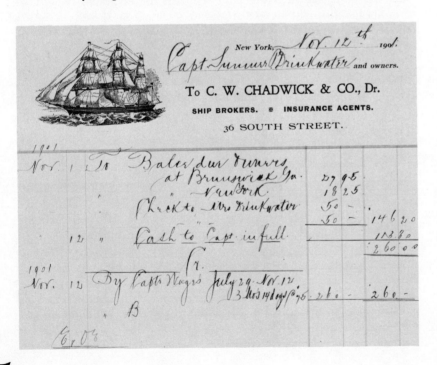

compliment, "enjoyed beautiful scenery." Now, twenty-two years later, it was fall again.

Openings for employment often occurred when a ship's regular captain was incapacitated right before a voyage and a substitute was needed immediately. Sumner had been given command of the *Lizzie Chadwick* under such circumstances; he had had to leave home the day the berth was offered to him. Competition for any command was tremendous, no matter how short its tenure. Although Sumner's original commitment terminated at Piermont, he agreed to stand by the vessel up the river to Catskill, New York, where he took on board his replacement and a cargo of brick.

Sumner did not return to Yarmouth immediately after the vessel brought him to New York City. Rather, he made the rounds of shipping firms and looked up old friends. A Captain Knolton of the schooner *Allen Green* wired for permission to have Sumner take his command for a voyage but he was refused. Captain Knolton, like every other shipmaster, was in no position to argue. The owners' whim was law. They wanted the man who knew their ship best and could get the most from her. Whatever reason Captain Knolton had for requesting leave did not impress the owners of his vessel.

Finding no opportunities, Sumner reached home on November 17, just in time to admire a dress Alice had been making at Hattie Poole's and to act as her escort at the supper social at the First Parish Church.

A house owned by Mr. Isaac Merrill, but built by Alice's uncle, Captain Joseph Drinkwater in 1844, stood a quarter of a mile before her family's homestead at the intersection of Gilman Street and Prince's Point Road.

Tuesday, December 10, 1901   Ther=38   Bar=29.66   Wea=Rain & fog
varriable winds   wind going round the compass
Repairing Sleigh
4 PM   was Called up to Mr. Isaac Merril's who had fallen Dead at his work Bench. Staid till the Undertaker arrived. Weather clearing.

Alice and Sumner had lived in her parents' home for nineteen years, and their two-family arrangement had grown to three when Jack brought Nellie into the household. Sumner did not note any discussions about moving, even after negotiations must have begun, but on May 19, 1902, the Drinkwaters purchased Isaac Merrill's property from his heirs in Boston. The deed was put in Alice's name; Sumner was at sea.

1902

Sumner was employed fairly steadily throughout 1902 as skipper of the coastal schooner *Lugano.* He made six voyages to New York from Maine on her between March 25, 1902, and February 14, 1903. Alice only accompanied him once because she was preoccupied with their new home and with family matters.

The *Lugano* was in East Boston on June 13 when Edith graduated with "marked ability & success" from Yarmouth High School. Sumner hurried home and bought a new suit for the occasion. Edith was one of fourteen girls and two boys honored in the exercises held at the First Parish Church, and Sumner presented her with a long gold watch chain meant to be worn around the neck. While Edith treasured this gift from her favorite uncle, she never had a watch for it and wore wristwatches instead.

On July 15, as Sumner was getting under way from New York harbor, he received word from Alice that her father was being buried that very day. Watson Gray Drinkwater had passed away three days earlier at the age of "72 years, 5 months and 5 days." Since Sumner remained with the *Lugano,* he did not reach home and Alice for another week.

Alice probably delayed moving down the street to their new home in order to comfort her mother, but on November 6, Sumner returned from the sea to find "Alice at our new home and Edith with her." They used the upstairs for their living quarters and rented out the downstairs. Far less jubilantly than they, Alice's mother, Sarah Staples Drinkwater, took possession of their former apartment in her home and yielded her place as mistress of the house to Jack's wife, Nell.

Sumner continued to apply for deepwater berths while in command of the coasting schooner *Lugano.* The name of N. W. Rice appeared frequently, perhaps more so than any other firm that Sumner jotted into his diary. Persistence paid off; on March 12, 1903, he was offered command of the bark *Benjamin F. Hunt Jr.* chartered to Buenos Aires.

For our purposes, Sumner's years with the *Benjamin Hunt* begin at the end of this voyage rather than at the beginning. Alice traveled with him on the eight-month passage, which began on March 25. On this, her last recorded voyage as the Captain's "Mrs.," they touched at Buenos Aires, Rosario, Rio de Janeiro, Barbados and Turks Island, at the southeast end of the Bahamas. Sumner's next letter to Alice came after the *Hunt* had arrived back in Boston bringing salt from Turks Island. As it was then already November 27, 1903, Alice had hurried ahead to Yarmouth to prepare for the holidays.

> East Boston Mass
> Tuesday Dec 15/03
>
> Dear Alice
> Yours of Sunday is at hand and I may as well write you again as I cannot tell just what day I'll be [finished]. . . . I shall come home over Sunday anyway & wish now that I had last Sunday. . . . If I had known Edith was likely to go in to a decline [waiting for me] I suppose I should anyway. But try & cheer her up even if you have to with false hopes. . . .
>
> I should think you might get Alfred [Edith's brother, their nephew] to do things for you that is needed & you needn't wait for me to get a couch. Get just such a one as you like & I shall be satisfied. . . .
>
> You say you have spent a lot. So have I. Bought an Overcoat yesterday. Couldn't stand it in my thin one. It's awfully cold here now.

Well, I guess you'd think I needed looking after in more directions than one. There is quite a charming young lady next room to Julia [an elderly cousin] & she has been in every time I have been up. I rather think she likes me pretty well. I carried a basket of fruit—grapes, candy, etc. one eve & she was enjoying it with us, saying she allways shared Julia's nice things. Then I am quite a frequent visitor at Uncle John's [John and Hattie Staples—probably Alice's uncle, as her mother's maiden name was Staples]. And if I told you where Aunt Hattie & I had been, you would be well, I don't know how you'd be. But there's lots of things you never learn at school.

Glad Lucy is to make a long visit. You'll have to have another small bed in the attic if they come to see us. Tell her she better sell her hay if she can get a fair price for it. If not I can take it & sell the whole [mine & hers] together.

We finished discharging today & have towed to East Boston to have some work done on the vessel. The copper has got to be repaired & some small matters attended to. She is chartered at 7.50 per m. [$7.50 per thousand running feet of lumber of any size] & will follow the Johnson in loading [a ship they met in Auckland in 1897]. . . . The Goddard [owned by N.W. Rice also] is for Sale.

The Salt overrun 1046 Bushels with 168 Bushels dirty. The Towell only overrun 27 bushels & had 928 Bushels dirty. They told me I had the cleanest cargo that had come to Boston for a long time & hoped I would bring another. I said Nit= but thanked them. Shall probably settle freight tomorrow & . . . I hope I can settle the voyage.

Capt Lewis don't want me to come home till we tow up to the Lumber berth. Thinks a fortnight [at home] ought to do me so I think he expects me to go again. But I have thought if they sold the Goddard they might give the Hunt to Capt Duncan [the *Goddard*'s captain would have seniority]. So to inquiries or inquisitors you don't know whether I am going again or not.

I don't see how we can get to the Lumber berth before Friday.

Now I must write to my Dear dispirited niece & try to extend a few gleans of hope for I should feel so badly to find the roses faded.

You can write again. If you think of anything you want, let me know.

lots of love
Sumner

The *Johnson* finished taking on lumber and yielded her berth at Mystic Dock to the *Hunt* on Friday, so that Sumner was able to leave Boston for Yarmouth the next day, December 19. The second Christmas in their own home was bittersweet for the Drinkwaters; while Sumner had been given command of the *Benjamin F. Hunt Jr.* on her next voyage to Buenos Aires, Alice apparently had decided not to go with him. Still, the season was merry: Edith called the day after he got home, and Lucy and her three children arrived for the holidays.

Alice accompanied Sumner back to Boston on January 10 and remained with him until his departure for Buenos Aires on Monday, January 25, 1904.

THE YEARS WITH
THE <u>BENJAMIN F. HUNT JR.</u>
1904-1908

"Them that has, gets."

1904

N. W. Rice Co., the Boston firm that employed Sumner, was not a shipping house but a leather-trading company. Neimiah Webster Rice, its founder, had had a general-merchandise, hardware business in Portland before moving to Boston in the late 1880s to participate in the River Plate Trade. Once as familiar a name to Yankees as the China Tea Trade, "the River Plate Trade" between Argentina and New England had begun in the 1880s. These two market areas were perfect complements. Argentina needed lumber thanks to a boom in British and European immigration and investment; New England hurried to supply it. Their ships returned full of hides and wool—valued commodities in America's Northeast. Boston was a bustling shoe-manufacturing center at that time. Individuals and firms involved in this trade had shares in the fleet that carried its cargoes. The *Hunt* and the *Goddard* were only two of the vessels N. W. Rice managed over the years, and N. W. Rice was only one of the merchants involved. Because these merchants stayed with sail rather than investing in steamships, the River Plate Trade, which continued through World War I, extended the lifetime of many great sailing ships.

When Sumner talks about the "over run of the log" in the following section of his letter to Alice, he is referring to a "patent log," a device towed off the stern of the ship which measured and then recorded its speed. Going back before Columbus' time, seamen literally cast a small log overboard from the bows of a vessel and counted the number of seconds that passed until it reached the stern, making their calculations in that way. Just preceding the "patent log" that Sumner used, the "chip log" was commonly used. The chip log was a disk of wood or, more often, a quarter disk that was streamed astern for fourteen seconds by sand glass, and the length of line that had run out was then pulled in and measured. It was marked at intervals with knots—these were what were measured. Hence, "knots" have come to be used as a unit of a ship's speed. Eventually the patent log evolved, which was read on a kind of clock face with a moving hand. However, even these devices are consistently off by a certain percentage, and Sumner's log evidently records more distance than the vessel actually covers. Since the instrument's error is consistent, Sumner would know the correction factor.

Bark Benj=F Hunt Jr   at Sea Feb 7th/04   Lat=31–40N.
  Long 35–42 W
Letter No 1 (1)
Dear Alice
Thinking You may be begining a letter to me (which shows you my thoughts are with you), I think I will comence one as you will be pleased perhaps to compare this voyage out with the last one of which you doubtless have much better recolections than I do.

The Fair wind which wafted us from the Harbor of the Hub [Boston] was not of long duration. The following day it died out to a calm followed that night (Tuesday) with a short S.E. gale. We were then about half way from Georgia Shoal [east of Boston] to Cape Sable [Nova Scotia]. . . . From Sat. Jan 30th to Yesterday Feb 6th we had very changible winds, gales & constant cloudy weather with heavey rain at times, very high Sea most of the time & no observation for that time or 6 days. Yesterday our Sights proved that we were nearly 100 miles ahead of our reckoning, not allowing for the stream [prevailing currents] & the over run of the log. I suppose of course that was much pleasenter then being behind.

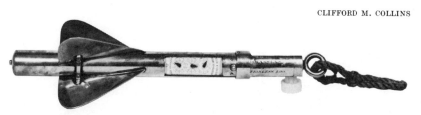

Sumner's patent log.

The *Benjamin F. Hunt Jr.*

Yesterday we took the stove down, cleaned & Blacked it & put [it] away for all the voyage, I hope. Today is the only nice day or the first I should say since we sailed, sunny smooth & fine with moderate northerly wind, Ther up to 70. . . .

Now bye bye till some other time   Lovingly

Sumner

Evening

It's so pleasant to what it has been that I feel rather lonesome, more so than any time since I came out. I thought of you monday P.M. as on your way home & imagined when you got home about 6 I was off Cape Cod, probably some East of it. The Pilot left us at 945. We were quite a while getting the Anchor.

2 Men froze their fingers quite badly going aloft without Mittens. They have been pretty sore since I had to open 2 fingers & they will lose the nails but they are getting most well now. . . . The mate seems to be all right. 2nd mate nothing extra but is willing enough. Crew is much as usual, part of them very fair kind of sailors, on the whole better than the last voyage. We had a lovely Sunset & I took a sight & have been working it & wondered why you wasn't picking out the Logarithm for me. I guess that's what made me feel lonesome.

Now guess I'll light a cigar & take a promenade.

Good night

S

Sunday Feb 21st   Lat 6-40n   Long 27 40 west

27 days at sea

Not to the Line yet & 2 weeks since I Laid this by. I wonder (as I do every day) what my Dear Wifie is about. Of course I imagine that a short time of each Sunday & doubtless of other days is devoted to her absent hub & today you are getting a letter about ready for a mail, no doubt.

. . . Today is really the most tropical looking we have had & the ther= has got up to 80°. . . . I have just last night changed to my lightest underclothes after a good Bath & the steward has fixed up my large berth with cool sheets & I slept fine last night. Today he has cut my hair & I have cut the Mates.

The Pussy Cat is well & just as usual, comes in & looks in the mirror & swells up & then I plague her & perhaps get a scratch once in a while.

We have our Sails nearly all repaired now. I have worked quite a good deal on them as there are only 2 decent Sewers. [Sewing a fine seam on canvas was an art acquired by only a few old salts who did so sitting on deck in the sun, relieved of more arduous duties.] The rest work aloft on the riggin & the mate keeps them at it & keeps up the dog watch. I don't believe there will be as many stay by [for the return voyage] as last time. I hope not. The Steward is keeping all my clothes washed as fast as he finds any. I tell him he needn't do it but he seems to want to & seems to have plenty of time. He gets on easy as can be

& everything so much nicer than the last cook. It does seem singular that we couldn't have had such a one when you were with me.

Parlor at Gilman Street.

It seems a long time since we came out though only 4 weeks tomorrow. . . . I can hardly think that you are probably setting by a coal fire & perhaps none to warm & looking out on a winter landscape, the Earth clad in virgin whiteness & have been noting the church goer & listening to the tinkle of Sleigh Bells making their sunday music. I wonder if you have learned the sound of the Adams [new neighbors] bell yet so you don't have to know when they are passing. I wonder too if you are very neighborly & if you are planning any change in the Lower part of the House? I think I feel most lonesome when I look up at the Picture (as I have fixed it up on the wall to look at). I often imagine I can look in through the windows & guess what you are about at different hours of the day as I compare my time with yours. At present about 1 P.M. with you & you're just through cleaning up from lunch & will set down to write a little or if the day is nice & fine go down home unless [your] mother is with you keeping house then you may call over to Aunt Nell later on. Well I'll rest a while or I'll have so much that you'll get tired reading it. So bye bye

Lovingly Summie

Evening

Have been writing up my log & thought I would add a line to this & mention that I have fixed over the mattress. I cut off 6 inches on one side laying back the tick each side & then when I got the stuffing cut out, just lapped one part over the other & sewed it up. It fits the berth fine & is all right only up level with the top of the Bunk Board but I shall make a nice Shifting Board for bad weather [so he wouldn't fall out].

Good night. Wish you was in the Berth waiting for me to come to Bed.

Sunday March 6th L= 8–10 South
Long 35=35 West

Isn't it awful? Two weeks gone passing with continued light winds, Calms & Rain-Showers over 14° or 893 miles behind the last voyage. If this isn't discouraging I don't know . . .

We have had a serious misfortune. On Tuesday about 5 P.M. we were struck by a sudden squall. It had been raining all day & a light Easterly breeze & I had not thought of a squall & had all sail set. Away went the Jibboom & fore topgallent mast [affecting a total of six sails]. Such a mess but we got them down from aloft & everything cleared up Friday & sent down the Mizzen Top mast & have got it nearly fitted for a fore Top gallant mast & will have it up tomorrow, I hope. So you see we are still more crippled. . . . Of course we shall lose quite a number of miles a day till we get in Order again. [The wild pitching of the vessel made it too dangerous to hoist the new masts aloft and the emergency was to occupy eleven days.] . . .

Made a small sale [Slop Chest merchandise] of 4.$^{30\ cts.}$ worth including 3 Bar more of soap. That's all now. Lovingly & longingly

S—

The *Hunt* was seriously threatened on March 1 when a squall broke off the top section of her foremast as well as the jib boom, and the crew had been working desperately ever since to secure the bark. The repairs to the jib boom were now complete. Holes had been bored into at the right intervals for the head stays. These had been set up and the jibs hoisted on their stays once again.

Evidently, according to this next letter, the Drinkwaters' fence near Captain Young's property didn't meet the State of Maine specification: "horse high, bull strong and hog tight," and needed to be repaired. The Drinkwater property at that time consisted of three acres around their home and three acres diagonally across Gilman Street and up the hill toward the Indian Cemetery. (The Indian Cemetery is named for Yarmouth pioneers killed in Indian raids.) Sumner seems to be referring to that separate piece of pasture, because Captain Young lived nowhere near his house. The Youngs' house was built up the hill near the beginning of Gilman Street on the site of the old Meeting House under the Ledge, which was torn down in 1839. The stone lying before its east door, which in Sumner's

day was in the Youngs' front yard, may still be seen today. Gilman Street is named for the Reverend Tristam Gilman, the first minister called to Yarmouth to lead services in the old church.

"Nick" Bucknam, his cousin, is now one of the Drinkwaters' closest neighbors. The Bucknams' house still stands across the intersection from the Drinkwater place, although both places no longer belong to those families.

Ervin Doyle was a bachelor who lived with his mother across Gilman Street from Alice's family homestead. He was a butcher as well as a farmer and would drive around Yarmouth with his wagon picking up pigs. He had a piece of pasture over on Cousins Island and would hire the boys of the village to swim his horse and cow across

Sumner and Alice's new home, c. 1902.

Casco Bay in the summer. Sumner's sister Eunice was married to his brother, Will Doyle.

"A square face" refers to the four-sided, square-faced bottle in which Holland gin, a popular drink among foreign seamen, was available. These bottles originally were used to contain cheap "trade gin," used for barter with Africa and Polynesia.

Sunday March 13th   Lat 19–04 South   Long 37–46
. . . Just on the edge of Abralhus Bank

Well my Dear a few more lines again today . . . & almost as still & quiet in the Cabin as though at anchor on South Boston flats & naturally a rather lonesome day. I had my usual Sunday ablution. Changed the Bed linen & co. . . .

. . . I imagine I have letters on the way & perhaps nearer to me than I know of . . . I wonder who is staying with you. I Presume a female of some kind. I hope you will See that the Fence between us & Capt Young is repaired so as to give him no trouble. I don't suppose if you let Nick the Pasture that he'd repair that Part of the fence or not as that is from the Road down towards the Gully. I expect you have had something coming in from the Hay ere this as most likely Ervin has sold more or less of it.

Tell Nellie I have enjoyed the Luxury of her Sisterly Kindness & the chickens were just fine & heartily enjoyed. She may know that at least once on the voyage she was very pleasantly Remembered. I wonder if she is hen or Rather Chicken farming this spring.

If you have Father & Mother up to visit you anytime you can treat Dad to something from the [liquor] Closet. You want to send him a square face or 2 during the spring & Summer. I shall quite likely bring home something in that line. Does Mr. Young come down to see you often I wonder, or is he going west as he Talked?

Well, I hope I may be able to write of a better week next time.

My sale last night was over $8.00 but only 1 Bar Soap. Kitty has caught 2 big Rats during the week. No more this time. Lovingly Sumner

Sunday Mar 27th 04

Well My Dear Alice
. . . Have Packed my Grip all ready for morning—suit of underclothes, 2 white shirts, night dress, 4 collars, 3 Pair cuffs, 3 Pair hose, 2 ties, ½ doz Handkerchiefs, tooth Brush, Soap & 3 towels, letter paper & envelopes, fountain Pen, Toilet Paper, Cuff studs & Collar Buttons, Brush & Comb, tooth Brush & Picks & Ship Papers, letters

& co to go in later, Razer strap & tobacco, silver mounted pipe & Diary. Thought it might interest you or at least amuse you. S—

When Sumner mentions "Mr. Hunt's folks" he no doubt means the firm of Charles Hunt & Co. that is sending lumber to Buenos Aires on the *Benjamin F. Hunt Jr.* The similarity in surnames suggests that this company owned a share in the vessel, although the leather-trading company of N. W. Rice managed her.

The bark *Benjamin F. Hunt Jr.* was built in 1882 in Newburyport, Massachusetts. At 1,132 tons, she was almost twice the size of the *Grace Deering.* More of Sumner's correspondence exists from the *Hunt* than the *Deering,* yet at no time did Sumner speak affectionately of this ship. The *Hunt* was considered a fine vessel, but perhaps he couldn't get the trim little bark that he'd commanded earlier out of his mind. Or he might have guarded himself against attachment to the *Hunt,* fearing that she was only a temporary

command. Another possibility is that seafaring, in general, and his ships, in particular, may have become a sensitive issue with Alice. As early as their 1900 trip to Rio, she wrote Hattie Poole that she no longer cared for going to sea. Sumner may have been feeling pressure from her to remain at home.

Sumner's contemporaries considered the Drinkwaters "well-off." They purchased a home and six acres of land and they had no dependents. Nevertheless, in Maine people don't put on airs and Sumner never seems complacent, although he does try to convince Alice to indulge herself. They did not keep permanent help, but the Adams boy up the street (belonging to their newest neighbor) came by to do heavy jobs for Alice, and she had a strong support system in her extended family. After all, between the two of them they were related to nearly everyone around.

A constant current runs through Sumner's letters concerning Alice's health. She had been delicate since their courting days, when

Launching of the *Benjamin F. Hunt Jr.,* 1881.

she suffered from severe headaches. In addition, she had asthma, and she often broke out in hives, which she attributed to her nerves; excitement on one day predictably meant blinding headaches the next.

Josh, Sumner's younger brother, became the first carrier on Yarmouth's rural free delivery route in 1903. Before the introduction of paved roads, Maine's fifth season, "mud months," used to occur between winter and spring. They provided Josh and others who regularly had to get from place to place with a formidable challenge. Officially Maine now has four seasons, like everybody else, but some corners of the state deny it.

Josh's mail route was twenty-four miles long and he scheduled it so that he would be in the area of his home near lunchtime for a change of horses. Then he'd continue on, often until after dark. Since the fields, now wooded, were open then, Hattie Josh could tell his wagon by its lantern from quite a distance, and she'd have a hot meal waiting for him as he stepped through the door. Although Josh lived until 1951, he never owned a car.

No 2   Hotel Provence
                                            Buenos Aires
                                            Eve March 31st 04

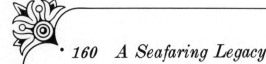 My Dear Alice
     I will write a few lines as there is no where to go for Amusement & so long & nice a letter deserves quite a lengthy answer, more especially as I shall give you more of my thoughts & time which of course is your due, than if I had been earlier remembered by my family. . . . But as for that they have all forgot me but you, so that I am feeling very Tender towards you, grateful for a love that forget-me-not. I hope you are aware today of my safe arrival as I asked Mr. Hunt's folks to wire you when they heard. . . .

     I am stopping ashore . . . as the expense would be very little different than the getting back & forth from the ship. As I knew I should Hate myself off there alone . . . I concluded to stop ashore even though I would spend a few dollars (which I think one is entitled to after spending 2 months tied up alone at Sea.)

     I have really missed you this voyage more than you may think. If one never had his wifie with him, all right, he wouldn't know then the difference. But having you one voyage & then going alone makes it doubly lonesome & it's a lonesome miserable life at best.

     I am glad Mother S[arah, Alice's mother] is staying with you so much . . . & wish she could be content to make her home with us. I am sure she could live more at ease & not work as she does at home. . . . With the cold winter you are having I am glad you are running both fires. I was afraid you would not & also very glad you do not lug wood up stairs. You know I do not want you to do it or any work like that & I want you to send all your washing out & of course Mother's too. You must tip Pat [Adams] once in a while or if he won't take Tips, think of something to give him.

     I have read quite a good deal of the Papers & enjoyed them. I can sit in the Hotel Parlor & read when I feel like it. . . . Enjoy it more away than at home as the Talk of the town doesn't seem so frivolus somehow away & it's pleasent gleaning the news.

     . . . I don't know if I mentioned in my first letter how close the 2 passages were . . . we anchored at 3 A.M. of the 28th 63 days lacking 6 hours, the other passage (you made with me last year) 63 days lacking 2 hours. I find lots of Capts in telling of their quick passeges reckon when they got into the Bay or to their first anchoring.

     I am surprised to hear of Mr. Alden's death although he told me once he didn't expect to live long & didn't care a dam if he didn't. I want to take up every thing about the people that you mentioned. I am always sorry to learn of the death of those we know & glad that those that were sick are mending. . . . I expect Josh is having it pretty hard getting over his route. [With the mud] he will need 3 horses, I should think. . . . Do you think Capt F will take a young wife? Funnier things have happened. So you have an Electric bell. Quite Toney, ain't you?

. . . I am very glad you are having another treatment & pleased to note your encouragement. I hope you will give it a good trial & don't look at all at the cost. Put that out of mind entirely. Cannot he treat you for your Hoarseness as well?

Speaking of the pasture, I know Nickie would feel awfully disappointed if he didn't have it. Of course you will do as you wish with it but I would tell him before letting it that you have a better offer for it & give him a chance to say if he would pay an equal amount.

. . . There are no Capts I have got aquainted with here just now so it's rather dull . . . The Schooner Melba arrived here 2 days behind me, 66 days from New York, but has gone up to Rosario to discharge. [Her master] Capt Dodge was ashore last night & stopped here & we were together that eve & went to a Spanish Theatre. . . . Dennis Long come up to the Hotel last night & went out with us to the Theatre. He has a great fund of amusement in him, lots of Irish wit & most as good as a threatre himself. He enquired after you as also several others. The Counsul & his wife are both unwell . . . and going on to the states for awhile & I don't beleive she will come back if he does. I think he is hoping to get a transfer to some other place. They both wish me to send regards to you.

No more tonight. Wish you were here   Lots of love   Sumner

Although Sumner teases Alice in this letter about her flagrant misconduct with the dentist and other men, he almost certainly never questioned her fidelity. Not only was Alice living in the bosom of *her* family under *his* family's watchful eye, but as a Yankee of that era, Alice would care more for her own standard of behavior than what her neighbors might say.

Sumner's life may seem to have been less circumscribed than Alice's, yet for the kind of man he was, it really wasn't. The women he met briefly in port whom he may have befriended were wives of acquaintances, and his diaries give no hint that he ever misbehaved. The fantasies we see glimmers of are quite another thing.

One of the family stories might serve to illustrate the morality of their day. An ailing maiden lady received a house call from a doctor who began his examination by taking down her statistics. Things proceeded smoothly until he asked if she had ever been married. She said no, and he then asked if she was a virgin. The lady shot upright in her sickbed and snapped at him, "Young man, in my day the one meant the other!"

Sunday April 3rd
Well My Dear

I am glad you are remembering me. A mail came yesterday but did not get delivered till this morning & I have been up to the Consuls & got your letter No 2 & no others. . . . I guess they have all forgotten me but you. . . .

. . . Well, the first item that interests me is having gentlemen callers varnishing for you [while] you [are] Tucking Drawers. Did he admire the Tucks & I wonder if the Desk was the only Article that got varnished that day? Anyway it was a nice Job to have done but I don't see where he got payed for it as a Pint of varnish at $6.00 per gallon would be 75 cts. I guess Mina [wife to the gentleman caller] & I will have to see about it when I get home. I wonder how her rheumatism is getting on. If she has another attack when I am home I'll prescribe for her. Perhaps a massage treatment would be beneficial.

Now the next in order is having new teeth for nothing only if you will let him do it & then go on to tell me you have accepted his offer & even ask me if you didn't do right. "That takes the cake." But no joking I could not tell for the life of me if you had a full set or only an upper or lower set. Anyway I would have them now if they trouble you. You didn't expect the ones you had to [last] for only a year or so & expected to have new ones . . . As to your asking me if you done right, I should say allways pay for value received. But if he thinks he didn't give you that in the first set why you may feel justified in accepting his offer. I wouldn't suffer with toothache anyway.

I am pleased to have you write so cheerfully in regard to your improvement under Dr. Podor's treatment. . . . Do not look at the expense part of it. You know, my Dear, that I should not care if you spent a Hundred Dollars or several of them, if we have them, for your comfort & health as well as pleasure. It will be your own fault if you do not enjoy your share of what comes to us. Probably I'll spend more for cigars & going about here than you'll spend all the time I'm gone. It will do us no good in the next world. Still I do not intend to be foolishly extravagent but of course one can't be among ship masters in Port without spending a few dollars unless he wants to be termed a hog or a [dead] beat. . . . If you could find a cure for your humor [depression], that also would improve your health as well. I hope my next letter [from you] will be as happily encouraging as this. . . .

I am surprised that the House of N. W. Rice sent you a check without notice from you but glad they did . . . but they may have concluded you were diffident about asking for it.

I am glad someone is taking up our needs in the way of town improvements & glad you signed the paper. I hope he will get his article through. I wonder if Mr. Adams will interest himself any in town matters. . . .

. . . No I ain't jealous of the Capt. He wouldn't do much mischeif, I don't believe. He would be afraid of having his heart affected under shuch great Excitement.

. . . I am verry verry sorry to hear that Nellie is so unwell. I hoped she was benefited by that Dr. she went to but fear not. I am sorry, & sorry too that you & she are not more sisterly as you were when she was so sick & I was on that last voyage to New Zealand.

I hope John will get through the cold strong winter without mishap. It certainly ought to be well over by this time. Now good night

Lovingly Sumner

Hattie Josh.

Sumner quips to Alice about their niece Edith's beau, Will Rent. Actually, Will lived with his own family in Cambridge near her Uncle Edwin's store. Edith's Uncle Ed was Hattie John's older brother, and he made his living selling butter, eggs and cheese. Edith was visiting them when she first met Will, and although she was quite young, she never forgot him. Will came running into her uncle's place carrying two horribly dirty kittens and Edith hated cats the way most people hate snakes.

"Elizabeth" was Sumner's niece born to Joshua and Hattie Josh on August 12, 1902. Hattie Josh, unlike her daughter Elizabeth, who had plenty of space to run in, had been a city girl, confined to rolling a hoop around the Bunker Hill monument near her home in Charleston, Massachusetts. After she married Josh in 1894, the couple made their home with his parents, Margaret and Nicholas. Hattie Josh was never popular with the Drinkwater family, none of whom came from *Boston.* A prim woman, she held herself quite straight and she disapproved of nicknames, although she put up with being called Hattie. Having selected her daughter's name, she informed the family of the choice and admonished them that her child was to be addressed at all times as "Elizabeth." Nicholas successfully side-stepped her and called his beloved granddaughter "Baby." But Woodbury, May's easygoing husband, who loved to tease, decided to meet Hattie Josh head-on. One day when Hattie Josh opened her door, he was waiting to greet her, "Hi, Hat. How's Liz?"

Hattie Josh was not deterred by her in-laws' chuckles and she reacted instantly when outsiders began calling her daughter "Liz" at school. She swept into the principal's office and explained to him that her daughter had been named *Elizabeth,* her name was to be pronounced *Elizabeth,* as well as spelled *Elizabeth,* and used as such —or else.

"Holy-stoning the cabin floor" was a backbreaking job. The steward would have been kneeling on a short section of padded board and pushing large pieces of broken grindstone back and forth over a section of the floor that was kept covered with wet sand. Subsequently the sand would be removed and the wood allowed to dry clean and white before a protective coat of oil, varnish or paint was applied. Out on deck, surprisingly, a thin Stockholm tar was the standard preservative.

On board again
Monday eve April 4th
I find a mail goes Wed= morning for the steamer that the Consul is to go on. Was up there [at the American Consulate] this morning & got a letter from Edith. A very nice long affectionate letter. So I'll have to forgive her not having one here on my arrival. . . .

I guess Edith's Rent is quite in love with the occupent if not the occupent with the Rent. I guess he is with her most of his spare time. . . . Elizabeth is not able to walk yet. Well perhaps she'll runn enough to make up for lost time when she does get going. . . . We came into the Boca [for discharging] this P.M. . . . We are tied part way up & will get up to Berth tomorrow, the same place where we discharged

Edith Drinkwater.

last time. . . . The vessel looks very well below & on deck. The steward has everything in fine order. He has been holy-stoning . . . the cabin floor & it looks white as can be. He has the curtains up & the Berths all made up in real Steam Boat fashion, the spreads on all three & Blankets rolled up & laid diagonally acrost. Every thing is shining & the decks have been cleaned, the spars painted & the Blocks aloft, the running gear all flaked up & down the shrouds & stopped clear of the rails & all in very nice order. I think she will compare favorably with any ship in Port.

The 2nd mate wants to leave & I guess I shall let him go. He isn't up to much. I hope the crew will all skip. There isn't but one I would care to keep by.

Well dear I think this must do you this time. Shall write often, most likely every week, but think I must finish Edith's letter or she will be disappointed as I was not to get one from her. Give my love to Mummy Sarah & say that I hope to find her Just as lively as ever . . . & living with you & that she won't run off home Just as soon as I get home. Love to John & Nellie & also to Capt Adams & his good Lady, especially his good Lady, & all the family you see as well as remembrances to neighbors & Friends. . . .

With lots & lots of love & longings from your own

Sumner—

Sunday April 10 1904

My Dear Alice   No 3

I will write a few lines this eve and only a few. The mosquitos are so troublesome. They have got in quite plentiful though I have screens in. I use the netting to sleep under & so get clear of them through the night. There is a mail due tomorrow from the states so shall expect more letters. . . .

We begun discharging of cargo wed = morning 6th across another Bark. Getting along fairly well. 6 men & the 2nd mate have disappeared. . . .

There is nothing special to write except an Accident happening to the mate which I didn't speak of in my last letter and which came near being very serious if not fatal. He was working on the broken Jibboom & had one of the men at work with an axe not far from him. The axe sliped or glanced from the stick & the mate being stooped over with a mallet & chisel, the axe just went over the top of his head. The end of the blade cut a nasty wound in the Top & back of his like this. Had it gone a ¼ inch deeper, it would no doubt have killed him. He had to be taken ashore to a doctors & have it dressed. He remained ashore that night but the Dr. allowed him to go on board the next day. He had to put 6 stitches in the wound but the mate is doing nicely now. The Dr. has been on board . . . & thinks there is very little danger now of any bad result. It was a close shave. I cabled notice to the Owners as there was no agents here.

Monday eve

We have quite a hole in the between decks tonight . . . Another man has deserted, only 3 now. No business is offering & F. C. Cook & Co. do not think they will be able to load us home. Very few freights offering & poor rates make the prospect any thing but encouraging. There are lots of sail vessels here too which makes matters still worse. . . . Marko the calker brought Fruit & Flowers yesterday. I am going to have him calk the main deck. He will begin about Wed. 13th. He was surprised that you were not with me. . . .

Yesterday was Presidential Election here. Seems Odd to have Elections on Sunday.

Mail not in so will wait till tomorrow. A mail goes Friday so have plenty of time. . . . Wish you were here. Good night.

The passage below about the rental of the field is remarkable. It demonstrates the traditional American attitude which originated with the settling of the country that men and women were equals in the job of living. Sumner held Alice as his partner, not the inferior that his English Victorian counterpart would.

From Sumner's comments it would appear that Alice seems to be feeling lonely. She has gotten on the wrong side of her sister-in-law, Nellie, and seems worried that her brother may be taking sides. Probably the incident with Nick Bucknam upset her, but it obviously bothered her that Nick had never paid them for his use of the pasture the year before. The entire burden of evicting undesirable tenants, obtained for them by her brother, has fallen on her in Sumner's absence. Actually, she had a reputation for being extremely courteous and self-possessed. Her composure was tested once when her friend Lizzie Glover, Hattie John's younger sister, stopped by with her two small daughters, Winifred and Doris. Alice had just finished preparing the downstairs apartment for its new occupants and asked eagerly if they wanted to see how it looked. They did. The apartment loomed large and empty, accentuating the sheen of the freshly varnished floors. Tempted beyond her control, the elder child took a little run and slid along the floor, scratching it badly. Alice couldn't keep from dropping to her knees to trace the marks etched into the floor, but she remembered herself and rose. Nothing, then or later, was ever said and Doris wasn't reprimanded, much to her sister's disgust.

Nicholas Bucknam, Sumner's senior by ten years, lived closer to the disputed pasture than its owners, the Drinkwaters, as it was directly across from his place. No doubt, his nose was put out of joint by Alice's decision, although he didn't have much in the way of livestock—a couple of cows, a few pigs and a horse. He was the tax collector at one time for the town of Yarmouth. His most obvious handicap was a stutter—until in his later years he lost an arm.

Almost the whole town heard about the putdown he got at church supper one night from Harry Porter. Nick never got fat, but he could certainly put food away. This particular night he was sitting next to Harry at a church supper and the burden fell on Harry to pass the food to fill up Nick's plate. After a while Nick became aware of Harry's reluctance to continue in this role, so he said apologetically, "I'm real sorry, Harry, but I've only got one arm." Quickly Harry responded, "I understand, Nick, but I've only got two."

Tuesday eve

I am now in receipt of your third letter & glad to get them so often. I will add a few lines to my letter every eve till Friday. . . .

Now about your talk with Nick. I knew he would be disappointed if he found you had let the pasture & said nothing to him about it. One day when he was talking with me at the front door, you most likely remember he said just as he was going away like this "I suppose I can have the pasture next year."

I said, "Oh, I don't know probably you can if everything is all right but Alice isn't going with me & will be home to look after things." That is very near the reply I made him. I meant when I said that if everything was all right, that if he paid for last year, no doubt, he could have it again. I suppose he took it for granted he could. I ought to have told him distinctly that he would have to make his trade with you but I never do just the right thing or say right out what I ought to. No, he did not ask me about the field by Capt Young's but in the future we will keep matters straight about it.

Funny Jack comes in so little but I suppose he is always riding & don't want to stop. So you have given notice to [our downstairs tenant,] Mrs. Tolman, to vacate. Well, I hope you won't have trouble with them. . . . I should think the new neighbors [the Adamses] were quite freindly with you. Hope you'll not fall out with them & when the cigars are gone, get some more. Does the Capt call alone often?

. . . I think I would rather not advise you about the hay but if the crop is good again this year, don't sell too cheap. You could estimate what last year's will net after Paying the cutting Insurance & co.

. . . Have not had an offer of business yet. I am thinking that I might have to go to the Cape [Capetown, South Africa] if nothing homeward could be had. How would you like that I wonder? . . . Yes, the steward goes right along the even tenor of his way & everything is in good shape & a good table is set, but I have had very little Company. He is very temperate, I think. I don't know if he has been ashore or not. The mate seems all right in Port so far, but goes ashore quite a lot evenings. He is doing all right I guess. Of course, I havn't let him do any hard work but he is able to tally cargo & look out for things generally. . . .

You see, I am very good, staying on board ship every night. It's a bit lonesome but I talk with the Watch man & smoke a cigar on deck for a while & write a little. . . .

Well, no more tonight. With much love your own Sumner. I'll have lots of letters to answer now. . . .

Thursday eve 14th
  Dear Alice
  Just a few lines more this eve.
  No prospect of business as yet. Have out 18570 pieces which is about ⅓ of the cargo, total 55346.
  Tuesday 12, quite a disastrous fire occured at Rosario about $1,000,000 damage estimated, largely covered by Insurence.
  Yesterday's report from the Far East is much in favor of the Japs. Hope they will clean out all Russia's fleet & be victorious.
  Well dear, no more this time. . . . I only wish you were with me. . . . With lots & lots of love to you & Mama & all. I am as ever your own   Sumner

Monday Eve 18th
  My Dear Alice
  Your 4th letter is at hand. Awfully glad you are writing so often, but singular I have not got it before. . . .
  You are very fortunate, I think, if you have really found a Doctor who can help your throat trouble & I am very glad indeed if it is so. . . . Rather than thinking you were getting into a scrape, I am thankful that you have grounds to hope & beleive you are getting out of one. That is the way to look at it & don't for goodness sake let the money

part fret you . . . & have your curtains & covers & Lawn swing & what ever else you want . . . The Lawn swing, by all means, I should be delighted to find one out in a shady place where I could enjoy a fragrant cigar when I get home . . . You want a new Hammock too & croquet set? I think [that] would be nice even if a little out of date & a big Red rocker such as they use out of doors for Mama S— . . . And don't get a cheap affair either. Yes, I will take pleasures out here in moderate amounts but you know I can never learn a miser's habits. It's not born in me. I don't care to cultivate it too much & don't want you to.

So Mrs. Moody [tenant] is up on her ear. Well, I hope you & she won't come to blows. It's a bit tough on you isn't it, Dear, to have to do all the disagreable parts of our business negotiations, but still I think you will be more sucessful than I might & will have your rights, no doubt. I don't see why she should have written Mother. I guess she is off her nut. You didn't say if you had got the March rent but presume you had and sent the [eviction] notice with the receipt. Hope you won't have lots of trouble with them.

I see you have paid Both Premiums in the New England [Insurance Co.] in full so that is all right for another Year . . . I got 2 bundles of Papers today, one with the town report in it. Thanks much for it. . . . I also got another [letter] from Edith with yours (same day) & surprised & very sorry to find Hattie John has had to have another opperation. She seems to have a multiplicity of misfortune. I do hope she will get through all right. Had she never told you about it? But you would have told me if she had. Well, good night Dear, with lots of love to You & Mama

Sumner

Pará, or Belém, is the capital of Pará, a state in northern Brazil. This chief commercial center and port of the vast Amazon river basin handles primarily rubber, Brazil nuts, cocoa and timber. Founded in 1616, the city was a military defense of northern Brazil against

French, English and Dutch pirates. It reached a peak of prosperity during the wild-rubber boom around the turn of the century. The abundance of rivers made the region a great haven for smugglers.

Cook & Co. was formed by F. C. Cook, who traveled to this River Plate area in the 1880s with Neimiah Rice to size up its market potential. N. W. Rice returned to set up his leather-trading company in Boston, while Mr. Cook remained behind in Buenos Aires to act as his shipping agent. Cook & Co. also represented other merchants trading in the River Plate region.

Wed= eve 20th

Dear A-

Just a little more as I have done a stroke today that I don't know what to think of. Have chartered the vessel, the only thing that has come up. Thought it best to secure it, of course with approval of Cook & Co, as I could not get time on it to cable home. It is to Load Hay at Rosario for Para which is most up to the Equater. You'll quickly find it near the mouth of the Amazon. That will be a Hot place but nothing bad, I guess. . . . Capt Johns . . . of Bark Aurion the only Capt I have took any liking too . . . has been there & says its all right & that he had as soon go there as Rio=

Now we shan't get away from here till the 30 or later & allowing 1 month to go up river & load, 1 month to go to Para, including down river, will bring me in Para, say, 4th of July. That gives plenty of time to get letters there in answer to this. In fact, I think you can have a letter waiting [for] me there easily & can tell the rest of my folks.

Don't Fret about my going there. Of course it will be Hot but I have got a clause that lay days at Para shall not exceed 15, so I'll not be there very long. Mail goes tomorrow noon.

So with lots of love
I'll close, yours lovingly
Sumner
American Consul Para
Brazil S.A.

Tuesday Eve April 26 '04

No 5

My Dear Alice

I'll be one ahead now, no letter this week. A mail is leaving here Thursday & will write a few lines. . . .

Everything is all right with us. Am feeling very well as I have been all the time except a few days of belly ache & diarrehea. I hope you are well dear. . . .

I have been to a Theatre lately, an English troop, play "Belle of New York," very good. It is to play here a month but different Plays. They are taking well, I should think, a crowded house and the styles or rather the Goorgeously dressed women was quite a show itself. I never saw such lovely rig outs anywhere I've been, lace & Jewelry & Silks in dazzling array. . . .

Have had to buy 2 new charts of cast & River of Para. This Capt Johns has been there 4 times & says it's all right & no more expensive than Rio, so hope there will be a little [profit] left for the Owners. . . . I am anxious to hear again from Hattie John as Edith wrote me the night after her mother had been opperated on [to remove a tumor from her left breast] and of course could not say much about it, only that the Dr said it was successful. Of course, so soon after, nothing reliable could be said but hope & trust she is recovering again. . . .

I intended writing home [to Father & Mother] again this mail but as I have written my sister May will wait awhile. Now I'll get things in shape for making up my statment [for the owners] and turn in with lots of Love & Kisses,

Your Own Sumner

Love and a kiss to dear Mama. Hope she is well & the Roads drying up so she can trip up to the villiage once in awhile & make calls. How is Nellie? My love to She and Jackie. Let's see, who else will I send a kiss? To . . . Mrs. Adams? Ah, no I'd hardly dare to. George [Adams] would go for me, but I don't know if I would be any more than square with him. Good night again.

Left to right: Doris, Hattie John, John, Edith, Lizzie and John. *Bottom:* Mrs. Hamilton, Winifred and Mrs. Glover.

Sumner speaks of John Glover's illness in the following letter. Thirty-four-year-old Mary Elizabeth Hamilton had married John Glover, three years her senior, at the Yarmouth Baptist Minister's parsonage in 1896. They had met in 1895, the same year Lizzie stopped teaching to stay home with her mother following her father's tragic death on the ice bridge. She had taught school for fourteen years. Her first position began precipitously when her elder brother, Edwin, who was teaching on one of the outer islands, Cliff Island, contracted typhoid fever and sent for Lizzie to finish off his term.

When she and John Glover met, he was working as the head carpenter of a syndicate building homes on Little John Island. He was of good Massachusetts stock, a direct descendant of the General Glover who supervised the Marblehead fishing boats that carried General Washington's troops across the Delaware for the Battle of Trenton.

Prior to John Glover's illness, the couple and their two daughters had made their home with Lizzie's mother, Nancy Hamilton. As John added his mother, Abigail Reynolds Glover, to the menage, the couple had two in-laws to cope with. At the time of Sumner's writing, John Glover had just suffered a stroke. He was ill for the next two years, having developed Bright's disease, the illness of the heart and kidneys which had taken Captain Webster's life in 1902. The doctor who treated John remarked to his family that he was the most "patient patient" he had ever had; Bright's disease usually made people very irritable. Lizzie and he had been married only nine years when he died in 1905.

No 7
My Dear Alice   Rosario May 18th 04
I am much pleased tonight to have your two last letters of April 3d, No. 7, & April 7th & 9th, No. 8. I have been waiting very impatiently for a week or more. I have also one from Edith . . . finished April 14th. She had just got one from you.

I was very glad to hear that Hattie John was doing so nicely up to that time & hope she is fully regained her health by this & will be even better than for a long time past. Edith wrote me of [Woodbury's brother] Ammi Hamilton's attempt at suicide, enclosing an item from a paper . . . It seems sad indeed, but hope he will recover, although the Item in the paper spoke very doubtingly. . . .

Now I must say firstly that I am very pleased you have got a vacant rent. (Aside from hearing that you were quite well . . . that did interest me most.) I am so glad they left with out causing you trouble. I am feeling very glad as in imagination I can see the rooms clear & the wood & carriage house emptied of all that mess. Even if you get no one you like for all summer, I don't care, I would not let it hastily. But I have no fears that you will without knowing pretty well what kind of people you are getting. You will be much more carefull than I should be. But do not let Jack think we were displeased with him for letting it [while we were down here last year]. He done what he thought for our interest & it's all right. We got 6 or 7 month's rent quite easily but I couldn't bear the Idea of their stopping indeffinatly & we being at home. So, for that reason, I'm awfully glad they are gone.

Now have any thing done you wish for improvements . . . this summer. I hope Jack will do well in his new departure & make a good landfall in the end. Seems like he is going in on quite a big scale. I am truly sorry to have you write as you do about Nellie. . . . Does she have a Doctor? My love to her & Jack with best wishes. Mr. Adams seems very attentive to you all or does he give [treat] all the neighbors alike? Very good of them. . . . I was surprised & sorry to hear of Mr. Glover's illness. Hope he will recover all right. I didn't have any faith in that Dr. Eastman. I didn't like the appearance of things at all as I guess I told you at the time. They were imposters, no doubt.

I hope you are not going to a similar one but I shouldn't suppose Dr. —— would recommend him if he hadn't considered him all right & hope that you will derive benefit from him. . . . I am glad . . . that your face [which often swelled up from hives] is better. That is the best returns you could wish for the expenditure.

Well, I can't say now when we shall be loaded but may before mailing this. There is no mail to the states for several days yet. Everything is going on smooth at present & I am quite easy in mind. I have not fretted any this voyage to speak of. Another of my original crew from Boston deserted a few days ago & one that shipped at B. Aires. I have only one of the Boston crowd [left] & mate & cook. They are all right & the Steward is really an exception. He is doing fine both in ekonomy & quality & neatness. If I have wished once, I have 100 times, that he had been with us last voyage when you were with me. To show you the difference, he hasn't used the 2 tubs of Butter—42 lbs that was gone last voyage when we got to B. Aires & other things the same & he is 4 months on board now & more now. . . .

I am wondering how you feel about my going to Para but hope you won't worry about it. Dr. Ayer, the Consul here, was there 3 or 4 years as Consul & says it's all right, of course hot. But if one is not careless, there is no danger of sickness. . . .

You will be much surprized to learn of the Death of Mrs. Meyer [the consul's wife at Buenos Aires who had just departed for the States by steamer], on the passage home & occuring so very sudden. I will enclose an Item cut from the Buenos Aires Herald. It seems very sad, indeed. She seemed so full of hope of better health to leave here. I doubt if the Dr. comes Back to take his new appointment of Consul General in July.

Well Dear, I'll put this by untill sunday.   lots of love
Sumner

Sunday 22nd 04

My Dear Alice
. . . I do wish they would finish us up so I could get out of this infernal country again. One gets tired of it after a few weeks. . . .

So Mama couldn't stand it any longer up with you. Well I'm glad she stopped so long through the cold & Bad going.

Of course I shall write again when ready to leave here & send the letter back by the Pilot.

No more this time. With much love & many wishes that I could see you or that you could be here with me. I am as ever your Loving Husband
Sumner

Sumner only noted the tonnage of the vessels that raced the *Hunt* downriver. In itself, this reveals nothing of their speed. There is a direct relationship between the length of the hull and the vessel's speed, but again, many variables must be considered, ranging from the hull configuration to the size of the crew handling the sails. Certain captains had a reputation for being drivers and getting every inch they could from their ship, and obviously the type of master a vessel had could greatly affect her performance.

The Argentine section of the Paraná River, down which they sailed, is hampered by shifting channels, sand bars and fluctuating river flow. This 2,000-mile-long river, first ascended in 1526 by Sebastian Cabot, the English explorer in the service of Spain, is the primary commercial artery of interior southeastern South America.

When Sumner later discusses his letters from Rosario and the Paraná River, he lumps them together as coming from the River Plate. Río de la Plata is the 120-mile estuary into which the Paraná runs after it joins the Uruguay River. Buenos Aires is one of its chief ports.

No 8
My Dear Alice

Rosario 29th of May 1904
Sunday Evening at Anchor in the stream

I think you will be interested in my Progress down River so will write a short daily Journal. I came on board last night with Crowley the Pilot also with Capt Witmore of Bark Mary A Law who as I have before mentioned is bound to Santos with Hay. We turned out this morning only to find a dense fog enveloping the river & calm remain-

ing all the forenoon untill 2 P.M. It cleared up then but remained calm so we made no start.

Capt Thurber of the Stillwater is at Anchor some 5 or 6 miles down river, his upper yards [sail framework] just showing above the low intervening islands. There will doubtless be a race down river as the three best river Pilots (so spoken of) are on the three vessels, all barks. [Of] the Law 890 tons, the Stillwater 1052 & the Hunt 1131 [tons], I shall expect the Law to win the race as she is considered a goer. We left Capt Dodge nearly Alone & feeling rather blue . . . He will be all this coming week finishing loading. I staid with him 2 nights. He wished to be remembered to you, also Mr. & Mrs. Ayer sent regards. The Consul gave me a nice Bundle of N York Herald from April 3d to April 16th inclusive & very systematically arranged as to folding & dates with a card bearing his compliments & a complimentary card of introduction to the Consul at Para, or rather Vice Consul, whose name is Julius F. Tiedeman.

I have exchanged quite a number of novels & Books with Newcomb [master of the *Johnson*] & Whitmore [master of the *Mary A Law*] as also Capt Johns at Buenos-Aires so have a good quality of Reading matter. I ain't so sure but I have swapped off one of Cousin Julia's but perhaps she will just as soon have another that she hasn't read.

Speaking of her, I imagine she may now be in Yarmouth & I think every day & dozens of times a day how I would like to be there myself & the picture that forms in my imagination makes me homesick—all most. I expect you have ere this got the lower rent all fixed & ready for a desirable tenant. I mailed you my 7th letter yesterday enclosing you a $100.00 U.S. Gold check or draft on the Farmers Loan & Trust Co. of New York, dated 28th May 1904, No. 39/57, Payable on demand. As I explained, I had drawn more than I intended & you will know how to take care of it all right. I was sorry not to get one more letter, but if more comes I'll get them in Para.

I have got several little remembrances at different times both here

& at Buenos Aires but nothing expensive, unless you'll think that to my Dear old Girlie is so. (But speaking confidentially, you know, as I have had a few little windfalls, it won't come [be declared] on my real Wage & Primage any.) The Ship's Expenses here this voyage doesn't vary $100.00 dollars from last voyage & I hope I shall find Para a less expensive Port than Rio.

Carluchi . . . the shipping master [crimp supplying sailors for crews] here that shipped my men last time & who I had engaged this time got 6 months in Jail together with his runner for beating a sailor & cutting him with a knife. So I had to get another [crimp] to ship for me, but I think I have a better crowd than last voyage & also a good second mate. I know you all ways ask about those things. We also have a dog which I may not have mentioned & 6 Biddies & a Rooster & the Kitty but no "Bar" [pet's name?] this time.

Well, Crowley [the pilot] turned in at 8 to be out early & it's now 9.30 so I will [too]. Tomorrow is Decoration day. I shall think of you & Mother S many times. I wish I was with you. With lots of love & Kisses to Mama too.

I remain lovingly yours
Sumner

Memorial Day exercises in Yarmouth during the eighteen-eighties and -nineties were the most impressive of the year. An almost religious seriousness pervaded the village. As many as sixty veterans might march between two bands with two companies of infantry as well as the local firemen supporting them. The parade wound over to the Baptist Cemetery. On their return, the military companies stacked their guns in front of the First Parish Congregational Church and everyone crowded into that building to listen to the martial music of the Yarmouth band and to orations given by some of the most stirring speakers in the state. (When the Yarmouth band was organized in 1866, its first instructor found only one member who could read music. The band went on to receive statewide recognition for its excellence.)

Monday Eve 30th May 04   Decoration day   Dear Alice

This has been an awfully lonesome day laying at anchor. Still a Perfect calm & thick fog till Past noon same as yesterday. I have read & smoked & walked decks & thought of home & you dear & this eve have been getting my Rosario Accts fixed up as I didn't get them ready to mail before leaving. Shall send them to mail by the Pilot.

This P.M. I worked or bossed for an hour or so the Building of a Potato Bin & Put my Potatoes in it. I have got 1½ tons this time. They were cheap for here & new so hope they will keep well. Paid $40.00 Paper a ton & last time I paid $60.00.

Well, Dear, I would like to know how you have passed the day. Pleasantly, I hope, yet with sad thoughts too in recalling Your Father [who had passed away two years before] & the interest he allways took in decoration day. [Watson Gray Drinkwater had served in the Navy during the Civil War.] I hope it has been a mild & pleasant one. With love as ever.

Good night
S—

The Drinkwaters seemed to be unlucky with the dogs they brought aboard ship. John used to tell the story of what happened when he decided to save money by not hiring a dock security guard to watch his vessel in Philadelphia. (Conditions differed in the ports —in some it was mandatory to take on a pilot, security guard, etc., and in others it wasn't.) On the second day in port, John left his first mate in charge of the ship with a revolver and a Newfoundland puppy. John had bought the puppy the day before as a surprise for his family. He returned some hours later to find the mate asleep, snoring, and the revolver and puppy gone.

Wed=   eve June 1st

A few more lines tonight. Anchored 3 miles above San Pedro. Have had a day Identical of yesterday . . . but what wind we have had has been fair. We are now ½ way down river. A little incident happened this morning that is all there is to relate today.

I don't recall if I have mentioned in previous letters that we had a dog which came on board in B. Aires. Quite a nice fellow with Black spots around & over his eyes. The Mate wanted him & I let him keep him. This morning just after getting under=way, he was running along the rail (a habit we couldn't break him of) when over board he went. We had no boat to put over & couldn't stop so watched him. He swam after us about 10 minutes & then turned off for the shore. The last we saw him, he was nearly ashore at San Nicholas so he will find new friends. I was glad he fell over when he did if he was bound to. I was getting quite attached to him though he & Pussy were good freinds too.

We are head ship to-night but only a mile ahead of Stillwater & 4 ahead of the Law. Have had a real summer day & now is dead calm.

Good night again   Sumner

On Board Bark Benj= F Hunt Jr
No 1   8 P.M. eve of Sunday June 19th/1904
Para

                                                 Lat 26°–00 South
                                                 Long=35–25 West
To My Dear & beloved Wife   12 days out
Greeting

Having you much in mind on this Pleasant Sabeth day (equally so I hope with you) I will give you just a few lines of thought as a begining of my next letter to you. Naturally and truely, as I trust you have faith to beleive, you come first as well as last (on my arrivals and sailings from Port) in letters, thoughts and affection to say nothing of the manifold thoughts & longings while sailing o'er the troubled waters.

Now You cannot find fault with that as a prelude to a letter from a devoted Hubby to a Dear Wife of nearly Twenty Two years, can you? And quite "Comme il fault."

My last letter to you was finished on the afternoon of the 7th . . . and given to the Pilot who left-us at 4.15. While we were at tea that night with the 2nd mate in charge & the lookout Blowing the horn, a bell was reported ahead. Allmost directly a light appeared on the Starboard bow . . . Proved to be the Station boat & such a shouting from the spanish Pilots to let go the "ankler!" [There would have been no time for the Spanish pilot ship to pull up the anchor. They were trying to unshackle it.] I was nearly Close hauled on the Port Tack but knew I hadn't time to Keep off [their vessel] so let her come close to the wind & just fetched by to windward. They on the Pilot station Boat hollered to beat the Band. I guess they were pretty frightened & it was a close shave.

. . . How lovely it must be around our little Habitation this month, every thing in summer bloom, the air rich & fragrant & filled with the song of Birds and rustling leaves of the orchard & Grand old Elms, & this Pleasant Moonlit eve rich in many beauties and the musical chirp of insect life. . . . This eve is just as lovely as the day with Nearly a full moon in the Eastern Quadrent of the Heavens. I can imagine it shining in your Eastern windows looking just as lovely as here & more so as the scene it beautifies gives it richer beauties . . . I hope you are enjoying it all with increasing bouyancy of spirits & good health which ought to come with "the Good old Summer time." Do you suppose I'll ever have a whole long summer at home? I imagine not for a long time. I expect you have it all ready for renting again before this. . . .

Caught a dolphin this P.M. & had him for Tea. Had my usual cleaning up Personally during the day & enjoyed being on deck with the vessel quite still & the day warm yet with some lonelyness & wishes that I was home. . . .

I have been reading lots since I came out—papers & novels—in fact, got my stock of reading Pretty nearly dijested. Have been all through the Papers & cuttings you sent & what the consul gave me. Got lots of ship news & war items. Hope the little Japs are keeping their end up all right. I should be sorry to see them wiped. I hope there is spirit enough in them to come off conquerors.

I have one smart young fellow among the crew, 18 years old, a Hollander. I have had him wash a lot of dirty clothes since we came out & he done it very nicely. I shall give him some more to do tomorrow. The steward is begining to clean House & has plenty to do. . . .

Well, I will tell you how Awful Smart I have been this week, have Painted the Store Room. Next week I am going to be More Smart & Paint the Pantry. Now this is really all I have got to tell you of the Past week. Only, I wish you was here.

Lots of love   Summie

Sumner has arrived at the Pará River, which is actually the southeastern arm of the Amazon. It is divided from the rest of that great river by Marajó Island.

"Fill away" refers to sails filling and the vessel gathering headway after changing tack.

4th of July Eve 04   Laid to off Salinas Point 30 miles
East of Entrance to River Para
My Dear Alice
A few lines this eve as it's 4th of July & I didn't write any yesterday. I was busy most of the day figuring sights & I should have kept you busy if you had been here & today too. So you see what you have escaped.

Well, I didn't get to Para . . . [today] as I hoped I might, but just got a Pilot on Board at dusk or about 6.30 P.M. We are now heading off shore & will not fill away till towards morning as it's not safe to run in the night. It's about 100 miles up to Para & hope to be up Wed 6th & I am awfully impatient to get more letters . . . This is not a nice place at all for a sailing vessel & I shall think myself fortunate if I can get in & out without mishap. I'll be glad to get clear of this Hay

for the Bugs are getting fearfully thick. You remember about them last voyage but they are getting everywhere now—so much longer aboard & so much warmer weather.

. . . I was up most of last night so you'll excuse a short chronicle . . . We have had . . . a very good passage so far.

I wonder how you have passed the day—pleasantly I hope. Been on some excursion or merry making of some kind, no doubt, you & Julia. Wish I had been with you. I am too sleepy & sweaty to write more so with much love & good wishes & plenty of Kisses I'll close.

Will have a bath & turn in.   Yours lovingly   Sumner

Tuesday eve 5th 04
At Anchor   In Para River   20 miles below the City
My Dear Wife
Just a few lines before retiring for the night. We kept away from Salinas light at 2 A.M. this morning & have sailed about 90 miles. Have had a strong head current most of the time since entering the river.

This P.M. it has been nothing but heavy Thunder Showers & some of the most wonderful & Magnificent displays of Electricity (or lightning) that I have ever Witnessed & I have seen it in many Parts of the world & at times when I thought its grandeur unsurpassed but this has far surpassed anything I have ever witnessed. Not so vivid & dazzling as perhaps we have at home at times but upwards of 20 & perhaps 30 different Chains of zig zag crinkly appearence like the candy we sometimes buy (I guess you'll know what I mean). All these different lines apparently shooting out from a common center in all directions occupying a whole Quadrent of the heavens from Zenith to the Horizon. I was greatly taken up with watching it for an hour or more.

We came to anchor about 6 P.M. Calm, hope to get up to Para tomorrow . . . It's not so Hot as last night & no mosquitoes yet. I imagine the Electricity has had a cooling effect on the Atmosphere. Well nothing special. Will have a light rub down & turn in. With love.

Sum

Alice and Sumner have been married for twenty-two years and remained childless. She is, by now, forty-two, and this letter of Sumner's is full of regret that their prospects for a family seem over. It is interesting that Sumner obviously takes no responsibility for their childlessness but does not seem to feel that Alice is barren. Rather, he seems to infer that it's been her choice not to have a baby. Little is known about Alice's attitude, although one of Hattie Poole's later letters to the family implied that Alice very much regretted never having given Sumner children. None of their siblings had many offspring. Actually, two of his sisters, May and Maggie, were also childless. Sumner and Alice had very different personalities, and she was remembered as being dignified and gracious with their nephews and nieces, where he was a tease.

The attitude toward childbearing was very puritanical in their time, as Sumner's comments reveal. Nellie delayed confiding in Alice until late in her pregnancy, when her condition could no longer be hidden. Sumner's responses to Alice's earlier letters showed that they were unaware of this pregnancy and thought Nellie was ill. While no one objected to children after birth, to the Victorian mind, pregnancy was proof of sexual intimacy, and women thus incriminated were best out of sight. A woman in labor was referred to as "sick." Sumner's comments to Alice make it obvious that there was much between them left unsaid. How this letter must have hurt her!

Wed=Eve

Well darling all safely moored at Para in the stream. Came to Anchor at 11 A.M. Got Dr's visit just before noon. P.M. ashore entered at Customs, tendered notice to Consignee, deposited papers at Consuls, cabled arrival & was the Happy recepient of 6 letters from my devoted wife . . . None from Father or Edith.

Well, Dear, I was awfully pleased to get so many letters & good news generally, that is best of all. I find one letter missing, No 9. Got 10 & 11 . . . The last one is dated June 13th which does not seem very far distant, less than a month old. . . .

About the renting of the House . . . I am very glad you have (& particularly so as you say you have) got good ones [tenants]. I must compliment you on your ability in that branch of business & if you are feeling satisfied with the Quality & Industrial Habits of your tenants, I can't see but you have really done a good financial stroke.

I suppose it's in order to take up & treat according to their magnitude the most important subjects of your letter first of which . . . is your good health. But as some events seem of unusual interest & You give me to infer that a delightfully pleasing event . . . a new acquisition to your [brother's] family . . . is likely to occur in the near future. I certainly feel that this is a subject of great as well as surprising magnitude & deserving of being at least second to be treated. Now I suppose unfortunately the letter that is missing, No 9, gives me the most important news since my leaving home & news in which I am highly & happily interested. What a surprise, truly, but I am awfully pleased & shall look forward to the event with much pleasure. It will be the best medicine that Nellie could have for the restoration of her health. I hope she may be able to look at it in that light & is happy in the thought of becoming a mother which must be . . . in the course of nature the sweetest & richest feeling of womanhood. My life would be quite full if I could receive such Joyful news of You. Let Nellie & John know, if you have made no secret of your having told me of their future prospects, how heartily I . . . congratulate them & earnestly wish for a happy & safe deliverence, the new being be all that heart could desire, even though it might have been unintentional (Just a little mistake) . . .

There would be only one thing that would give me more pleasure & that you doubtless know well—to find you, my Darling, in the same condition, but quite likely that is not to be & I'll be content.

So you are thinking the time long, before having me with you again. That . . . gives me to feel that I am missed even if not a model Husband. Well dear, I hope before the good old summer time is entirely passed for 1904 that I may be with you again & just get a bit of summer . . . merging with autumn perhaps but yet pleasent days to enjoy before Another winter.

I was very sorry to know that Dear Mother S. had been ill even for a short time but glad you could write that she was better. How pleased she must be at the thought of being a Grandmama. I know she is even though she might not say so. My love & a kiss of congratulation to her & for you. I wonder if I can think rightly that it's a pleasent knowledge to you & if you'll be pleased & interested. I can't help thinking that you will & that I can look for something very pleasent to me from the comming issue. Well, Dear, perhaps you'll think I'm too enthusiastic so will not write more about this though it's quite filling my mind tonight, so unexpected, you know. Tell Jack or Both of them I think they might have given a fellow a little Inkling or hint in some way.

There is a mail to leave on the 12 . . . due in N.Y. on the 24th. As I have plenty of time for writing up to Monday, will close for tonight. With more love than ever.

Sumner

Monroe Bucknam had a reputation for being "close." He paid the youngsters he hired to do odd jobs "in pennies." After they had finished raking the hay in front of his barn door, he would go over the area meticulously, picking up straws. In the following letter, Sumner comments about an incident involving his "Uncle Monroe." While this event amused an octogenerian that I was interviewing, it didn't surprise him and he told me, "Monroe Bucknam would if anybody could. That was just like him."

With considerably more than two hundred sea captains living in Yarmouth at this period, only outstanding shipwreck stories circulated at large. The experience of "Captain Frank" Young, who had sailed under Sumner in 1903, had a more interesting ending than most. Captain Young returned from his shipwreck unannounced and unexpected. Getting into Portland he found that he had missed the 10 P.M. trolley to Yarmouth and would have to stay overnight. Captain Young was too impatient to wait, so he walked the ten or twelve miles home.

This letter is a miscellany of comments on the news from home. Buried in the sundry items we see very clearly Sumner's insecurity about his future at sea. The same dynamics which came into play in the *Grace Deering* episode are threatening Sumner again: N. W. Rice, acting for the shareholders, might sell off their sailing vessels or a Captain Soria, whom Sumner has been replacing, might take over the *Hunt*'s command.

Sunday A.M. July 10th 04
My Dear Alice

I will add a little more to my letter today & be ready for the mail tomorrow. The Steamer that takes it is here, arrived last night. I wrote you in All 10 letters from the River Plate, . . . No 9 mailed May 28th contained 1st of Exchange Check . . . for $100.00 & I hope you got it all right. I think I asked you to answer it here. . . . I think if I don't hear from that, I'll send the . . . duplicate while here.

Uncle Monroe's Ill-ness certainly must have created Quite a sensation. To be looked upon as having departed this life & still in the flesh. I wonder what he thought of it. It's not often one has the privilidge of reading their Own Obituary.

So Capt Frank is really trying steam & got his certificate all right. I wonder if I could get one, thought I would quite as soon go windjaming for the Present. I am expecting to hear that Rice & Co have sold their fleet when I get home. In that case I'll be on the Beach & may anyway. . . . You don't say more about Capt Frank's supposed Engagement. . . .

. . . Kinder sorry you & Nickie fell out & I blame myself much for that. However, it may be best in the end. I suppose he would have

stuck us anyway but it wouldn't have been for much. You spoke of
. . . Ammi's Funeral so, of course, he never recovered from his suicide.
Another item lost in No 9. . . . Seems queer that Capt Prince is not
to have the command of the New Steamer. Some Political technicality,
no doubt . . . I have found your ad in Argus [the newspaper] you sent,
very good. It seems to Pay to Advertise.

I hope you have some one keep the Grass cropped short about
your Swing & Hammock so it will dry up early in the day & not get
your feet damp going out to them. Give my love to all the neighbors
who have sent like kind. [Tell] Mr. & Mrs. Adams (with an Equally
<u>rousing</u> Kiss to Mrs. A.) . . . that I hope that they are quite enjoying
their first Summer in our good old Eastern village. Say that I'm doing
as well as I can under a six or seven months' imprisonment.

I am glad you have done a little Gardening & have some Flowers
Growing. I have wondered often if you would do anything in that
line. . . .

We are to discharge in the stream & I like that. It will avoid much
trouble [as the crew will be confined to ship]. I hope to go ashore in
my Boat. We patched her coming up so she is quite a boat. I have one
man who is a carpenter & have had lots of little Jobs done in that
line. . . .

I shall keep in the shade & be careful so you won't need to worry.
It's not sickly at all here now & no cases at all of contagious diseases.
I have a bath every day. It's pretty warm nights but still not so bad
as I thought. I have my netting to keep out mosquitoes & flies so get
on quite comfortable.

As I'll probably add a few lines tomorrow, will close now with lots
of love, your own   Sumner

Sumner mentions writing to Alice again in his diary but the
letters are not extant. The remaining record of the voyage is from
his diary. As there was no cargo for charter in Para, the *Hunt* left
in ballast on July 23 and reached New York after a passage of

twenty-two days. Evidently some insect life remained from the hay
unloaded at Para because the *Hunt* was subjected to an hour's
extermination by officials on Staten Island before she was allowed
entry. Sumner proceeded into harbor, put the bark in dry dock and
sent for Alice.

She traveled with him aboard the *Hunt* from New York City to
Boston, where they found Captain Soria ready to return to command. On August 29, Sumner packed his things and left the ship.

The Drinkwaters reached Yarmouth on August 31, the day
before Nellie and Jack's baby, Malcolm, was born. Sumner ambigu-
ously noted: "much pleased with his appearance." As elated as they
were by the addition to Alice's family, they were concerned that
Hattie John, who had only recently recuperated from an operation
was due for another. She had developed a tumor in her other breast
and had a mastectomy.

Rather than look for a command—perhaps because he wanted
to stay at home for a while, perhaps because Alice was waiting for
him with a list of projects—Sumner threw himself into home altera-
tions. Many early Maine homes have a main house and a connecting
ell, or covered corridor, to the woodshed, carriage house and barn.
Sumner contracted with his relatives and neighbors to help him raise
a section of the ell one story which doubled the size of their apartment upstairs.

That same autumn Theodore Roosevelt was elected President
of the United States—without being indebted to Sumner, who, as
usual, voted a straight Democratic ticket, according to his diary.

1905

Sumner's friend Will Gooding, who had been captain of the
Grace Deering after Sumner, left for Seattle to work on a steamboat.
Sumner seems not to have given this alternative any further consid-
eration. Instead his diary indicates his preoccupation with painting
walls and varnishing their newly built kitchen cupboards.

By the time spring had routed winter, Sumner and Alice were
enjoying the conveniences of their renovated home and had settled

into the routine of village life. Sumner attended the town meeting which voted in a $250 addition to annual taxes—to be shared by the entire village—as well as $1,750 for streetlights to replace kerosene lamps. These lamps enclosed in glass lanterns on the top of posts had been lit for close to thirty years, each evening at sundown. The village lamplighter had made his rounds carrying oil cans and cloths to polish the glass-lamp chimneys, as well as a little ladder. The new streetlights would not need the same maintenance.

Sumner went to meetings at the Masonic lodge, "called down to the neighbors," and noted some dooryard calls—from visitors who stayed seated in their buggies rather than descend into the house. When the time came to garden, he plowed the field with a borrowed horse and shopped at an auction, the equivalent of the modern-day estate sale, for tools.

Thursday, May 4, 1905 Mild Fair S.W. Winds
    Went to auction of Greely Road on place of late William
    Blanchard with Mr. & Mrs. Adams

bought	shovel	35¢	pitchfork	35¢
	Barn fork	30¢	saw	55¢
	Planes	30¢	Top Maul [sledge hammer]	40¢
	Stand	50¢		

for a total of $2.30

He went bicycling, and hired out for odd jobs to his neighbors and friends as the weather grew warmer. After a long stretch of gardening Sumner complained of an "awful lame back." The town water source, the Royal River, became too polluted, so he repaired the old well curb. In the fall he made cider, bought a cow for $28, worked on his hen house and went gunning. Uncle Monroe Bucknam departed this life, for the second time, on October 31 and this time, did not return to read his own obituary.

Sumner had not been to sea all year, though he began sending out inquiries for a berth early in the summer.

1906–1907

Except for a letter Sumner sent Alice two weeks before the end of 1907, no records survived from these years. In that letter, however, he referred to taking out yachts. Whether he had found additional work coasting is unknown.

1908

Sumner's diary for this year is not extant and only the ensuing letters record his final voyage. These letters are the last in the Drinkwater collection. Clearly Alice and Sumner were selective about the correspondence they saved, since only the deepwater voyages are documented.

THE HAWKS NURSERY CO., Rochester, N. Y.

You will please furnish me with the following nursery stock, for which I am responsible and for which I agree to pay $..5..5.0...........in cash on Delivery during April or May, 190 7 Anything omitted to be deducted from bill. Any stock which does not prove to be true to name as labelled, is to be replaced free or purchase price refunded ; and all stock to be delivered in a thrifty and healthy condition but not warranted further than noted above. Standard Apple and Pear trees to be notles than 5 feet in height ; Cherry and Plum trees not less than 4 feet ; Dwarf Pear and Peach trees not less than 3 feet. In case specified varieties cannot be furnished, others considered by you as equally desirable may be substituted

This order is not subject to Countermand and this contract covers all terms, conditions or agreements between the purchaser and agent in relation to said order. The agent has no authority to change or deviate in any way from the printed conditions of this contract, or to collect any money or allow credit on this order.

Purchaser's Signature *S. P. Drinkwater*

Quantity.		$	CTS.	Quantity.		$	CTS.
7	Apple Trees........	2	50	Grape Vines......			
	Crab Trees........			Currant Bushes.....			
	Pear Trees, Stand...			Gooseberry Bushes...			
	Pear Trees, Dwarf..			Raspberry Bushes....			
	Cherry Trees.......			Blackberry Bushes...			
4	Plum Trees........	3	—	Shrubs..........			
	Peach Trees........			Rose Bushes.......			
	Apricots..........			Vines...........			
	Quince Bushes......			Bulbs...........			
	Evergreens........						
	Ornamental Trees..			Total.......		5	50

☞ SEE BACK OF ORDER FOR LIST OF VARIETIES

Purchaser's Name. *S. P. Drinkwater*
(Written Plainly by Agent.)

P. O. Address. *Yarmouth*

County *Cumberland* State or Prov. } *Maine*

Occupation *Master Mariner*

Location...........miles from Delivery Point. Direction.....*out*

Name of Street or Road and number of house. } *Gilman St*

Agent's Name *J. H. Bucknam*

(OVER)

At the end of 1907 Sumner was suddenly given command of the *Benjamin F. Hunt Jr.* when Captain Soria became ill.

He made arrangements through Hattie for Alice to receive the *Herald* while he was away. As the bark was managed by N. W. Rice in Boston, it would receive more coverage in a local paper. These newspapers were well used. Alice scanned them for reports of the *Hunt* before bundling them up to send to Sumner abroad.

The newspapers of that time did not enjoy widespread popularity and were considerably thinner than they are today. As this clipping shows, they interspersed their news events with advice of the type, if not the content, carried today in women's magazines.

Officially, Yarmouth had had a lending library since 1747, when a deacon of the old Meeting House under the Ledge left £30 to be used to purchase books that were to be circulated through the pastor. Yet by the 1890s, Yarmouth's Hillside Library had no more than 1,800 volumes and was open to the public in the old Baptist meeting-house vestry only on Saturday afternoons. Not until 1904 was a separate building established.

Buying books, individually, was expensive. As a result, most people didn't have much to read. Rehashing events was their main form of entertainment. This oral tradition passed on the extraordinary experiences of ordinary people. Unfortunately, these old stories, pitted against today's instant media coverage, are rapidly vanishing.

Monday eve   [Aboard the *Benjamin F. Hunt Jr.*]
[Boston harbor, Dec 17th 07]
Dear Alice
As we are in the stream & all ready for sea I will write a few lines. We towed out this morning early & I have been ashore all day clearing & getting crew on board. Look for a chance [favorable conditions] tomorrow.

John came off with me to stay all night. Shall go ashore tomorrow if I can, if there is no chance & will most likely get another letter. . . . I think I am well fixed up now & don't know of anything I lack.

Of course there will be little things that I will wish I had thought of but probably nothing but what I can get along without. . . .

Mailed you a Journal with Items of nonsense about the Hunt & Brynhilda's 7000 mile race & she a steel ship. You'll laugh at it. I don't know who has written such a mess but thought I would send you the paper. . . . I expect the Brynhilda will beat me some 10 or 15 days out so if you see her arrival & don't mine for some time, don't feel concern for she is a flyer. . . . Don't fret or worry about me for I am feeling well. . . . Coming away so unexpected & soon after being home so long

LUMBER VESSELS TO HAVE 7000-MILE OCEAN RACE

The prospect of an exciting 7000-mile ocean race between the British full-rigged ship Brynhilda and the American bark Benjamin F. Hunt, Jr., both of which will clear today for Buenos Ayres, is arousing much interest in shipping circles. Both vessels have been loading lumber at Mystic wharf for South America, and both finished taking on their cargoes last Saturday. While the Britisher is the larger vessel and is loaded with 1,390,000 feet and the American has a trifle less than 1,000,000 feet aboard, the Hunt is regarded as the faster of the two.

Capt. Drinkwater will go in command of the Hunt and Capt. Schmeisser will take out the Brynhilda. Capt. Soria, the regular commander of the Britisher, is ill with the grip and will be unable to participate in the encounter. The Hunt is owned by Portland parties.

rather worked me up so I felt it but I am myself again & find every thing pleasant. . . . Of course, I wish you were going but will soon get over being lonesome after getting away & well at sea. Have got lots to take up my mind in going over the Stores & Slops & clearing the drawers & lockers for they are pretty well cluttered up. . . .

I think . . . the mate . . . a Mr. Moran . . . will prove a pretty good man. He has that appearance. He has been in many vessels that I know & in the Ship Atlas 4 years which ought to be a pretty good recomandation. Hope he is all right in Port. Have a good cook I think & an educated cabin boy who seems willing & very polite & uses extra choice language. [He was] 2 or 3 [in his class] at school & is willing to work & learn & takes hold well, much superior to those we had. . . .

Was up to [your sister] Hattie's . . . The Herald office is moved way toward where she is [working as a stenographer] & I got her to fix the matter of the Herald [subscription] for me . . . You will get the first Herald tomorrow.

In fact I have hardly been off of Commercial St. . . . Been busy about stores, crew, getting Articles [crew's contracts] & co . . . Had no chance to go up town any except to N. W. Rice's . . . Mr. Chandler was very pleasant & agreable & talked with me a long time about the voyage, that I should do all the business of the ship away & could act my own pleasure as regards consulting with F. C. Cook & Co [for chartering a cargo] out there. I don't think they have so much to do with them as formerly. He said I was to remit to them personally. Of course, I do not wish you to speak of such things only I thought he showed more intimate spirit & was more social than when I was in the employ before. But he speaks of selling the vessel if they can get their price. . . . I have arranged with Mr. Chandler to send you $40.00 dollars a month & he will send the first installment Jan 1st.

If anything should come up in the way of a Yachting Berth why all you would do is simply answer saying I am at sea.

I am sorry, dear, you are feeling so lonely. You could have come if you had thought best but possible I may have her another voyage

& you may go then if I do. So don't be so down hearted. 6 months is only a little while. . . . Hope you will be able to get down to home once in a while during the winter. Be well & don't stay indoors too snug when the weather is good. Will write a few lines in the morning & if I should go out send it back by John.

No more tonight. With lots of Love & a bye bye kiss. as ever Sumner

. . . Everything seems so natural on board that it doesn't seem worth while to tell you anything about the vessel. The cabin is just as we left it except it shows the time in some ways. Those lounge coverings are soiled some. . . .

Don't feel badly. Think I am lucky to have so good a chance. [Poor] Capt Soria is in Hospital in New York.

Goodbye for now   lovingly yours   Sum

Sumner's correspondence to Alice sailing from Boston to Buenos Aires has been lost and only his letters to his parents during this part of the voyage survive. Curiously enough, the only journal to come down from his father was one Nicholas had kept just a few years earlier between the ages of seventy-five and eighty. Several of the people I interviewed described Nicholas at this time in his life as "always sitting in his easy chair, half asleep, puffing on his pipe."

1900
Sept. 11th   Wife 70 years old today & churned 10½ lbs butter.
    26th   75 years old today & dug 6 bushels potatoes. . . . I was born about 5 PM   Sept. 26, 1825.

Nicholas' concern for his eight children as well as his sustained interest in town affairs monopolized his five-year journal. The brevity of his entries, like Sumner's, leaves few clues about his attitudes and feelings, but overall, Nicholas' journal suggests numerous ways he influenced his son. They shared a love of nature, an independence

combined with responsibility and a seemingly unconquerable hardiness.

At seventy-five, Nicholas Drinkwater did not hesitate to walk over two miles to Yarmouth village to cast a vote for the presidential candidate William Jennings Bryan, or to attend a Masonic meeting of Casco Lodge. When the highest tide in years tore his wharf "all to pieces" in the winter of 1900 he repaired it, only to have it destroyed within the month and to repair it again. A few years later he wrote skeptically:

1902
Feb. 2nd [Candlemas or Ground Hog Day] This has been a very stormy day. Wind E. a gale with snow & then rain & at 7 PM a Thundershower.

"If on Candlemas day it doth snow or rain
Winter is gone & won't come again."

We shall see.

Nicholas Drinkwater did not just endure the elements, he left marginal notes when he stopped to watch the wild geese flying, measured the 3-foot 9-inch snow drift in front of his home, counted more than 50 robins in a morning and picked the first "dandy-lion" of spring. He was often called upon to survey property lines and take paying guests out sailing. If he wasn't tracing the family geneology, he might be pulling beans or gathering the best apples, having the fancy-goods peddler to supper or fixing the frozen water pipe in the barn. Doubtless Nicholas spent some of his time nodding off in his armchair, as his descendants remember, though he didn't make note of it.

Sumner compares coasting to deepwater sailing in this letter to his parents. He has changed a great deal from the man of 1899 who wrote that he didn't want to continue to go on long voyages without his wife.

"I should have been King" refers to the third-highest office in Sumner and Nicholas' Masonic York Rite Chapter, Cumberland Chapter #35, of which Nicholas had been a charter member, historian and High Priest. Sumner joined the chapter on February 24, 1892 and held the following offices: Master of the First Veil, 1894; Scribe, 1897; Royal Arch Captain, 1905; Principal Sojourner, 1906; Captain of the Host,1907; and High Priest, the highest office of the chapter, 1910. He never did serve as King.

At sea Wed=	Jan 1st 1908
Lat=	26–00
Long=	42–40

My Dear Parents Father & Mother—

I will begin a letter today to wish you a Happy New Year & hope you are both quite well & not having a cold winter but can keep warm & comfortable. I wish you could have some of the warm weather I am having & the day . . . pleasant . . . Ther=72 . . . with Easterly winds not very favorable as I haven't got as far East as I want to before making too much Southern. [If he went south too soon, he might experience difficulty working around the coast of South America.]

. . . Xmas day was . . . rather rough. We were then 1150 miles from Boston, our 8th day out & today we are a little over ½ way to the Equator & 15 days at sea.

I am feeling real well & not nearly so lonesome as I expected to be but then I have been quite occupied in mind in looking after the progress of the ship & fixing up things about the cabin to suit me & so have not been idle in mind at least. The time is going quite quickly. I have a good set of Officers & the crew are all young fellows. Though some of them are lacking in seamanship yet they are willing & active & everything is going on fine.

We are busy fair days in overhauling her spare sails, unbending her best ones & bending the poorest ones for summer weather which will grow warmer & finer as we get south. . . .

Alice sent me an Item, an Election of officers in the chapter. I suppose I should have been King if I had been home. Will have to start in again & work up if I stay home again after this voyage.

I have plenty of reading matter & cigars & so can amuse myself when I get lonesome. I feel that I am fortunate to get this chance. If I am going to sea I had rather go in this trade then coasting. It is much easier, nothing to fret about at sea. Just take things easy. Of course, one feels lonesome at times & wishes he could hear from home & know how you all are getting on, but 2 or 3 months soon slip by & then I'll get letters from home. I will hear from you sooner than you can from me, except notice of my arrival as I shall cable home on arriving. Well I will lay this by till later & add a little to the one I comenced to Alice Xmas & write more later on. So good night with love to all

Sumner

Margaret and Nicholas Drinkwater.

BEN'S PHOTO STUDIO

As Sumner wrote the following note to his mother and father on their anniversary, he must have recalled their fiftieth wedding celebration only three years earlier. It was an important landmark in his parents' lives and some of the grandchildren who attended remember it still. Sumner's sister Lillian, who brought her family from North Yarmouth, ten miles away, stayed overnight. Although the children were put to bed early, they realized it was a special occasion. Iva, one of Lillian's eight-year-old twins, still remembers the trip by pung (sled) which she and her sisters took to their grandparents' home on the Foreside. They were covered by a pungent buffalo robe, which had still not totally relinquished its original owner's odor. Her grandmother was the center of attention in her wedding gown, which still fit beautifully. She was so tiny that no one else has fit into it since.

The beds at the Drinkwater homestead had a wooden frame and rope fed through this frame to crisscross to the other side. It was this rope that supported the sleeper. The children were tucked together in one of these beds in a cold, frosty room. Sandwiched between two feather beds, they rolled together as the rope underneath sagged.

Although the grandchildren were not allowed to stay up that evening, Nicholas recorded the festivities in his journal dated 1900–1905. (Note that Nicholas also continued to use weather notations at the beginning of his journal entries exactly as if he were still keeping a ship's log—though it had been many, many years since he had been at sea.)

January 28, 1905 Ther 20 Cloudy weather with snow squalls
    Wind N
    As tomorrow is the 50th anniversary of our marriage the children have come to celebrate it. 7 children, 3 daughters-in-law & Edith's young man [Will Rent] & we had a nice supper, 25 of us. It was past 1 A.M. before they all left. Lucy could not come because Elden was sick.

In the South Atlantic

L= 20 00
Long 37 00
Evening [Jan.29]

43 days at sea
Dear Father & Mother—
As today is your [53rd] Weding Aniversary I will write a few lines to wish you much happiness & comfort today & that some of your children will be able to come to see you. Quite likely May & Eunice & Joshua who is with you everyday & perhaps if the day is fair & not too cold Maggie or Lillian or both may get down to bring greetings & good cheer. I hope & trust that you will have many more returns of the day yet to come & that another year I may not be so far away from home. . . .

Now wishing you much Joy. I will say good night.
With much love   Sumner

Although Sumner was pessimistic about beating the *Brynhilda,* he probably tried very hard. After all, if he could win against overwhelming odds, it might help his career. The *Brynhilda* was a handsome ship, and she held the record of thirty-eight days between Buenos Aires and Adelaide. For a period of years she came under the American flag and one of her captains during that time covered her so lavishly with white paint that she came to be called "the great white bitch."

Friday Feb 14 08
Dear Father & Mother
I arrived here [Buenos Aires] yesterday, 58 days. Found myself 6 days behind the *[Brynhilda]* . . . but a good average Passage. I am awfully disappointed & feeling uncomfortable in not receiving any letters from home excepting one from Edith dated Jan 18 . . . I don't understand why there are none from Alice. I was expecting at least 5 or 6 letters. However, a mail is due the 17th but I shall not get it before the 20th as I am Ordered to Rosario & will leave here tomorrow in tow.

I shall feel anxious as Edith wrote that you, Father, had been quite unwell in bed but were better the last she heard from her Mother. . . . I do hope I shall get letters soon as I get to Rosario & that I shall hear that you are quite well again.

I have lots to do today & a mail leaves in the morning so can only write these few lines. I am real well & hope & trust you are at home. With much love to you all.

Your affectionate son   Sumner

No 7

Sunday evening Feb 23, 08

My Dear Sumner
I am awfully sorry to have to tell you the news I must. Your father died this morning at 2 oclock. He had been gradualy failing all the time but friday he began to be worse & sat= morning they thought he was dying but he rallied again & lived 18 hours. Eunice & May were there all that night. He seemed to know them all & was not unconcious until the very last.

The funeral is to be tuesday at 2.30. They cannot keep him longer without embalming him & he was much opposed to that always, so your mother says & don't want to have it done. There is really nothing to wait for. We think without doubt that [your brother] John is in Portsmouth & Hattie John will go up & telephone him tomorrow morning. He can come right home. She will also send for Edith. . . . Your Mother is standing the strain <u>well</u> but is pretty tired & sleepy. Of course she hardly realizes it yet. We expected to go down tomorrow & fix up the house a little but they don't think there is much to be done, so we are not going. The kitchen looks terribly bad, worse than I ever see it before for Hattie Josh has been doing the cooking & hasn't cleaned up at all, I don't think.

Don't feel too badly darling. I know it will be a shock to you now that it has realy come, although in all my letters I have not given you much encouragement about him & you knew he was feeble when you left home. I am sorry it should have happened when you were at sea but all the others will be there I think. Lucy can come for the day if no longer. [Her son] Howard came this forenoon. He heard through his mother that his grandfather was just alive so started right off, but heard he was dead soon as he got here. . . .

Well Mrs. Willard [the downstairs tenant] & Mrs. Pickering [her housekeeper] were gone just three days & arrived home in a very dilapidated state & were both <u>sick</u> for a few days. They both looked like walking rag bags. Had their night dresses on under their dresses & hanging several inches below & partly in tatters where they had stepped on them.

Well dear in the excitement I had almost forgotten to say that I heard of your arrival [at Buenos Aires] last monday evening. Charles Hunt & Co. wrote me & sent it at 11 A.M. Sat. the 15th. It must have been at our P.O. sat. night but of course I didn't get it until monday A.M. but was much pleased to hear. You made a fine passage & the "Brynhilda" didn't beat you but very little. Realy you did better than she considering the difference in the ships. Your report was in the sunday Herald so I did not see it in my paper at all. But [her sister] Hat did see it & sent the item to me & I got it along with [the] Hunt letter. . . .

I hope someone will write a nice obituary of your father. I think they will have Masonic services but do not know for sure.

Lewis Bucknam wife has Diptheria & the house is quarantined. I believe she is not dangerously sick but they have two children that may take it. . . . We have very good sleighing now, about 6 inches fell one day & people are improving it. . . .

If you do go to a salt Island this voyage I hope you can bring home some more rum & gin. I don't know but you can get it in South America. Don't use much of such things yourself will you. I don't

think it would be good for you. I hope you will find some Capts there who you will like & some you have met before. It will make it more pleasant for you. . . .

I will finish in the morning as it is 9.30 & I am getting sleepy. Good night.

Monday morning 24th

Will close this up for Frank will come with the mail today & will be likely to be along earlier than Josh does. The snow storm did not amount to anything. This morning is fine with bright sun & Ther about 26. Hope tomorrow will be pleasant.

I am going up to the Village some time today & call into the Drs-office. I want to know if I am to keep on with my medicine. It has done me lots of good. I am feeling better than I have for a long time & I can walk so well without putting me out of breath that I feel pretty much pleased about it. So when you get home we can take long walks together. Will that suit you? . . .

Hattie has just gone up to the villiage to telephone John [to come on from Portsmouth]. Howard came up at the same time & they walked up together. I don't know whether the family will get flowers for the funeral or not. I think it would have been a nice idea to have got 82 white pinks [carnations]. Just now Woodbury [May's husband] called & thinks it will be nice to have an Anchor made of flowers & will go into Portland & get it this P.M.   I told him I would agree to getting anything that the others wanted. I must not write anymore. Most time for Frank [Josh's substitute as mail carrier].

Will write again next sunday as usual. With lots of love Alice

Don't let this bad news make you sick darling & take good care of your self. Not quite as long letter as I generaly write but I write so often there isn't enough to write long ones everytime.

I asked Nicholas' granddaughter Iva if she remembered the funeral service. She didn't. Later I discovered, in the only one of

Edith's letters which Sumner kept, that Iva and her sisters hadn't attended. Their mother, Lillian, hadn't felt their coats looked "nice enough." In every other way, Edith's letter was a duplicate of Alice's.

As was the custom, Nicholas was buried from his home and the family or close friends might have "laid out" his body. The casket was probably simple. An undertaker would have been on hand to organize the burial and supervise the ceremony. The minister would have conducted the ceremony in a room apart from the casket, and following the service, the casket would have headed the procession to the cemetery. After the burial the minister and close friends and relatives would return to the home. Everyone would have contributed to the meal served them by the family.

No. 8
Sunday evening March 1, -08

My Dear Sumner,

I am just begining a letter this evening instead of having it most all written. But I have had some one here all the time & have hardly been alone for a week or more. It has been only your family I know but they tire me in time.

John & Edith came last monday evening & Hattie John & Alfred were here. Alfred went down to Nell's but the other three stayed here all night. John went back to Portsmouth thursday & they were all here a good part of the time. John came [from the barge] with his old coal dusty clothes on & Edith brought his best ones that were at Edwin's. He had to take a bath & be mended up & borrowed some things of yours. So got along somehow.

Tuesday was a nice day & the funeral was largely attended. All the children but you being here. Lucy (& 2 of her children, Muriel is ill) Howard & Eldon came. There was 18 teams in the procession. Did you think there were so many relations? Your Aunt Alexina & Zena Marg came, but Annie Noyes was not over. They think she did not get the letter. The time was so short for anything.

Your father looked very nice indeed & had a nice couch casket. There was two floral pieces, a pillow from your mother & a large Anchor from all the children. Alexina brought a wreath. I am going to send a pressed violet or two that was among the flowers. I had a horse & sleigh from the Russells with a driver who took Mother & I. He was buried in his family lot in the S.W. corner of the Ledge cemetary. I think dear you would have been satisfied with everything except the looks of the old kitchen which is a disgrace to Josh. I saw Ben Lord among the Masons. . . .

During the first year of the Civil War he was chased for three days by a rebel privateer and he had a Negro cook who had run away from Jeff Davis' plantation and who was in the most abject fear of being captured, as he declared he would be swung from the yardarm as soon as they found him. The terrified darkey did not eat or sleep during the chase but passed most of his time praying and when the privateer was finally distanced insisted his prayers saved the ship, but Captain Nicholas thought the way the crew kept every inch of canvass shook out had something to do with their escape.

As a shipmaster Captain Drinkwater was what was considered 'lucky,' both by ship owners and sailors, and so much faith did owners have in his luck or care that his ships were often sent out lightly insured or not at all. In his long career he only lost one ship, which was lured from her course by false lights shown by wreckers as the ship was steering among the Bahamas Islands, but his good luck happened to be fully insured and no lives were lost.

The captain appeared in the court against the wreckers and they received a speedy and deserving dose of Spanish justice. Captain Drinkwater's house was a veritable museum of curiosities that he had gathered in his many voyages to many lands.

FUNERALS.

Capt. Nicholas Drinkwater.

Captain Nicholas Drinkwater whose funeral took place Tuesday from his late home at Princes Point, Yarmouth, passed the greater part of his long life on the water.

His first voyage was made to the West coast of Africa when but 14 years old and in a subsequent voyage made to the same place years after he took out the first shipload of manumitted slaves sent out from Baltimore by the Colonisation Society.

I know it will interest you to know that Mr. Ennes read a part of the poem, "Like him who wraps the drapery of his couch about him & lies down to peaceful rest" at the funeral. He talked very nice & gave quite a little history of your father's life. I will send several different pieces that has been written. Some are full of errors.

Mr. Brewer has taken the last of the hay, about ½ ton I guess. They have not paid for it yet but will soon. It will be nearly $50.00 in all they have paid us. I am too tired & Sleepy to write more tonight.

Alice complains of being tired, and the funeral was no doubt quite a strain, given her delicate constitution.

She did her duty as a daughter-in-law, but she must have felt superfluous among Margaret's many daughters. Alice never spent as much time as Sumner did with his folks. Nicholas' diary records frequent visits from Sumner when he was home and, generally, Alice did not accompany him.

Mud season is on in Maine and the walking is difficult.

Monday morning, Mch = 2

Now dear I will write more & have it ready for Frank as he comes along much earlier than Josh. Josh is taking two weeks off & Frank takes the route. It is a nasty day snowing & raining & I think it will be most to bad walking for anybody to get here today & I shall be glad. The Obituary I send, Edith wrote for the "Argus." I will send others with the papers.

Capt = Crickett [of the *Grace Deering* days] is in the Florida Keys. Vessel leaking & damaged. Must either tow to Balt = or disq = into another vessel. Pretty expensive job won't it be? I suppose he was loaded with Phosphate rock but do not know. . . . We heard today that Ed White was here in town & living at the poor house is destitute & blind. Just think of it. . . .

Can't you bring some of those long stem pipes, T.D. pipes, I guess they were, that Geo- Allen [a good friend] liked so well. He is always telling about how nice they were. I believe you got them in South America somewhere didn't you.

You would be surprised to see the pile of Ashes Mrs. Pickering [the housekeeper downstairs] has dumped on the floor down in the play room. Their iron barrel has been emptied only once since you went & all the rest has been piled on the floor. It is not only an awfully nasty mess but is dangerous as I have known all the time. Yesterday Woodbury noticed it & said I ought to put a stop to it before it was to late. If it was known, our insurance would not be worth much. There is not need of their doing so. It is only laziness.

I believe I wrote you that Frank Bucknam had failed. Well we hear it contradicted but that he has been closed up on account of selling liquor.

I don't know as I have said much about your Mother, but she is about as usual. I haven't seen her since the funeral but shall go down some day soon when the walking is suitable. Of course she will be pretty lonesome & will miss your father terribly, but I think she will go ahead & do just as she always has. She went right back up stairs in her room to sleep. She is real spunky I tell you. I suppose of course you will have letters on the way home long ago to your Father but as you always write them together, it will be all the same.

I hope I will get a letter by the 10th. Am awfully anxious to here from you & hope dear it will be good news I shall here. I shall write again next week & I suppose I can ans= your first letter anyway. I hope you won't think of going over to Africa any way. . . .

I can't write a very long letter this time for want of material so this is about all. But you will get so many from me you won't want them too lengthy. I don't know how many of [the street] car men have written if any but think some of them will surely.

With lots of love   Alice

Alice and Sumner corresponded independently of each other. Her first letter, which he has just received, took almost six weeks to

catch him so it will be a while before he is informed of the events occurring today at his father's home.

At the time Alice wrote, Muriel, his sister Lucy's daughter, had gone into a decline. Muriel is remembered as a very pretty girl who had a childhood sweetheart, Angus Wilson. For years they waited to see if her health would improve so that they could marry. Three years after this letter, when Muriel was twenty, they finally married. She died six weeks later.

Galuchi, a crimp, would have to be more circumspect in luring Sumner's crew members away at this point of the voyage than he would have had to be at the end. Although it was usually a strict rule that no one was permitted on deck until the work was finished, the crew paid off and dismissed, it generally took a strongly armed man to keep the boardinghouse keepers from clambering over the side of the vessel. If their attempts to reach the sailors were frustrated, they tossed small packages onto the deck which contained their cards, cigars, or even small bottles of liquor. Much like sideshow barkers, the crimps would keep up a running line of talk as they called endearments to the men and promised them a paradise of earthly delights. No matter how badly the sailors had been previously used by crimps in other ports, they predictably responded to such persuasion. After a short spree ashore, the duped seamen would be put aboard an outwardbound square-rigger at so much money a head.

Sunday Feb 23d
Dear Alice   On Board still in the stream. Have got no orders for docking. [Reached Rosario February 20] & got your first letter It was mailed at Yarmouth Jan= 14th & I don't see why it was not at Buenos Ayres. I am sorry to hear of so much sickness at home, so many of you with colds & Father Sick a bed & Muriel been worse than when I came away & yourself, dear, having more trouble with your breathing. I suppose I should be scared to death if I was sleeping with you & shall probably worry about you a good deal. I am glad you went to Dr Bates . . . I have no great faith in Doctors as a rule but think Dr Bates prefferable to any in Yarmouth.

I am glad you think Father is better. It must make it hard for Mother as you say. Hope she will not get sick. Hope all the sick ones are getting well again. Poor Muriel is really having a hard pull. Hope indeed she will come out of it & get well & robust again. Lucy does seem to have lots of trouble come to her.

Well, as the old fellow said of his wife I am a little bit peculiar myself. Had kind of a colicky spell since Monday—change of food & water at Buenes Aryes, I guess. . . . but lots better to day. . . .

So you don't want me to go to Africa but if I could get a good freight it would only make the voyage a month or 6 weeks longer. I should not go if there is anything north . . .

Yes the Cabin Boy is all right, a fellow that has quite a good Education & has been a salesman for a shoe Manufacturer. Just what he is here for I don't know. Was not sick at all & is all right so far. How it will be when we dock I don't know with any of them. It's then when the trouble begins. This morning the mate has reported 4 of the crew missing all ready. I expect that Galuchi [the crimp that was jailed when Sumner was there in 1904] got them in the night. I don't care if they all go. Better for the owners & better for me. 2 of them I had cut down to Ordinaries.

Hope you will give the apples away if they are rotting. Wish I had had time to have sent a Barrel or 2 up to the vessel & I might have got some over to Nick or Wallace. Give Mabel some or any one who is a mind to come after them, except dealers. I wouldn't give them to any one to sell that wouldn't give you anything. . . .

Well no more now. Lots of Love to you, Mother & all the members of both families. Should be glad to have you here but it's pretty hot & uncomfortable.

Yours as ever   Sumner

Wed Feb 26 08

Just a few lines before mailing. We just got to discharge this morning. Docked yesterday. Think they are going to take it away fast when they once get at it.

I spent last evening on board the Snowden with Capt Toye & Mrs. T. She wishes you were with me as she is about the only Female here except a Norwegian Capt who has his wife, but she doesn't speak but very little English. Capt Toye & Wife have been married 23 yrs & have no more to show than we have [childless]. . . .

I wish I knew what I could get Edith here in case she goes & does it [gets married] some time this coming Summer. Think I shall get some thing anyway & I want to get something for you. It's hard to know what to select but I don't mean to leave much of my earnings out here. Any way what Capts I have fell in with are quite temperate so that is an advantage. Don't have to spend much in sociability. This place has changed a good deal on the waterfront. Where we Loaded Hay when you were with me is build up with a fine bulkhead for the distance of a mile, I should say. I am laying very near where we did the & go to town the same way up over the Embankment. Well dear, hoping this finds you all well at home, I'll close for this time.

With love & kisses & a big one to Mother S
as ever Sum—

Obviously, Sumner still does not know of his father's death on February 23.

Rosario March 8/08

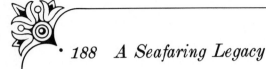

Dear Father & Mother

I will write you a few lines today as a mail is leaving on the 10th direct for New York. I sent a letter from B. Aires. On arriving there was ordered here & had got only one letter from Edith there in which she mentioned she had heard that Father was not well but knew very little about it. I got letters from Alice & also one from May after getting up here & was sorry to hear that you had been quite unwell for some time & not able to be up & had had Dr Bates. In [Alice's] last letter she wrote that she had been down to see you & that you seemed comfortable but was in bed upstairs & had a fire up there & seemed to have things comfortable. I shall hope to hear you are much better in my next letter which I hope to get this week. I hope when it will get warm & spring like, you will be up about again as well as usual. . . . I am getting on quite well in discharging & will probably finish about the 13th or 14th. Business is very dull & I have not been able to find a freight yet. If nothing comes up when she is disq= will sail in ballast for Barbados & most likely take salt home from Turks Island. In that case I would probably be home in May.

The past week has been one of festivities, called Carnival week, a Catholic affair which occurs in all Spanish Countries the week preceeding Lent. Business slacks up although there are but 2 days that are Legal Hollidays.

The Hunt is the only American vessel here so that I havn't much Company, although there is one Capt [Starrit] of Maitland, Nova Scotia here that I have met before. My first Officer is Proving as good an Officer in port as at sea so I am fortunate in that way. The 2nd is inclined to drink but not quarrelsome. I may pay him off. 4 of my men deserted while at anchor in the stream. The rest are very sober fellows for sailors & are working steadily every day discharging. Have a good Cook & Cabin boy & can take things quite easy & comfortable. The weather here is pretty hot & mosquitoes pretty troublesome but I keep well screened about the cabin.

What a terrible fire Portland has had, too bad the City building is burned. I see by the papers Alice sent that the greater part of the records were saved which is fortunate. There is little of interest to write. I will enclose a couple of views of the water front showing the . . . apologies for wharfs for discharging & co.—although there has been a good deal of improvement since I was here over 3 years ago.

Now I will close hoping that you, Mother, are keeping well & not having to go up & down stairs to much & that Father is much better. Shall write again before leaving. I think of you a good deal & shall hope for good news soon. With much love to you both

Sumner

The *Hunt* at dock.

Sumner's following letter is one of a pair, since Alice's answering letter was kept. These two letters are unique because they provide the only actual dialogue in the Drinkwaters' surviving correspondence.

From Sumner's comments it would appear that the Drinkwaters had become estranged from Mr. Adams since his voyage of 1904. However, Sumner must have retained a soft spot for Mrs. Adams because he recorded her death in Bath, Maine, in 1917.

As Sumner lists the mail he has received, he mentions a letter from his brother John, who had returned to the sea after an abortive attempt at farming. Sometime following John Glover's death in 1905, John left the sea to help Hattie John's mother, Nancy Hamilton, run her farm on Cousins Island. Mrs. Hamilton had sold off a lot of the shore acreage of the 120-acre property to summer people which she later regretted. John tried farming for a year but it was not something he enjoyed. His mother-in-law once observed that he had "no patience with animals."

Her remark didn't surprise his family. John was seven or eight years old when he was sent to bring the family horse up from the pasture. Greatly put out by the errand, he muttered as he went, "I wish that old horse was dead." During a storm the night before, the horse had sheltered under a tree and was struck by lightning. So when John reached the pasture he was greatly shocked to discover that his wish had been granted. John always ended that story with the admonition, "Just be sure when you make a wish in life, that it's something you really want."

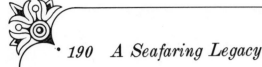Tuesday P.M. March 17th 08
My Dear Alice   Just 3 months since I left Boston & now 3 P.M. I am on the way down river. Glad to get away but with rather sad feelings for I shall feel through all the passage that when I hear from home again . . . I must expect to learn that Father will have gone from us. I know such things must come to us all. It has to you, dear, & must to me. I feel somehow to day as though it had all ready come. . . .

Your letter was gladly received but fills me with sad restless feelings to hear of all your wrote. I havn't let myself think but what I might get home again & find all there but now I feel that it can not be so. Capt Cleaves' death seems very sad & sudden to me to read of, Fannie [the captain's wife & Sumner's former schoolteacher] must be feeling dreadfully. And Mr. Adams is gone too? Well when one is gone, we must cover their faults with the mantle of charity & let them Rest. . . . I hope Dear Mother will keep up as long as she is needed but I feel she would not stay with us long after Father is gone. [His mother, Margaret Hannah Gray Drinkwater, lived six more years, to be eighty-four.] Well dear, I won't let myself fret too much about it so do not worry about me. I am glad . . . that you are feeling so much better especially with your breathing & that you are able to walk so well. It had been a long time since you had walked to the foreside, I guess, not since you were down there with me in the Fall. . . .

Now I'll go up on deck for awhile & see how she is going
Sumner=

The *Adolph Obrig* that Sumner mentions apparently went down "with all hands" as she rounded Cape Horn. There were many icebergs sighted in the area that season. One was reported to be 500 feet high and 50 miles long.

Sunday P.M.   Mar 22nd
Dear Alice
I will write a few more lines to-day. We are now near Martin Garcia Island with fresh S.E. wind & will have to lay at anchor till it changes as S.E. blows right up through the narrow channel just below the Island. . . .

I don't know if I mentioned that my 2nd mate deserted. Have a new one, pretty good, I guess, not as good as the other, but he went right to drinking soon as we got to the dock & begging me for money. When I gave some the third time, I told him he would get no more & the next morning he didn't show up & his things were gone. The rest all hung by & worked cargo all the time (except 4 I mentioned) & didn't go ashore much, quite temperate fellows as were the Mate & Cook & [Cabin] Boy. So I have 4 new men & 2nd mate, not so many deserters as I expected. . . .

Perhaps you may have seen an account of the missing of <u>Adolf Obrig</u>. Think she was reported missing before I came away. The Capt of her was Mate with Capt Don Nichols [on the *Emily Reed*] when we were in Singapore. His name was Ross. He had his wife with him. . . . You asked if my Eye bothered me. Well it does a little but not to hurt. I suppose I ought to have had glasses fitted before I came away but concluded I would do nothing out here but wait till I get home. I don't have to use the right one taking sights so that is all right & I don't read much. Have read the papers & Slips you sent. Didn't get the last ones, doubt if I do now. . . . Well bye bye. Till a fair wind.

Love from S—

Sumner mentions his wages. He earned $100 a month, a portion of which was forwarded directly to Alice. In addition to this set figure, Sumner's renumeration included the proceeds from the "slop chest" merchandise he sold to the crew as well as "primage," a percentage of the freight money, which in this case seems to be 5 percent.

Tuesday Morning 24
Got my letters all ready last night in case the Pilot should leave during the night but had a thunder squall & then calm & had to anchor. Got underway at 3 oclock . . . My Pilot is a hustler & keeps her moving when he can make an inch. . . .

I feel sorry to come away in Ballast & only Earning monthly wages. If I had got a Hay Freight of 4000.00 Dollars, it would have been 200.00 Dollars in my Pocket, but I will make 100.00 a month if I should come clear home in Ballast. I will mention that my acct shows 243.00 Dollars charged against me, 200.00 of it I have sent to you so there would be $179.00 due me on the commission outside of the monthly wages. $60.00 from slops. So if I was ordered to Boston in Ballast & got home in 5½ months I should earn over $600 dollars but hope I'll get a salt freight or something. A salt freight will give me 150.00 more.

I hope Dear if you felt there was any thing you could get or do Father & Mother for their comfort you have done so & I think you would. I am [worrying] how mother gets enough good food if she had to give up all work down stairs & of couse she would. I hope she would have enough nourishment. Of course, she wouldn't eat much. . . .

3 P.M. breeze S.S.W. & raining with thunder in the west. Pilot says I will have a fair wind. He will leave in a little while now. Got flag up. Boat to come for him. So will say bye bye with lots of love & Kisses. Love to Mama & all Yours as ever.

Sumner

In Alice's answer to Sumner's preceding letter she refers to the passing of John Dexter Cleaves. He was formerly master of the schooner *Essex* and one of Sumner's earliest employers. Sumner sailed under Captain J. D. Cleaves at the time he began courting Alice. Winifred, Lizzie Glover's younger daughter, remembers Captain Cleaves's funeral. She was ten years old when she walked over the ice from Cousins Island with her family. The people assembling on the Foreside for the service were "just black specks against the snow. Someone kept his hat off at the burial, got a cold, contracted pneumonia and died."

Jessie Simonton, Hattie Poole's niece, was sixteen at the time of this letter and battling tuberculosis. As she now says, "They called it tuberculosis in those days until it killed you and then they called it consumption." It had killed her brother, Charles, six years earlier.

Jessie has never forgotten her wine-and-egg diet. The doctor prescribed 1 Tablespoon of wine to be mixed with a raw egg, and as her appetite declined he increased the frequency of the dose. He expected her to take this concoction twelve times a day but she balked beyond seven. After Sumner returned from this voyage he personally delivered the wine to the family and Jessie remembers both him and "Aunt Alice" very fondly. "It was a long way over to our house," she says "and they had no horses." When the local doctor could do no more for her, Jessie was sent to the tuberculosis sanatorium at Hebron for fourteen months. After she was cured she entered training to become a nurse for tubercular patients. Her life plans changed abruptly when her mother died and she had to return to Yarmouth to care for her family.

No-16

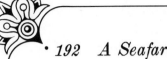

Sunday 4 P.M. April 26

My Dear Sumner -
I will begin my sixth letter to Turks Island. Got your last one from Buenas Ayres sent by Pilot, the 22nd almost a month after you sailed. You are now 33 days out & I hope are getting pretty near Barbados.

We are having a pretty warm day, the warmest yet. But there are hardly any signs of summer. The grass is beginning to turn green but trees around here have not begun to leave out. The Peonies are comming up, & have been a long time & were covered with snow twice but did not hurt them.

We have had a very exciting afternoon. Soon after noon I noticed a smoke over by Yorks hill & soon see that it was a big fire. The Alarm was blowed & soon there were crowds of people on the road from the village & every where. Mother & I went up on the hill where we could see it plainer. It was a fire that the [trolley] cars set in the grass somewhere, so we heard . . . I knew if it got started & the wind got more S.W. it would swipe us all out. As it crossed the road . . . so many

men & boys . . . fought it well in spite of the strong west wind . . . it was finally put out on a point down by Broad cove.

Mrs. Willard [the downstairs tenant] has a new housekeeper. An Irish woman but a very good one she seems. A widow who is poor & hasn't a home & don't mind about trifles & I think will stay a while. Any way I hope so sure so Mrs. Pickering can't come back. . . .

So you got more letters by staying ashore that night. Yes, you must have been surprised to here of John Cleaves' death. Just one more letter would have told you of your father's death. But as it is you would be expecting it I know.

Hattie Josh told me that since your mother had come back from Mays she had seemed much more like herself. She is well as usual I think & will get more used to being without your father in a little while & will get back into the same tracks. For some time after he died she didn't do anything about the work & seemed terribly dull & unnatural but she will get to feeling more contented all the time.

I am sorry dear that your eye troubles you. You must have glasses as soon as you get home & most likely [you] will have to wear them all the time. Anything will be better than losing the sight of it which I am afraid you will do if you are not careful of it.

The notice of the interest on your loan on the ins= policies has come & it is due May 15 & amounts to 26.75. I didn't know just what it was. One of them will soon be paid up for good which is some comfort. I am glad you have been prudent this voyage for I have spent quite a lot & am going to spend still more.

Shall get an Oilcloth as soon as Jack can fix the floor which will be in a week or more. He must finish the work he is doing on the front door at Fels then make some chicken houses for him as he has got a big Incubator going.

Last week Mother & I went to Portland. She got several things. I got me a pair of boots & a pair of brown shoes & stockings to match & a black skirt to wear with the silk waist I made in the winter which will make a very pretty suit for some occasions. . . .

MARION KNIGHT REED

Charles and Lillian Drinkwater Crockett.

I haven't heard a word from Hattie John since I wrote last. Should think she or Edith would write once in a while. I expect your thin underclothes will be all worn out by the time you are back. I might have put more suits in your trunk well as not. . . . Capt. Crickett got home a week ago. I don't believe he will make another trip in the Schooner. There are five six-masters [six-masted vessels] in Portland now & they make quite a showing in the harbor. About all are in the stream.

Hat Poole was down one day last week. She says Jessie Simonton is quite miserable, has been sick all winter & Dr. Gardon of Portland says her lungs are diseased. Suppose she will go in consumption like Charlie, her brother. I sent her up a bottle of wine, some we have had years. The Dr. said she ought to take raw eggs & wine. They have eggs but the wine they can't get her. . . .

[Your sister Lill's husband] Chas. Crockett is quite sick again. Lill is just the same. Her foot does not change any.

No more now & may not send this for a few days.

Edith was devoted to her Uncle Sum, and Alice was her favorite aunt. Alice's comment on Edith's wedding probably derives from her concern for her sister-in-law Hattie John. After all, church weddings were only just coming into vogue. Most of Alice's contemporaries had been married at home or at the minister's parsonage. Hattie John fought successfully against cancer until 1926. Her husband was absolutely devoted to her, and after her death he spent a great deal of time wandering along the shore on Cousins Island trying to find just the right natural stone for *his* grave. He had a passage from *The Rubaiyat* inscribed on it: "With all life's problems still unsolved, we have to go." He was premature in his preparations, as he lived until 1940—until he was almost eighty-five.

Charles Crockett, whom Alice mentioned in the preceding letter, met and courted Sumner's sister Lillian when she was visiting her older sister Maggie in North Yarmouth. Maggie's homestead burned down sixty years ago, after she and her husband had died, but the

Crockett home has only just left the family. Charles suffered most of his later life from an injury he had received in his early thirties due to the negligence of a road crew. He was unaware that a horse-drawn road machine had been by his place putting in ditches to drain the roads. Although the crew was required to fill in the trenches by people's access ways, it had not done so. Charles Crockett rode away from the barn with his horse and wagon heading for town. He didn't see the ditch until it was too late to avoid it and he was thrown from the wagon. He was bedridden for a long time afterward, had periodic relapses, and never totally recovered.

Wednesday evening Apr. 29

Dear Sumner-
Well I told you that Chas. Crockett was sick again but I didn't know how bad. Today I have been up to his funeral. He died sunday. Your Mother & Eunice went up monday morning as soon as they heard of it & have stayed since. Eunice will come home tomorrow but your mother will stay a while with Lillian. Lillian is taking it pretty hard but she is very courageous & will get along all right. She says her foot is better. [Ten of us] went up on the 2 P.M. train & there were teams to take us all up to the house & to the cemetary & then back to the 6 oclock train again . . . The neighbors lent their teams for the purpose & we were very glad to ride as the mud up there was terrible, much worse than any I have seen down here. May could not go & Lucy did not come but wrote Lillian. Muriel is better & sits up now.

I had a postal this morning from Edith. She says her mother is no better. They are at Edwins [Hattie John's older brother in Cambridge]. Hattie John was carried from Gertrude's [her niece] in a carriage. It looks to me as if Edith's church wedding would slump through. I hope she will give it up & be married without so much fuss. She had a letter from you last week & was going to write to Turks Island right away. John must be in Boston today as he [was reported] passed the Vineyard monday. . . .

No more tonight dear. Think I will mail this tomorrow then not write again until I know you have arived at Barbados—which ought to be very soon now. Good night. I sent some papers this week.

Thursday morning 30th
Will write just a line & send this on the way. It is quite a warm day but some cloudy. I am at work cleaning the sitting room what little it needs. Mother is bound to have a hand in it so she is cleaning the windows. Then I shall give it a good sweeping & call it square. I shall get the Art square [a floral rug, usually 9 by 12 feet] in the dining room up tomorrow & put it out on a line to clean. Then I shall only have the front hall up stairs & down to do which will close up my cleaning for the summer. . . .

Well I will write no more now. I think I will wait until you arrive in Barbados before I send another letter.

With lots of love   Alice

Take good care of yourself & be sure & not load too deep with salt. Hope you will find some vessels there & will like the Capts= So good by for a short time.

at Sea Sunday April 5th 08
Lat-29-00 Long 43-00
11 days out

My Dear Alice
This is my first attempt at writing since I came out. We have had such miserable weather . . . nothing but head winds [coming from ahead of the vessel] for 8 days & 2 of that a gale N.E. 1 day under Lower Top-sails & we lost 100 miles. The past 3 days has been favorable but the chance of a good passage is slim now. . . .

Our old Black cat deserted at Rosario & so we have but two Pets now. I didn't get any Hens. I thought they were so dear 1.50 a piece

Paper & just as well perhaps. You see I am trying a different pen, the other was scratchy & coarse. But the Mate says a squall is making up to windward so I'll go up & take a look & continue later. S—

Sunday 19th 08   Lat By D.R. 1.24 North   Long 38-20 west

Well Dear, a few more lines as Sunday has come round again. I suppose this is Easter Sunday whatever that may mean, but it don't make any difference to me. I shan't appear out with a new spring Bonnet. If I did it would get wet for it's rained about all day & has for that matter all the week. The Mate is wild. [He] only got one really decent day last Monday for painting. I think if we had kept the Hatches off all the passage we should have had the Lower hold just about full of water. I never seen so much rain in any passage I have made, but have had a fair amount of wind . . .

Last wed= noon I shipped a course for the "Rocas" [a string of closely spaced small coral islands off Brazil] intending to make it to verify the chronometer. But it shut in thick, rain & squally about 4 PM. I kept off 2 Points as I wouldn't take the risk of running for it [and wrecking the vessel if the chro= were inaccurate] & so passed well to westward of it. I havn't had a direct observation since & I imagine I am really farther west than I have recorded her as I know there is a strong N. W. Current.

The Mate has had the men in the hold when not raining too hard, getting it cleaned up for Salt but I expect he'll be crazy if he don't get some pleasent wea= soon to finish up his painting. I have got my water closet arrangements all fixed up & the brass knobs for turning on the water & lifting the trap all polished up fine & the woodwork varnished. So you would just take comfort when you had to use it if you was here. Don't you wish you had come? . . .

My light under clothes are getting rather shabby. I expect the boy scrubs them rather hard. I have discarded 1 Pair of drawers & another I have cut off the ankle bands & made short-legged & have cut off the sleeves of 2 under shirts. Just as good this Hot weather. You see I am practicing economy. May get some at Barbadoes. . . . I hope next Sunday I will be quite near Barbadoes. Lots of love S—

Dear Alice, I have more than realized my hopes of Last Sunday & find my self at anchor at Barbadoes. Came to anchor just at dusk. Had a fine week & I feel quite pleased to find the Bark Snowden here. Arrived here yesterday, the Pilot tells me. I had no Idea of taking up with him as he left Rosario 8 days ahead of me & [paid about $700 to be] towed down River at that. I'll have to tease Capt Toye a bit tomorrow when I go ashore.

I shall hope to get a letter from you . . . Of course, I shall be glad to get one but still I rather dread to though I never did before. But if bad news awaits me why I must try & be reconciled to it & not let it worry me too much. . . .

Now I'll say good Night & see what the morrow has in store. I don't like to think about it. With lots of love. Yours as ever, Hope you are all well as usual.   Sumner

Monday evening 27th   A few lines this eve all though I have been writing quite long Letters to N. W. Rice & Chas Hunt Co. I see your letter is No 13 & I got 6 at Rosario, 3 you have written to Turks Island & this makes 10. So there must be 3 more at Rosario or following me. . . .

I suppose you have written to Turks Island & told me more of the particulars of Father's death. Of course, I could hardly expect anything different & had made up my mind that it would be so. I must try & feel reconciled to it. I can't realize it as I shall when I get home. I hope Mother is bearing up under it & not down sick. . . . I am sorry to learn that Muriel is so bad, poor Girl. I don't see what can be her real trouble. It seems so singular a disease. I am glad you are feeling so nicely.

Will add a line tomorrow as I'm sleepy. Bye bye love Sumner

. . . Tuesday 28 2PM on shore & about to go on board to get under way. . . . Give my love & sympathy to Mother when you go down & tell her I think of her a great deal. . . . So bye bye again. Till you hear from Turks Island. Lots of love & good wishes to all.

Sumner

Thursday April 30 08 3.30 P.M.
In the Caribbean Sea Lat 15-54 Long 64-51

My Dear Alice

I will begin another letter today as it's so fine & smooth here in the Caribbean Sea, just as it was 5 years ago when you were with me & we were passing over this same track nearly. I am a little South of our track then, about 30 miles. I am also at noon, 85 miles ahead of where we were in the same time from Barbadoes that passage. . . .

I will tell you of my being on shore at Barbadoes Monday which I should have enjoyed much more than I could after reading your letter of April 7 which told me of Father's death. Allthough I was expecting to hear of it when I got there, it's a hard thing to realize & I don't beleive I shall fully untill I get home.

I found Capt Toye & wife, Capt Lee, wife & daughter (about 13 or 14) of the Barkentine Skada, Capt Marrel, wife & boy (of 4) & Capt McBride of the 4 masted Barkentine, Kings County with Wife & 2 boys (of 4 & 7or8). Capt McBride was in Company with us in Auckland in the Golden Rod [1897]. You will remember him. He is much the same in looks as I remember him except his hair is quite Gray. They have 2 fine boys & Mrs. McBride is lovely. I think we took to each other. Anyway we seemed to be together a lot & she went shopping with me next day for a little while. As Hattie Poole says she was awful good to me.

Well we all went to the Victoria Hotel & had our dinner. Just 12 of us sat down to a private Table in a room by ourselves & enjoyed a fine dinner. How strange is life. We fall in with Captains & think

perhaps we will never meet them again & then after several years fall in with them in unexpected places. . . . Goodbye for now

Sat=morning 6 A.M.   Wind still very light, weather fair & pretty Hot 80.

We have been pretty busy . . . getting the hold ready for Salt & it's looking pretty clean & nice. Have been down looking it over this morning. I shall not load her at all deep though the wea= ought to be mild & settled by the last of May.

In some ways I like the Idea of coming to Portland & in others I don't but it's all right either way, I guess. We shall go in to Central wharf I think as the cargo is to Lord Bro=

I got a few things at Barbadoes & will probably get a scolding for spending money. Got you a bit of a present & Edith I think but havn't decided yet & a few little curios. More later.

Sunday 3d   Still light Easterly winds & fair weather. Not going more than 4 knots but hope to get over tomorrow. I have been trying to write Mother today but it's awful hard for me to. I don't know what I ought to write her. I know how hard she will take poor Father's death & I don't know what I can write of cheer or comfort. . . .

Will write a little more tomorrow & go & have a bath. Bye bye.

Nellie and Jack had had a second son, Russell, on February 21, 1907, three years after Malcolm's birth. If, as Alice suggests, Nellie was eight months "along," and only just now mentioning it, she miscarried. Russell developed pneumonia following measles and died at the age of seven, in 1914. Nellie was inconsolable and always blamed a nurse who had told her to give the child a cold bath during his illness. After Russell's death Nellie continued to set a place in front of his highchair at the family dinner table for over a year.

Edith Janette Drinkwater married Will Rent in the Cousins Island Chapel on the only rainy day of the month, June 8, 1908. The chapel had been built by her Uncle John Glover's crew in 1895, and theirs was the first marriage to take place there. It had been decorated the day before with ferns, garden roses and daises, but the ferns wilted over night. Her cousin Gertrude dashed out in the rain to gather fresh ones at the last minute.

Margaret, Sumner's mother, had given Edith her own lovely blue-and-gold wedding gown because she was the eldest granddaughter, but of course, it was too small. Instead, Edith wore a white dress made of very fine batiste with insertions of the Grecian key design.

Everyone ignored the steady drizzle, and even the lack of ice cream for the reception's refreshments failed to dampen the spirit of fun. The steamer that serviced the island was supposed to bring the ice cream from Portland. However, the crew forgot to leave it off on the Cousins Island wharf, and it accompanied the steamer on her circuit out to Bustins Island.

Edith and Will Rent had three children in their thirteen-year marriage before Will was run down by a car as he stepped off a trolley in Portland in 1921. Edith died of cancer in 1933. She was fifty years old and had not remarried.

Although she was the first bride to grace the Cousins Island Chapel, Edith was by no means the last. It is today a popular place to hold weddings even for people from "off the island." I would have been married there fifty-eight years after Edith if rain had made it impossible to hold my garden wedding in Sumner's backyard.

No 7 to Turks Island

No. 17

May 1st 08

Friday evening

My Dear Sumner—

I said when I closed your letter yesterday that I would not write again until I knew of you being at Barbados. I got a letter by Josh yesterday morning from N. W. Rice saying "You were there & left for Turks Island the 28th." I think most likely you only stopped at Barbados one day & then proceeded. You were 34 or 35 days on the passage which was pretty good. You couldn't have had much calm weather in the equater. I was sorry I had my letter all ready to send but as it was I let it go. You may get these last two in the same mail. I hope I shall

Cousins Island Chapel

Cousins Island

Maine

Built by the people of Cousins and Littlejohn Islands in 1894

They built the chapel on the highest hill,
Midst pointed firs, white birch and golden rod.
Those Island folk whose toil-worn hands are still,
Because they felt the need to worship God.

"Unto thy temple, Lord, We Come" they'd sing,
Those valiant Islanders in days of yore;
Have we not, too, the same great need to bring
Our praise to God, as those who've gone before.

Sunday Services held from July 1st thru first
Sunday in September inclusive.

Cousins Island Chapel.

get a letter from Barbados some time next week. Hope to here you are well & all right & got several letters that followed you.

Last night we had a heavy S.E. gale & rain but it cleared up this forenoon & has been pleasant & very cool this P.M. . . .

I took a walk down to Jack's towards night after the squalls had let up & Nell says there may be an increase in her family by the time you are back.

Nell has had a letter from Hattie John. She sits up some but cannot walk & is terribly weak so she sweats all the time. She will be lucky if she ever gets any better.

I am thinking that some of Edith's [wedding plans] will slump through.

. . . I wrote a line this morning to Lillian thinking she & Mother would like to know of your arriving at & leaving Barbados. I am going up there [North Yarmouth] for a couple of days pretty soon. She will be terribly lonesome after your mother goes home. I don't know how long she [your mother] will stay up there, perhaps all the spring if she was contented to stay. I expect Lill would like to have her all the time for company & she would have a much more comfortable home than down to the old house. She has grown terribly deaf. One can hardly talk with her.

Well dear there isn't realy much to write about but I will finish this to mail monday. So good night.

Alice mentions "Will Gooding," one of Sumner's colleagues who sent them a bottle of Mount Pelée's ashes from the *Deering*'s deck in 1902. In those days every child in the village of Yarmouth could recite the details of Captain Gooding's grueling shipwreck. He was with his first command, the *Tewksbury L. Sweat,* built in 1874 in Yarmouth, when a typhoon struck on a passage between Australia and Hong Kong. The bark hit the Suzanne Reef at midnight on April 9, 1889, and he and his nine men took to the 16-foot boat with no more provisions than a compass and chart. Reaching the island of Pozant in the Caroline Islands, they were welcomed by natives (actu-ally cannibals), herded into a hut and fed breadfruit and coconuts.

Three weeks later Captain Gooding, who was permitted to explore the island under guard, found an iron kettle and located its owner, a thirty-seven-year-old Englishman who had been left off on the island by a schooner and forgotten. Although Charles Irons did not wish to return to civilization, he helped the others to do so. As the cannibals would agree to releasing only a few of the men, these few obtained the help of a missionary on Truk, 150 miles away. The missionary traveled with them back to Pozant and won the release of the rest of the crew. Returning him to Truk, they then continued on to the island of Ponipa, 450 miles farther away. There they were given passage on a vessel to Honolulu, from where they easily reached San Francisco and cabled home.

Since their ordeal had occupied the better part of a year, they had been given up for dead by most people—except Mrs. Gooding. When pressed to accept the captain's insurance, she maintained that he was alive and would return to her. When the shipowners received Will Gooding's cable, *"Tewksbury L. Sweat* total wreck. Wire funds for crew," there was considerable rejoicing in the community.

While I was awed by Captain Gooding's adventure, the cannibals he encountered seemed quite amenable compared to those that played host to an ancestor of James Monroe Bucknam, Sumner's late brother-in-law. This Bucknam ancestor, marooned after a shipwreck with no other survivor than his mate, was unable to kill the officer after the cannibals had begun to eat him. The poor man had been taken from the hut they shared, had had his leg removed, and the wound cauterized, and was returned alive until they were ready for another piece of him. The mate had hidden a knife and beseeched Captain Bucknam to dispatch him, but even so, the captain could not bring himself to commit murder. He waited while the wretched man killed himself and then used the knife to break out of the back of the hut. Captain Bucknam managed to elude the cannibals, was rescued by a vessel and came home to write down his story. Unfortunately, the family's copy of it has been lost, and while the details are vividly recalled, names and dates are missing. However, the little green book still existed in Sumner's time. No doubt he read it.

Monday morning May 4
Just a line before sending

A lovely morning & I have quite a big washing underway & it is a nice day to dry them. Hope you are having a good passage & that I will get a letter from Barbados in a few days. . . . Will Gooding told Jack you might go over to Turks Island in four or five days with a good chance but I think a week will come nearer it. . . . I will write once or twice more as you will be likely to be three weeks loading I think we were that long last time. Hope you will load at Grand Turk as it is much the best place I am sure.

No more now.
Lots of love   Alice

Sumner did not load at Grand Turk, the island's capital, as Alice had hoped, but at East Harbor. He asked if his father had been buried "under Masonic honors." This ceremony would have been a short colorful memorial service performed by the officers of his lodge in full regalia following the funeral service.

East Harbor   Turks Island
May 7th 08

My Dear Alice
I will write a few lines between day light & Dark. We got over here Tuesday morning after my sending your letter ashore Monday night (which I hope you will get next Tuesday). Got no salt that day. Begun loading Wed= morning & have in tonight 11 000 bushel, about ⅓ cargo.

Tuesday night the 4 master [sunk astern off Puerto Rico] came in to Anchor, the Lydia M Deering, & I called on the Capt last eve, Capt Gammage. It called up old memories to go on board & think that was Capt Will Hamilton's home for several years. I was on board of her only once while he was master of her—in Salem. She looks well yet.

. . . [I got] 5 [of your letters] in all here. None have caught up with me yet of those written to Rosario. I am quite disappointed that you wrote nothing of Father's Last days or any particulars of when he was buried, if from the old home (I imagine he was) or if under Masonic honors. I thought as you concluded that I didn't hear of his death before leaving Rosario you would say a few words about it. But never mind. I know he is gone. I have been trying to write mother a few lines. It's rather a sad duty but feel I must write. . . .

I don't know sure about that Hay Trade with Ervin but I wouldn't have him worry & suffer over the loss of a dollar for anything so let it go, though I think that the Hay was to square the Bill. . . .

What a lot of Yarmouth people have dropped away since I left home. I can count 7 & perhaps there are more. . . .

If you have Ervin plough, tell him to plough as much, more than last year. Possibly some of the roots will come out that wouldn't last year. No more. Can't see.   Sumner

Sat eve on Deck just after supper, having my smoke. This is the only cool part of the Day. Yesterday & today we have had a fresh S.E. wind & so choppy that there has been no salt shipped to day & yesterday. They knocked off soon after Dinner.

I have been on shore with Capt Gammage from 3 to 5.30 P.M. Just for fun we went to see a little vessel that is building here & he wanted to go & see a colored woman that he was to the wedding of quite a number of years ago. She is a widow now & sick. It's just awfull to see the Poverty among the Negroes. We saw a little pair of darky twins 2 weeks old in a hut close by the widow's. Cunning little things. I am going to take her ashore a can of milk tomorrow if I go. She says she hasn't milk enough for them Both. She has 6 beside the twins. It was real amusing.

Yesterday we went on a picnic with [the] Consul & wife [sister to an owner of one of the saltworks] & her sister & brother way out across the Salt Ponds to the hills & had a lunch. We drove out with 3 different teams. Liked to done Capt Gammage & myself quite up in the hot sun & rough road but the natives here don't mind a thing like that. . . . There were 4 young girls on the trip so of course I enjoyed it.

Tomorrow we are going to church. The minister has been up & called on us. Dark again.

Sunday 10 Awfully Hot. Capt Gammage & self went on shore to meeting. Had a great time. They have a queer little church & the whites & colored mix right together & sing & pray together. I rather like the white people for that but it's awfully Primitive & even amusing to listen.

The minister was very social when he called & joined me in a social whiskey & smoked a cigar while making his call. I imagine he may be off again. I wonder what our ministers would think of that? Yet they may have their nips if not in a social way. . . .

Guess I'll say bye bye & go & cool off   Yours as ever Sumner

Thursday noon All cleared from customs & hope to get away soon.
With much love,
Sumner

Sumner encourages his mother to stay with one of her daughters instead of remaining "alone." This sentiment is very revealing, since Margaret shared the family home with Josh, Hattie Josh and their child, Elizabeth.

Thursday May 1st 08

My Dear Mother
I feel today that I must begin a letter to you allthough a sad duty & knowing how little comfort can be conveyed to you in a few written lines. I know I ought to have wrote you ere this on my passage up from the river. I wrote to you & father . . . before I got the last 2 letters from Alice telling me how sick Father was & how fast he seemed to be failing. So I had to come away with anxious feelings bringing only

sad uncertain thoughts & I could not seem to bring myself to write you allthough you were so much in my mind & thoughts all the passage. . . .

I have been thinking so much of Father to-day as I am passing along the South coast of Porto Rico & can see with my glasses into the Port of Ponce where Father has been as well as other Ports in this Island. I can not help thinking that perhaps he has passed many times along over the same track of waters that I am sailing now in years gone by, & it gives me many sad thoughts.

I can only realize in a measure how hard it is for you, dear Mother. Yet I hope you will bear up bravely & try to think of those things which will be the most comforting. Perhaps the greatest is that you have been spared to take care of him so many years & minister to his wants untill the end. This I know is a great comfort to you & many other things also, the many years you have been blessed with together so far above the average & the many years that have passed without a broken link in our dear family chain. How few families so large have been so blessed—so many children growing up to man & womanhood without many blemishes of character to mar your quiet Life. All these & many other thoughts as your mind reverts to the past will I hope & trust, aid in comforting you in these troubled hours of bitter trials.

Alice's letter spoke of your being over to May's & I felt glad. I thought you would feel better there & I hope you will stay with her a long time. It seems better for me to think of you with your eldest daughter. It seems more fitting than at home alone with your thoughts & where there is so much to constantly recall the great loss that has come to us all. All the children were home at the last, I hope, but possibly John & myself unless Lucy could not get down. Poor little Muriel, it does seem hard that she be so afflicted while so young [seventeen].

How very sad Capt= Cleaves death seems. I was much shocked to read of it only a little more than a week before dear Father's. You,

Mother dear, & Miss Soule seem all the older ones left to us on the dear old Foreside.

Well, I will not try to write more now. Shall hope to be at Turks Island Sunday or by May 4th & will try to write more there so will close for now but my thoughts are with you very very much=

Your affectionate son   Sumner

Sumner speaks of "Will Hamilton," Woodbury's brother. Woodbury chartered his sailboat to interested parties locally and was not interested in a career as a merchant seaman. However, his elder brother Will had been well respected in that profession.

Sunday May 10 at Turks Island

Dear Mother   I will write a few lines more from here. I got here the morning of the 5th. Had very light winds the last 2 or 3 days. We have about ½ cargo of Salt & I hope will be loaded this coming week. There is a mail to go sometime this week so must have letters ready. It is 90° in the shade & never gets below 80°. It's the hottest month here of the Year. There is but one other vessel here & that is the 4 masted Schooner Lydia M Deering that was built for Woodbury's Brother Will= She is loading for N York. I have been on board & it recalled memories of the past thinking of Wood's Bro=   & the years he had spent in the vessel as a home.

The Capt [currently in command of the *Lydia M. Deering*] & I have been on shore this A.M. & went to church. The English episcopel has about 5 or 6 white families, the rest colored and is very primative in appearence. Quite amusing but all very serious & earnest in their devotions. . . .

When I have had my thoughts with you at home as I so often do, the feeling come to me that I can hardly realize that Dear Father has gone from us. Perhaps I shall not fully realize it untill I get home again. Then I know I must.

No more now   Sumner

Tuesday eve 12th

Dear Mother   Just a few lines this eve. I hear a [steamer] goes from Turks Island Thursday & a small boat leaves here tomorrow to Take the mail over to connect with the steamer. Will close some of the letters I have underway to send by her as there will not be another mail for 10 days or more. . . .

[Last Saturday] it blew so fresh that the Lighters were unable to come along side so we lost the day entirely. . . . We shall finish loading Thursday 14th & get away the 15th I hope & shall see you again if all goes well about June 1st. Till then, Dear Mother, will say good bye. I think of you a great-deal & know how lonely it is for you, but hope you will not be sick. Try & be comforted with thoughts of the past. I feel that I have not written much that will bring you real comfort. I wish I could but you will know how often I am with you in thought & all the rest of the family. Give my love to them all & I hope they will excuse my not writing. It's so hard to try to. With much love I am, my Dear mother, your affectionate son Sumner

BEACHED
1908-1932

"Fish or cut bait!"

Sumner's arrival in Portland with salt from Turks Island was probably close to his reckoning of June 1, 1908, "and the apples be in blossom when I get home." As he never hurried to make inquiries about a berth after a long voyage, he probably enjoyed Yarmouth that summer. He may have had some yacht charters in the fall, but he never went deepwater sailing again.

He had not expressed any thoughts of retiring in his letters from the bark *Benjamin F. Hunt Jr.* Therefore, the decision must have been reached sometime after his arrival home in June 1908. What possible reason could have turned Sumner from his life's career? Despite the difficulties of finding a deepwater command, he had seemed fairly confident of his future plans in his letters from the *Hunt.* There could only be one explanation: Sumner left the sea to be with Alice.

Alice's journal of 1898 and her letters of 1908 could have been written by two different women. Now she was acerbic, where before she had been funny. On the issue of Edith's wedding, she could only empathize with Hattie John. She seemed to have forgotten the ardent girl of her youth who had written in Sumner's diaries. Her health was probably worse than she indicated in her letters to Sumner, for she died less than seven years later. Her death certificate stated that she had had a history of angina pectoris, valvular heart disease and asthma, which could explain her shortness of breath and difficulty in walking. Much as Sumner loved the sea, he loved his Alice more. He stayed home and became a trolley-car motorman. The *Grace Deering* sank after being converted to a barge; Sumner was more flexible.

He applied for a job at the car barn in Yarmouth village for the Portland Railroad Company trolley lines on April 12, 1909. "Was so glad went but so sorry." While he was relieved to have work, he could be nothing less than stricken to leave a career which had been passed down to him from his forefathers. What challenge could running a trolley car provide a man like Sumner? On his ships he had had complete authority over his men and their destiny, as well as the cargo and the vessel herself. The trolley run must have seemed a parody of the voyages he had made through the salt seas. How did

Alice's last photograph.

THE YARMOUTH HISTORICAL SOCIETY

a deepwater man feel greeting his peers who were still mariners when they climbed onto his trolley on their return from the world? During the eighteen years and two months he remained with the streetcar company, he left home once, for a two-week winter vacation in St. Petersburg, Florida. However, every motorman and passenger alike knew that he had once been a deepwater man.

Alice Gray Drinkwater died on April 29, 1915, at the age of fifty-three. None of the diaries for the years 1910–1915 survived, but the pain Sumner felt at his untimely separation from Alice laced his entries in 1916. This period of his life was easily recalled by the pupils in the one-room schoolhouse around the corner from his home. Sumner was a great favorite, supplying refreshments and favors for their holiday parties, and allowing them to fish in his pockets for candy almost every day on his way back from work. One pupil, now in her eighties, recalled that for several days he didn't come by the school because his wife had died. "And when he did come again, he looked so sad that we felt sorry. He was such a nice man." Here is a poem which Sumner clipped from the newspaper at this time:

The Ledge schoolhouse built by Will Doyle.

Monument Square, Portland.

YOU OR I

If we could know
Which of us darling, would be the first to go,
Who would be first to breast the swelling tide,
And step alone upon the other side
If we could know!

If it were you,
Should I walk softly, keeping death in view?
Should I, my love, to you more oft express?
Or should I grieve you, darling any less?
If it were you?

If it were I,
Should I improve the moments slipping by?
Should I more closely follow God's great plan?
Be filled with a sweeter charity to man—
If it were I?

If we could know!
We cannot darling; and 'tis better so.
I should forget, just as I do to-day,
And walk along the same old, stumbling way,
If I could know.

I would not know.
Which of us darling, will be first to go.
I only wish the space may not be long
Between the parting and the greeting song;
But when, or where, or how we're called to go—
I would not know.

John, Sumner's brother, had accepted work as a first mate on a merchant steamship. We know that Sumner had some offer from his old shipping firm of N. W. Rice in 1916. That firm still had vessels sailing to the River Plate, although they had sold off the *Hunt* in 1912. His diary indicates that Sumner thought it over for a few days and then declined. Perhaps he had been a motorman too long.

However, one factor in his refusal was probably his second marriage to Mabel Fels Grover, which took place that summer. They shared sorrows; Mabel had lost her first husband. She was childless, alone, and had become a good friend of the Drinkwaters' before Alice's death. She evidently never challenged Sumner's continued affection for his first wife—which was wise, for Sumner never forgot Alice Gray. His later diaries are filled with accounts of his trips to the cemetery to bring her flowers, and he often noted the occasion of her birthday or their marriage.

November 21, 1932   50th Anniversary of my 1st marriage to Alice G. Drinkwater.

While Sumner never loved any woman the way he loved Alice, he was content in his second marriage. Indeed, he must have been more than content, since Mabel bore him, when he was fifty-eight, the daughter he had always coveted.

Because Sumner's diaries were limited to his actions, his fantasies proved elusive. From interviews I learned that he had had afterthoughts about N. W. Rice's offer and had spoken about taking some of the trolley-car men on a voyage to South America. This poem survives from the trolley-car period. It was written on September 10, 1917, over two years after Alice's death, and shows some of Sumner's old whimsey.

SUMNER'S POEM

This is the truth as I'm alive
After leaving Portland at two forty-five
On car two hundred and forty-one
Outward bound on the Yarmouth run.

As Motorman Drinkwater, seven hundred and four
Attempted to close the Vestibule door.
The roller being rusty in want of grease
He did on the door his strength increase.
The consequence was as it came to pass
It shattered to atoms the inside glass.
Altho his wages are not verry large,
He is perfectly willing to stand the charge.

Sumner was sixty-eight in June 1927 when the Portland Railroad Company discontinued its two-man cars and encouraged the older motormen to retire by raising the pensions to $33.32 a month. It was Sumner's second confrontation with progress.

Eighteen years and two months of running a trolley did not make Sumner a motorman any more than contracting out for carpentry jobs with his brother-in-law had made him a journeyman.

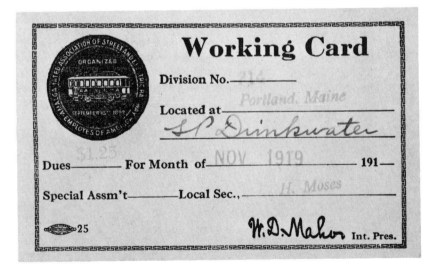

Working Card

Division No. _____

Located at _____ *Portland, Maine*

S P Drinkwater

Dues _____ For Month of _____ NOV 1919 _____ 191—

Special Assm't _____ Local Sec., _____ *H. Moses*

25 *W. D. Mahon* Int. Pres.

Sumner and friend.

Sumner had succeeded in his profession before the world took it away. The other car men always called him "Cap," short for Captain, and they told this story about him:

One winter evening Sumner Pierce Drinkwater, motorman number 704, was operating the trolley on the twelve-mile run from Portland to Yarmouth. The weather was cold and the passengers on the road had a half-hour's wait between cars. On this particular night Sumner's partner was Cornelius McGerrigle, a man who regularly accompanied him as conductor.

At Falmouth Town Landing, a few miles south of Yarmouth, Cornelius noticed that the streetcar had passed a woman who had been waiting by that station and was now frantically waving her hand. The conductor pulled on the bell rope to get the motorman's attention. Startled by the sound, Sumner brought the trolley to a stop—well past the indignant woman.

The conductor hurried forward, pitching his voice so that the passengers seated in the car could not hear. "Cap, Cap, you went right by that lady waiting for us at Town Landing Station. What's the matter? How come you did that?"

"Did what?"

Corn said, "You didn't stop for a passenger back there. How come?"

After some thought Sumner said sheepishly, "You know, Corn, I forgot where I was. I wasn't watching out for passengers tonight. My eyes were on the North Star."

About the Author

JULIANNA FREEHAND received her B.S. degree from the University of Maine in Orono in 1963, before serving as a Peace Corps volunteer in Senegal, West Africa. She studied Comparative African Literature at the University of Wisconsin and in recent years has been working as a free-lance photographer and publisher, specializing in turn-of-the-century photographs. She is the author of *The Westchester Treasure Hunt Tour: Treason in the American Revolution,* the story of the capture and hanging of Major John André. Currently Ms. FreeHand is at work on a book about the main streets of Westchester County, New York, and on a photographic study of women, *Elizabeth's Dream.*

Julianna FreeHand was born in Portland, Maine, and although her family moved to New York a few years later, she returned each summer to her native state. With her husband and three children, she divides her time between Croton-on-Hudson, New York, and Eugene, Oregon, where this book was written.